GUARDIANS OF THE LIFE STREAM

Shamans, Art and Power in Prehispanic Central Panamá

by
ARMAND J. LABBÉ

with a Foreword by
Peter Keller, Ph.D.

This project is supported in part by
a grant from:

NATIONAL
ENDOWMENT
FOR THE
ARTS

and
THE FLETCHER JONES FOUNDATION

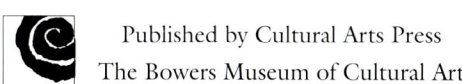

Published by Cultural Arts Press
The Bowers Museum of Cultural Art

Distributed by The University of Washington Press

Copyright © 1995 by the Bowers Museum of Cultural Art. All rights reserved. This book may not be reproduced in whole or any part by any means, whether mechanical or electronic, without the written permission of the Bowers Museum of Cultural Art, 2002 N. Main Street, Santa Ana, California 92706, except for brief passages used in a review.

ISBN 0-9633959-3-9

Printed in Hong Kong

Published by
Cultural Arts Press, BMCA

Distributed by
University of Washington Press

Project Director and Art Direction
Armand J. Labbé

Project Coordinator
María Teresa Inga

Photography by
Ognan Borissov (5-8, 10-12, 17, 20-22, 24, 25, 27-30, 38-50, 54-57, 59-62, 65-73, 77, 78, 83-86, 89-94, 97-107, 109, 110, 112, 113, 115-118, 125-127, 129, 131, 132, 135, 138-140, 142, 144, 146)
Armand J. Labbé (1-3, 8-9a, 16, 22a, 23, 31, 32, 35, 36, 51, 58, 79-81, 122-124, 133, 136, 141, 143, 145, 147)
Warren León, Jr. (13, 18, 19, 33, 37, 53, 63, 64, 74, 76, 87, 88, 95, 111, 114, 119, 121, 130, 137)
Lois Ellen Frank (29a, 29b, 37a)

Digital Pre-Press and Pre-Press Production
Borissov Photography

Illustrations by
Joseph Kramer

Design by
Barbara Smiley, Smiley Graphics

Printing by
Kay Lau & Associates

Manuscript Preparation by
María Teresa Inga
Jacqueline Bryant
Ximena Minotta

Editor
Aleida Rodríguez

Research Assistants Coordinator
Jacqueline Bryant

Research Assistants
Kirby Beneville   Chris Mulroney   Anna Sanchez
Steve Foote   Adriana Orozco   Christa Smith
Nancy McIntosh   Stacey Olin
Lydia Morimoto   Alexis Pavenich

Art Object Preparation
Teresa Ridgeway
Alice Bryant
Timothy Campbell

Art Object Care, Management and Logistics
Timothy Campbell

Back Cover
STANDING SHAMANIC FIGURE
Conte Style. Central Region, Panamá.
c. A.D. 600-800. Fired Clay, Paint.
13" h.
Only the impressions of the figure's arms and hands are visible, as if the figure was wearing a costume or garb. The surface designs represent tingunas, shamanic emanations characterized by claw elements and terminating in a stylized bird's head.
Anonymous Loan, Los Angeles.

```
972.87 L115g

Labbé, Armand J.

Guardians of the life stream
```

*This book is dedicated to the people of Panamá,
past and present.*

ACKNOWLEDGMENTS

The present volume could not have come to fruition without the dedicated and concerted efforts of a large number of individuals and institutions. First, credit is due to Peter Keller, executive director of the Bowers Museum of Cultural Art, and to Ruth Seigle, president of the museum's Board of Governors, for committing the institution and its resources to this project.

We would like to extend a special thank you to our many friends and colleagues in Panamá for their cooperation, encouragement, and support:

Richard Cooke, of the Smithsonian Tropical Research Institute, who facilitated our visits to the important excavations under his direction at Cerro Juan Diaz in Los Santos and sites at Natá, and who reviewed the manuscript and made invaluable comments on attributions, dates, and other technical aspects of the text; Laurel Anne Breece, currently excavating at Natá, who coordinated our visits to the excavations and research laboratories in the Azuero Peninsula; Licenciada Marcela Camargo, head of the Dirección Nacional de Patrimonio Histórico, without whose foresight and commitment this project would have remained incomplete; Licenciada Ana Matilde Conte de Mosquera, director of the Museo Antropológico Reina Torres de Araúz which provided exceptional artworks for inclusion in this monograph, and whose generous expenditure of time and support is greatly appreciated; and Mr. Jacinto Almendra of the Patrimonio Histórico, who generously gave of his time and expertise and assisted in the selection of artworks from the Museo Antropológico's collections.

Sincere thanks are due to Alan Grinnell of the University of California, Los Angeles, who participated in every stage of the research, both here and in Panamá, and whose deep and considerable knowledge of all things Panamanian was a joy, inspiration, and beacon that kept our research focused and on course. We also extend a deep appreciation for his in-depth review of the manuscript and insightful commentaries, and for the many hours spent assisting us with difficult attributions.

Our research findings would have been impossible without the ability to study a large number of artworks. Many thanks to the museums, foundations, institutions, and private individuals who made or offered to make their collections and resources available for study. We are indebted to the following institutions and individuals:

Gordon McEwan, curator of New World Art, and Brian J. Lang, New World Department of the Denver Art Museum; Jane S. Day, chief curator and curator of Archaeology at the Denver Museum of Natural History; Nancy Rosoff, assistant curator at the National Museum of the American Indian Research Branch, Smithsonian Institution; Frank Norick, principal museum anthropologist, Phoebe Hearst Museum of Anthropology, University of California, Berkeley; Charles Stanish, Department of Anthropology, the Field Museum of Natural History; Anne-Louise Schaffer, assistant curator of the Art of Africa, Oceania, and the Americas, Museum of Fine Arts, Houston; Cheri Falkenstein-Doyle, registrar of the Southwest Museum, Los Angeles; James A. Greaves; Ed Thomas for sharing his insights on vulva imagery in dual-spouted vessel forms; and Susan Lerer for her unfailing support and illuminating commentaries on the text.

This publication and the Panamá Project exhibit – Between Empires: The Artistic Legacy of Prehispanic Panamá is supported in part by a grant from the National Endowment for the Arts. The Bowers Museum of Cultural Art would like to thank the NEA for their generous assistance and encouragement, without whose support this monograph and project would have been greatly diminished.

Special gratitude is expressed to the Fletcher Jones Foundation for major funding of this publication. The Fletcher Jones Foundation helped the Museum respond to the National Endowment for the Arts Challenge. The Foundation's gift made it possible to publish this book and have adequate funds remaining for other aspects of the Panamá Project, such as the concurrent exhibit on Panamanian art, as well as supportive education programming. Thanks is also due to the Collectors Council of the Bowers Museum of Cultural Art.

Funding for this project and monograph has come from many other sources. Sincere gratitude is expressed to Mr. and Mrs. Larry W. Wendt, who tirelessly helped in securing necessary funding and who coordinated visits to many private collections; Gregory and Mechas Grinnell, Norma Kershaw, Throckmorton Fine Art, and the many other contributors and lenders in Santa Ana, Los Angeles, Carmel, San Francisco, and other parts of California, New York, Florida, Texas, New Mexico, and Arizona who wish to remain anonymous.

The project was also supported and enhanced by the participation of many staff members of the Bowers Museum of Cultural Art:

Tere Inga, administrative assistant of the Division of Research and Collections, and the project coordinator, who kept the project on track and orchestrated the participation of scores of individuals in between those moments when she wasn't processing and correcting the manuscript; Jacquie Bryant, curatorial researcher and Research Center coordinator, who supervised a small army of research assistants involved in procuring books, articles, and unpublished conference papers germane to our reserach and which formed the basis for the research bibliography; Tim Campbell, collections manager, who professionally organized, maintained, and provided for this project access to the hundreds of Panamanian artworks on loan to the museum; Teresa Ridgeway, registrar, and Alice Bryant, assistant registrar, who coordinated the delivery of artworks to and from the museum and who spent many hours making condition reports and other necessary documents; Jim Stathakis, director of Administration; Pat House, director of Development and Marketing; Janet Baker, chief of Education and curator of Asian Art; Paul Johnson, curator of Exhibit Design; Jim Sherman, development officer, who assisted with the NEA grant; Ximena Minotta from the Education Department, who assisted with data entry and wordprocessing; and Chris Mulroney, intern from California State University, Fullerton, who assisted in examining public and private Panamanian collections in the American Southwest.

I would also like to thank Paul Apodaca, curator of Native American Art for the many hours of intellectual sparring and honing on a wide variety of subjects pertaining to Native American culture; and Raymond Yellow Ears (Navajo), the late Hubert Honani (Hopi), and the late David Villaseñor (Huichol/Otomi) for sharing their insights into Native American religions.

Armand J. Labbé

TABLE OF CONTENTS

Acknowledgments
5

Foreword
8

Preface
9

Brief Chronological Outline of Panamanian History
12

Chapter I
Introduction
15

Chapter II
Central Panamá: A Ceramic Art History
23

Chapter III
The Central Region
Changes through Time: An Art Historical Overview
51

Chapter IV
Neotropical and New World Shamanism
67

Chapter V
Mapping and Structuring the Shamanic Universe
77

Chapter VI
Paradigms and Models: A Key to Understanding
the Inherent Dualism of the Shamanic Cosmos
87

Chapter VII
Context and Meaning in the Art of Central Panamá
103

Glossary
123

Photo Listings
125

Index of Photos According to Appearance in Text
148

Bibliography
149

FOREWORD

For years, scholars and collectors alike have admired and questioned the uniquely stylistic patterns found in the ceramics and goldwork of precolumbian Panamá. Even so, until the publication of this monograph, *Guardians of the Life Stream: Shamans, Art and Power in Prehispanic Central Panamá,* there existed no comprehensive reference book on the art of Central Panamá that contained a systematic analysis of the art and nomenclature in the context of time. Prior reference texts on the art of Central Panamá avoided these very important issues. This monograph not only contains the latest nomenclature but also organizes this according to proper time frames and specific cultural contexts.

This monograph represents a continuation of the research that Armand Labbé began in the 1980s with his work *Colombia Before Columbus,* in which he analyzes the iconography of precolumbian Colombian ceramics. The connections between Colombia and its neighbor to the north, Panamá, are well established. His new research places the iconography used to decorate the beautiful ceramics of Central Panamá within a specific cultural context and goes on to offer interpretations based on his very careful analysis of neotropical ethnographies. Of particular interest to North American scholars is Mr. Labbé's model, which explains the basis for classifications made by indigenous ethnographic groups from the Southwestern United States through tropical South America. Related to this is a treatise on neotropical and New World shamanism, which forms the basis for interpretations given in the text.

Thanks to Armand Labbé's exhaustive research, these spectacular artworks from Central Panamá can be appreciated not only for their aesthetic merits but for their ideological context. This is done dramatically, using approximately 140 full-color plates of actual masterpieces gleaned from public and private collections across the United States as well as significant contributions from the Museo Antropológico Reina Torres de Araúz in Panamá.

Guardians of the Life Stream: Shamans, Art ,and Power in Prehispanic Central Panamá is a major undertaking that will have a significant impact on our appreciation of these precolumbian masterpieces from Central Panamá. None of this research, nor the publication of this monograph, could have been possible without the support of many individuals, corporations, and foundations. First and foremost, I wish to express my gratitude to the National Endowment for the Arts, for their initial Treasury Grant and to the Fletcher Jones Foundation for their major funding. The Bowers Museum Corporation is also to be thanked for its major sponsorship, as well as individual grants from Gregory and Mechas Grinnell, Norma Kershaw, Mr. and Mrs. Larry W. Wendt, and Throckmorton Fine Art.

I trust that everyone interested in precolumbian ceramics from anywhere in the New World, but particularly from Panamá, will take full advantage of this unique opportunity to gain important insights into one of the world's greatest ancient cultures.

Peter C. Keller, Ph.D.
Executive Director
The Bowers Museum of Cultural Art

PREFACE

Panamá has long remained neglected in literature dealing with the precolumbian art of the Americas. In comparison to the art of México, Perú, Ecuador, or Colombia, it is all but unknown to the general public. Even within scholarly circles, the available reference texts are scant and the information hopelessly outdated. The present volume seeks to bring to the scholarly community as well as the general public a reference text that not only makes available the latest findings in terms of chronologies, art styles, and developmental sequences but also offers an interpretative framework by which this art can now begin to be understood.

The art of the Central Region of Panamá must rank among the highest aesthetic expressions found anywhere in prehispanic America. It is surprising, therefore, to realize how little attention has been placed on this rich and important chapter of New World art history.

As used in this volume, the Central Region of Panamá refers to a cohesive cultural region and includes all of the territory now encompassed by the Panamanian provinces of Coclé, Herrera, and Los Santos, most of the provinces of Veraguas and Colón and part of the western reaches of the Province of Panamá, including extensive stretches of the littoral of the Bay of Panamá.

Given the depth of time encompassed by our inquiry—about twenty-five hundred years of continuous art history—we should expect that the cultural boundaries of the Central Region differed somewhat from period to period.

The earliest goldwork in Panamá is in a style known as the Initial Group, which dates circa A.D. 1–500. Many of the forms of the Initial Group are similar to forms found in Colombia and in parts of Costa Rica. The Costa Rican examples are generally later than those of Panamá, while the Colombian forms appear to be contemporary. Another stylistic group, the International Group is also found from Costa Rica to the Quimbaya region of Colombia and dates in Panamá from about A.D. 400–1100. Although the prevailing opinion among researchers is that Panamá's goldworking technology was initially inspired by or introduced from the south, likely Colombia, there are many questions left to be answered. The Panamanian dates for the Initial Group forms—animals with curled or upturned tails, spiral ornaments, and joined bird forms—seemingly are at least as early as for those found in Colombia. Later Panamanian gold styles such as Conte (c. A.D. 400–1100), Parita Assemblage (c. A.D. 700–1520), and Veraguas-Gran Chiriquí (c. A.D. 700–1520) reflect an internal Panamanian evolution of the goldworking tradition. The saurian emanations seen on an Openwork Group gold frog pendant documented in this volume are reminiscent of similar forms apparently of later date found in the Tairona goldwork from Colombia.

Our exploration of the art of the Central Region of Panamá is focused primarily on the ceramic arts, although examples of prehispanic Panamanian goldwork are included to illustrate the consistency in ideology and iconography between the two mediums.

The chronological sequences and ceramic typologies for the Central Region continue to be revised even as this volume goes to press. The dates employed herein reflect the latest archaeological findings and radiocarbon dates, much of which derives from as-yet-unpublished findings by primary researchers in the field. Those familiar with previously published periodizations and chronological parameters for the better-known ceramic styles will probably be surprised at the degree of revision that has taken place. We can only caution that revisions will undoubtedly continue to be made based on new findings in the field and at research laboratories.

The picture that is beginning to emerge from the available data, however, is not consistent with the view that Panamá was a cultural backwater area dependent on cultural stimuli from neighbors to the south or north. With respect to the graphic two-dimensional designs used to decorate a large variety of vessels in the early centuries A.D., Panamá emerges a leader and innovator, evincing technical and aesthetic mastery of the medium, superior in many respects to all other painted-ceramic-producing regions save that of the Maya of México and Moche of Perú.

Much of the iconography used to decorate the gold and ceramic artworks can now confidently be ascribed to shamanic imagery that in many instances is still current in extant indigenous neotropical groups. This rich and relevant ethnographic base, in conjunction with information gleaned from archaeological and ethnohistorical sources, has served as the basis for interpretations given in the text.

While the artworks reproduced in this volume can be appreciated for their exceptional artistic and aesthetic merits alone, irrespective of their ideological significance, we feel that the ideological content of the designs are an intrinsic dimension of these works as cultural art. Cultural art history seeks to uncover the cultural context and relationships that underly specific artistic forms and designs. Why was this art made? By whom was it made? How was it used? What was its meaning, relevance, and significance to the people who made it? What criteria, if any, did they use to determine whether this art was effective or ineffective, significant or insignificant? These are ongoing questions in our research.

No single volume can hope to be comprehensive with respect to the subject of Panamanian precolumbian art. Our intention has been to establish a framework that could be used in the development of a true art history for the Central Region of Panamá. The fundamental basis for such an art history must rely on the developmental sequences established by disciplines such as archaeology. These are delineated in Chapter two. Additionally, any analysis of the art must rely on a number of method-

1. Current excavations at Cerro Juan Diaz, Los Santos, Azuero Peninsula conducted by the Smithsonian Institution and the National Geographic Society under the direction of Richard Cooke.

2. Ceramic vessels in situ, Cerro Juan Diaz, Los Santos, Azuero Peninsula, Central Region, Panamá.

ologies, which will yield criteria by which the art may be viewed individually and as an integrated tradition. Our approach is componential and comparative. The ceramic art tradition of the Central Region has been divided into a number of discrete styles. Each style in turn has been divided into a sequence of design fields, designs, motifs, and design elements. This approach allows a discrete analysis of any design, determining which components in the design are derived from a particular style or chronological period, thereby establishing the relative affinity between styles and stylistic changes through time. Such an approach orders the database and makes it amenable to a variety of statistical methodologies.

Chapters four through six establish the basis for our interpretation of the ideological significance and cultural context of the artworks, leading to the interpretative framework developed in Chapter seven. Just as stylistic categories and chronological parameters are revised and adjusted with the insights gained from new findings, interpretations are subject to a similar flux. This is the nature of any scholarly endeavor.

Excepting minor modifications noted in the text, we have retained the basic stylistic nomenclature devised by the primary researchers working in the Central Region. The chronological parameters used are based on the as -yet- unpublished periodic tables devised by Ilean Isaza, as recommended by Richard Cooke, noting as always that these are subject to revision, although they appear to be the best estimates currently available.

We have also chosen throughout the text to use the spelling "precolumbian" rather than one of the more awkward spellings of this term currently in use, such as *pre-Columbian*. We feel that the term has sufficiently been accepted in general parlance to warrant a lowercase adjectival form, unencumbered by an emphasis on a specific historical personage, especially since much "pre-Columbian" art continued to be made long after Columbus's encounter with the New World. In some parts of the Americas, contact with Europeans did not occur until long after this event. Consequently, unadulterated, unacculturated, precontact indigenous art continued to be produced and deserves to be referred to as *precolumbian*.

3. View of shaft graves, Cerro Juan Diaz, Los Santos, Azuero Peninsula, Central Region, Panamá.

BRIEF CHRONOLOGICAL OUTLINE OF PANAMANIAN HISTORY

1502–04 Columbus's last voyage to the New World. It is during this expedition (1502) that Columbus first explores the Caribbean coast of the Isthmus of Panamá.

1503 Spaniards abort attempt to establish a settlement at Belén, Panamá.

1508 Although the Spaniards have not yet occupied Panamá, Diego de Nicuesa is given a grant of the lands on Tierra Firme known as Veragua, which refers to large tracts of Panamá located west of the Gulf of Urabá. Nicuesa is unsuccessful in physically securing his grant.

1510 The Spanish town of Santa María la Antigua is established on land expropriated from the Indian town of Darién.

1511 Balboa begins his land exploration of eastern Panamá, visiting a number of chiefdoms, including Ponca, Comogre, and Pocorosa.

1513 Vasco Núñez de Balboa becomes the first European to officially come upon the Pacific Ocean discovered by Native Americans many thousands of years before.

1514–19 Spanish forces, under Pedro Arias de Avila (Pedrarias Dávila), captain general and governor of Castilla del Oro in Darién, launch a series of raids against Panamanian chiefdoms. The first attacks are against the chiefdoms of Comogre, Pocorosa, and Tubanama, all of which had been friendly to Balboa.

During these campaigns, Gonzalo de Badajoz, with part of the Spanish forces under his command, collects a hoard of gold from defeated and intimidated Indians. Badajoz himself, however, is routed by native forces at Coiba and his hoard of gold taken from him.

Toward the end of the campaign, Pedrarias grows ill and turns command over to Gaspar de Espinosa, who launches a brutal campaign against the local chiefdoms. Espinosa is generally credited as the European "discoverer" of the Azuero Peninsula. Spanish forces eventually prevail and the native populations of the lowlands, west of the Gulf of Panamá, are subdued by 1519.

1519 Pedrarias founds the city of Panamá.

1739 After 1739 Panamá becomes a part of the viceroyalty of New Granada.

1821 Following the Central American revolt from Spain, Panamá becomes part of the newly liberated Colombia.

1903 Panamá gains independence from Colombia. Months later a treaty is signed with the United States granting the U.S. rights to the "Canal Zone" and permission to build a canal connecting the Atlantic and Pacific oceans.

1914   The 40.27-mile-long canal is completed.

1930–33   First controlled excavations in Panamá conducted by the Peabody Museum of Archaeology and Ethnology, Harvard University at Sitio Conte, province of Coclé, under the subsequent direction of Alfred M. Tozzer, Henry D. Roberts, and Samuel K. Lothrop. Lothrop publishes his findings in two volumes: *Coclé: An Archaeological Study of Central Panamá*, Part 1, 1937; and *Coclé: An Archeological Study of Central Panamá*, Part 2, 1942.

1940   The University Museum, University of Pennsylvania, under the direction of J. Alden Mason conducts excavations at Sitio Conte. Important finds, including the famed elite burial named Burial 11, are uncovered.

1950s   Panamá Archaeology Society uncovers numerous sites in the Central Region, many outside Coclé, containing polychrome ceramics. Many of these sites are excavated by P. Dade.

Controlled excavations are conducted in the Parita Bay area by Gordon R. Willey and Charles R. McGimsey III. Their findings are published in 1954 as *The Monagrillo Culture of Panama, Papers of the Peabody Museum of Archaeology and Ethnology*, Vol. 49, No. 2.

1964   John Ladd, who conducted an analysis of the ceramics excavated by Willey and McGimsey, publishes his assessment in *Archaeological Investigations in the Parita and Santa Maria Zones of Panama, Bureau of American Ethnology*, Smithsonian Institution, Bulletin 193.

1967–70s   La Mission archéologique française au Panama under the direction of Alain Ichon conducts a series of important excavations at a number of sites in the southern portion of the Azuero Peninsula. Although Ichon writes up his findings in 1972, they are not published until 1980 (*Archeologie Du Sud De La Peninsule D'Azuero*, Panamá).

1970s–80s   Richard Cooke conducts systematic excavations in Coclé Province.

1990s   Ongoing excavations in the Azuero Peninsula under the direction of Richard Cooke, sponsored by the Smithsonian Institution and the National Geographic Society.

GUARDIANS OF THE LIFE STREAM

CHAPTER I

GUARDIANS OF THE LIFE STREAM

4. Polychrome Jar with Split-Image (Frontal and Lateral) Saurians

CHAPTER I

INTRODUCTION

Every culture contains within itself its own peculiar statement concerning man, cosmos, life, and the human condition. Particularly in cultures lacking a written language, such statements are encoded and enshrined in their art. The language of preliterate art tends to communicate by means of symbolic metaphor, expressed iconographically. Metaphoric symbolism, as used by preliterate societies, generally favors the evocation of streams of culturally related images and ideas.

A point of consideration in viewing ethnocultural art is the relationship of art and artist to the culture as a whole. In many societies the artist is often either a practitioner of the sacred—a priest or shaman—or an agent of such. In these societies, art is used to communicate shared perceptions about the nature of man, the natural world, or the cosmos. It also functions as an integrative force, identifying the individual with the culture as a whole. Even when it is employed to acquire and manifest personal power, as in magic or sorcery, culturally recognized imagery is always used. The artist's freedom lies not so much in creating new artistic canons and metaphors as it does in manipulating and expressing culturally prescribed rules and imagery. An understanding of such art depends, in large measure, on uncovering and identifying the hidden laws that govern the art and in deciphering the iconography employed. This cannot be accomplished without recourse to ethnography, assisting us in determining which metaphors are used and what aspects of culture, myth, or cosmology are being communicated.

And although these observations are true with respect to art in general, they are particularly true and relevant with respect to the cultural art of the Americas prior to European contact in the late fifteenth and early sixteenth centuries.

The earliest European reactions to the indigenous art of the Americas was either to view it as the expression of heathens wallowing in ignorance and idolatry or, like the more sophisticated German artist Albrecht Dürer (1471–1528), to marvel at its artistic virtuosity and exotic aesthetic splendor, as occurred when Dürer first set eyes on the gifts Motecuhzoma had given Cortés.

The European conquest of the Americas—and the subsequent social, political, and religious campaign to convert indigenous societies to European ways, values, and perspectives—succeeded in large measure in destroying many of the great artistic traditions of the Americas. Although some groups have retained the core of their cultures intact even to the present, exceedingly few have managed to do so in any form approaching a precontact state.

For centuries following the conquest, all things indigenous were either ignored, held in low esteem, openly despised, or expropriated. While in real life indigenous peoples were almost universally marginalized, in literature they were paradoxically sometimes idealized and romanticized.

Following the various Latin American revolutions of independence from Spain in the early nineteenth century, the seeds of interest in the lost and ruined civilizations of the Americas were sown by traveler-observers such as John Lloyd Stephens and Frederick Catherwood, who published their observations of Maya ruins in 1841. A host of explorer-observers followed.

Scientific interest in precolumbian cultures and antiquities began to take root in the late nineteenth century, although systematic archaeology would not get underway for decades in most areas. Early scientific excavations of the first half of the twentieth century were handicapped in several ways. Archaeological methodology was still rudimentary and unrefined, absolute dating techniques such as C14 were nonexistent, and theoretical interpretative models tended to be linear rather than holistic and more often than not reflected the cultural conditioning and ethnocentric perspectives of the researcher. Another disadvantage was the paucity of ethnographic data on surviving indigenous ethnicities that could be used to shed light on the vestiges of culture being unearthed by the archaeologists. Moreover, multidisciplinary approaches to research and interpretation were not yet practiced. Not until the latter half of the twentieth century would these play a significant role in prehistoric reconstruction.

The artworks uncovered by both looters and earlier investigators were looked upon as alien trophies or exotic treasures. The archaeologists were generally content to view such works as stratigraphic time markers used to correlate chronological changes in culture or document the movements of groups and cultural traditions through time and space.

Interpretations of designs or motifs remained little more than convenient and unconvincing labels, that referred to artworks or compositions as this or that god. These labels often held implications far removed from the original intent of the prehistoric artist.

There were, of course, notable exceptions. Smithsonian archaeologist Jesse Walter Fewkes, working in the American Southwest in the late nineteenth and early twentieth centuries, questioned whether motifs and designs found on prehistoric Hopi Indian pottery excavated in northeastern Arizona might have symbolic significance or be keyed to indigenous mythological or cosmological lore. He had the good fortune of working in an area where the prehistoric cultures unearthed by archaeology were at least indirectly related to surviving groups still living in the same region.

This early pioneering work was largely ignored by most archaeologists, who preferred to believe that such correlations and reconstructions were futile, too esoteric, unsupportable, or irrelevant to the more mundane questions addressed by archaeology, questions that addressed tangibles such as subsistence, settlement patterns, demographics, burial practices, architecture, or commerce.

In defense of the earlier, conservative, academic stance it should be acknowledged that the ethnographic database was not yet in place. It was being generated at about the same time that systematic archaeology was getting underway. The prevailing practice among professionals, at the time, was to work in small groups of isolated specialists sharing the same discipline and applied to the same field of research. There was little dialogue among archaeologists working in separate regions, let alone meaningful exchanges between archaeologists and ethnographers.

It was not until the late 1970s, twenty years after the establishment of precolumbian art history as a distinct and accepted discipline at American universities, that researchers began reexamining precolumbian artworks from perspectives inspired by the new databases, emerging from the recently generated ethnographies. It was now becoming possible to access ideological, philosophical, and cosmological dimensions of precolumbian cultures. A window had opened on the precolumbian mind!

Ethnographic research relating to neotropical Indians revealed a rich and sophisticated understanding of the natural world and the nature of nature. It also indicated that certain individuals within the indigenous communities were the keepers, users, and disseminators of knowledge and rituals. Such practitioners played a role similar to that ascribed to religio-philosopher-healers found in indigenous societies over much of the globe. Although each society has its own name for these individuals, the term *shaman*, a word likely derived from the Tungus word *saman*, of northern Asiatic derivation, is the most common term used in both the popular and scholarly literature to refer to these practitioners.

The significance of shamanism to the study of neotropical precolumbian art lies in the large body of artworks seemingly directly or indirectly inspired by shamanic traditions. For this reason, an understanding of neotropical and New World shamanism offers us the best possibility of interpretative access to precolumbian artistic traditions, particularly those most likely to have been influenced and derived from shamanic perspectives.

The ceramic art of the Central Region of Panamá constitutes one of the most aesthetically rich, enduring artistic traditions found anywhere in the Americas, covering over eighteen hundred years of unbroken art historical development. This tradition has been divided into a number of styles, which in turn are correlated with chronological archaeological periods identified by researchers working in lower Central America.

Any approach to the complex art of the Central Region of Panamá must be analytical, componential, and systematic. Compositional art comprises discrete units that work together to create a total effect. Among these are form, color scheme, design elements, motifs, and layout.

It is important that we establish clear definitions for the technical terminology employed. Form is meant to convey the shape and configuration effected by the ceramic artwork. Color scheme includes both the color of the background and the color used in line drawings or as infill.

Design elements are simple irreducible configurations used as unitary building blocks in the formation of design motifs. Design elements are to design motifs what letters are to words in phonetic languages. Design motifs, therefore, are units of design composed of two or more design elements. They may be compounded with other design motifs to create designs. Design motifs are to designs what words are to phrases, sentences, and paragraphs. We should note, at this point, that many design elements, in and of themselves, often have a significance similar to a unitary motif, in the same manner that the letter *I* is both a letter and a word in English, or the letter *Y* is both a letter and a word in Spanish. It becomes apparent, therefore, that design may be either a simple configuration or a complex composition, comprising two or more integrated or repeated design elements or motifs placed within the confines of a restricted field.

Design layout signifies the spatial manner in which the design is distributed over the medium. For example, design may be spatially distributed within linear bands, may cover the entire surface of the object, or may be dispersed in a bilateral, trilateral, or quadrilateral format.

When certain design elements or motifs are repeated in certain combinations and are expressed in the same format or layouts, repeatedly, on a particular medium such as pottery over an extended period of time, such designs are said to constitute a design style. An artistic tradition is comprised of a number of interrelated styles persisting through time.

When certain design elements and motifs represent or suggest something by reason of relationship, association, or convention, they are said to be representational or symbolic. Symbols are often keyed to different audiences, and the same symbol may convey different levels of meaning. Symbols often have a hidden or esoteric significance, which is usually only understood by certain individuals within a society, such as priests, shamans, or initiated members of the group. They may at the same time retain a more generally recognized, exoteric significance for the uninitiated laymen. Simple decoration, devoid of cognitive content, merely represents an aesthetic dimension of art. It has the same relationship to cognitive art that an empty seashell has to the animal that once lived within it. Aesthetics has its own dynamics and a relevance peculiar to the individual psyche of the perceiver. It can be moving and uplifting, a great catharsis, an alluring beauty, which holds the mind entranced. It is an experience in its own right. But there are other dimensions to precolumbian Panamanian art that can only be accessed by the informed mind. An understanding of cultural art requires that one not only enjoy the beauty of the flower but also marvel at the seed that produced it.

In the pages that follow, we will examine the ceramic art of Panamá from the perspectives generated by contemporary scholarship, seeking to place this art in a rich, relevant, cultural context. We will explore the possibility of ordering the available data for the purpose of gaining insight into the laws and artistic canons that governed this long-dormant, little-understood tradition. We shall also attempt to retrieve meaning from imagery that, until recently, could only be appreciated for its formal qualities and aesthetic merits.

5. Polychrome Olla with
Bilaterally Spaced Saurian Heads
at the Neck

6. Polychrome Olla
Decorated with
Large Shamanic Egglaying Birds

7. Polychrome Figural Jar
with Dual Handles

CHAPTER II

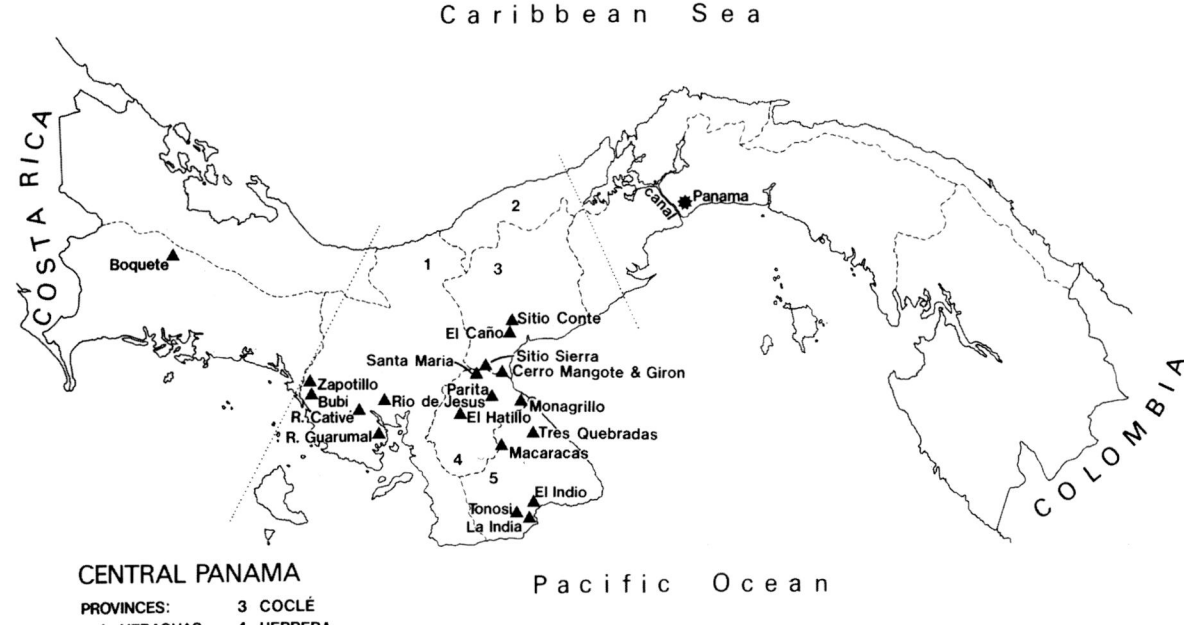

CHAPTER II

CENTRAL PANAMÁ: A CERAMIC ART HISTORY

The earliest ceramics found anywhere in Panamá date to 3000 B.C. in the archaeological sequence. This early ceramic period appears to represent a continuation of previously established cultural patterns.

From 5000 to 3000 B.C., hunter-gatherer peoples, adapted to tropical forest lifeways, began cultivating local palms and some tuberous plants. The archaeological record suggests that seed crops such as maize were also being cultivated but did not play a significant role in the local economy. Hunting was focused on deer, raccoons, small reptiles, and birds. Fishing was part of the subsistence base in areas with reasonable access to the sea or inland estuaries. Shellfish and crab formed part of the diet.

Pre-ceramic peoples in the Central Region appear to have lived in relatively small hamlets. It is estimated that over two hundred of these small-scale interrelated hamlets and other sites existed in the Santa María river basin alone (Cooke and Ranere, 1992b:269). Trade over broader regions is also evident. Hunting, food preparation, and other subsistence activities relied heavily on stone tools. Other materials, such as bone and teeth were also employed in tool making, but not extensively.

A number of different burial practices are noted, including primary flexed burials and bundle burials. Some researchers suggest that these may represent two stages in the burial process rather than two distinct burial types (ibid. 265; Stothart, 1985).

Monagrillo Ceramics (3000–1100 B.C.)

This pattern of culture persisted well after 3000 B.C., which marks the introduction of ceramics in Panamá. The earliest ceramics are in a style named Monagrillo, after the site on the Gulf of Parita in Herrera Province where this pottery was first found. Monagrillo pottery appears to represent a local development rather than an introduction from outside Panamá. Some researchers initially saw a connection between Monagrillo pottery and some of the early pottery found in Colombia and Ecuador. Others, however, have argued that Monagrillo is

8. Hill Country, Azuero Peninsula, Central Region, Panamá.

9. Tonosí River, Tonosí, Azuero Peninsula, Panamá.

sufficiently different from the Colombian or Ecuadorian types to be viewed as a local Panamanian development (Cooke and Ranere, 1992b:270). It is always possible, nonetheless, that the idea of pottery making could have diffused into Panamá from Colombia or Ecuador and engendered a local adaptation and development of the basic concept. The available evidence, however, supports the thesis of local development, given the concentration of the earliest Monagrillo-type sites in the Azuero Peninsula of the Central Region.

The overwhelming evidence of Monagrillo pottery is in the form of broken, scattered sherds and fragments rather than complete vessels. Vessels are rather rudimentary forms—bowls and jars lacking either bases or collars and varying in surface color, depending upon the local clays used and the firing techniques employed.

Vessels were fashioned using the coil-and-scrape technique. Firing was of low temperature, which has contributed to poor preservation. The earliest vessels were either undecorated wares or were decorated with incised or punctated designs. Punctate patterns appear to have been effected using awls, shells, and other sharp instruments. Incised decoration consists mainly of irregular curvilinear or rectilinear elements. Later, red paint, usually in the form of lines and bands, was added to the decorative inventory and combined with earlier decorative techniques to create the total design.

Although population density seems to have been on the increase in the Central Region in the centuries preceding the introduction of pottery, the process accelerated greatly thereafter. Between 2000 and 1000 B.C., there is evidence of increased levels of deforestation, apparently brought about by the intensification of slash-and-burn agriculture. Certainly by 1000 B.C. and earlier, maize agriculture had become an important component of the subsistence base.

The period between 1000 and 300 B.C. was one of rapidly increasing population in the Central Region, not only in the coastal areas but also in the piedmont and higher elevations. Burials now included deep shaft-and-chamber tombs. By 1100 B.C. Monagrillo-type ceramics ceased to be manufactured.

The ceramic record for the period 1100–300 B.C. is sporadic, incomplete, and as yet poorly documented. Modeling as a decorative technique is introduced. The new wares characteristic of this period are better made than the Monagrillo types.

The ceramics made between 1100 and 900 B.C. are technically very similar to the previous Monagrillo wares, differing mainly in certain modeled motifs and in the addition of necks. These have been studied by Isaza (1994) who feels that they may represent a transition between Monagrillo and the earliest bichrome and trichrome painted wares. These wares are still under study and poorly documented in the literature, therefore, it is perhaps premature at this point to link them to the subsequent painted wares.

10. Bichrome Jar: Mythic Theme Incorporating a Serpent, Birds, and Beetle

Sometime around 900 B.C. pottery appears with black painted designs in the form of rectilinear and curvilinear geometrics. The designs are painted against the color of the vessel ground. These early black-line wares are not discernibly related to the Monagrillo ceramic tradition. They may, however, be ancestral to the La Mula wares, which gave rise to the Aristide Style, which then contributed certain spatial and organizational traits to later painted wares, traits such as confining designs within circumferential bands and dividing designs into symmetrically arranged zones (Cooke, 1985:34). The Aristide Style is characterized by a black-on-red scheme utilizing geometric elements such as chevrons, T elements, scrolls, and other configurations, including crosshatching. The Aristide Style persisted till A.D. 300. Over part of the period A.D. 200–300, it was contemporary with another style known as Tonosí.

(100 B.C.–A.D. 500)

With the Aristide and Tonosí pottery styles we enter cultural periods, that are better documented archaeologically than any of the preceding periods. There were numerous settlements and villages along both major and minor rivers in the Central Region. Archaeological surveys have identified many of these along the Santa María drainage, as well as along such rivers as the Río Parita, Río Grande, and Río Caño. Some of these sites—such as Sitio Sierra (about A.D. 100–400) excavated by Cooke, and Sitio Girón, excavated by Willey and Stoddard—have undergone systematic scientific study. Farther to the south, near the tip of the Azuero Peninsula in the Río Tonosí region, a number of significant sites were excavated by Alain Ichon, including the important sites of El Cafetal and El Indio.

The archaeological data indicates that the Central Region was marked by continued intensification of subsistence efforts. Deer, rabbit, nine-banded armadillo, tree duck, turtles, frogs, iguanas, and a variety of riverine and marine species were exploited at Sitio Sierra, a Río Santa María site. Hunting was done with nets, snares, and, possibly, wooden spears with hardened tips. Fishing was as important a part of the subsistence base as it was in previous periods. There is evidence, however, that fishing was also taking place at sea, not just along the estuaries and littoral, as fish that avoid muddy waters, such as barracuda, were also being caught. Agricultural staples remained essentially the same, with maize now decidedly an important part of the diet.

The building types at Sitio Sierra appear to have been oval, rectangular, or round in floor plan. The variety of floor plans could reflect a variety of house types or it could indicate buildings of differing

11. Bichrome Jar Decorated with Three Birds

functions: dwelling, storage, or religio-ceremonial. The walls utilized cane or palm wood in their construction. The roofs and walls also appear to have been thatched.

Cooke reported finding a cemetery containing twenty-five individuals in flexed and primary positions beneath a roundish structure at Sitio Sierra. Carbon-14 dating seems to place at least some of the burials at around the first century A.D. The associated funerary pottery, however, are Girón and Escotá Aristide-type wares, small scarified jars, and plastically decorated vessels (Cooke, 1984a:282–286). Tonosí polychrome sherds are found in house floors and rubbish heaps. Farther south, in the Tonosí Valley area, some burials contain luxury items in gold, tumbaga, mica, agate, serpentine, and bone. In the Tonosí region, the most important ceramic ware of this period is a tricolor ware, which defines the Tonosí Style. Vessels in this style have been found outside the Tonosí area as far west as the Gulf of Montijo and as far north as Nata, in the province of Herrera. The color combinations vary from black and red on white to black on red with white outline, although a variety of other schemes are known, including red and black on red and some simple bichromes.

The Aristide and Tonosí Styles

The predominant vessel forms in the Tonosí Style are globular and subglobular jars, usually with very foreshortened necks and slightly flaring, or flat-topped rims. One of the most distinctive forms is a double vessel that appears to incorporate a shouldered jar for the lower half and an open-bottomed bowl placed above the jar. Designs on these vessels are vertically positioned and often extend along both the lower and upper portions of the vessel. Some of the double jars are decorated with a large hieratic standing figure with hands upraised. This figure is rendered as negative design, using the white ground color as the predominant body color (see Ichon, 1980: pl. XXIa). The body covers both lobes of the double jar. The bottoms of double jars, however, are undecorated. Designs are generally bilateral, in the sense that similar motifs are repeated on each side of the vessel.

The designs are usually laid out within bordered circumferential bands. Compositions vary, although some constitute genre scenes within the Tonosí Style. Among these is a looming mythic figure (Fig. 12) characterized by large concentric eyes, frontal facing pose, with hands upraised and a band of vertical hourglass motifs on the chest and abdomen. Equally distinctive are the two long tails that loop around the vessel, encircling long-legged birds. Commonly, numerous parallel-lined rectangular and lozenge-shaped panels are used as background decoration. Although we cannot determine the specific meaning or significance of this composition, the iconography is clearly mythic or shamanic and, given its frequency in the art, held great relevance for these people. Many of the vessels have had the necks and rims cut away (Fig. 12), a practice that appears to have been part of a funerary ritual.

13. Short-Neck Tricolor Jar with Paneled Design: Composite Creature Combining Bird and Serpent with Possible Astronomical Significance

12. Tricolor Globular Jar or Olla: Mythic Figure with Birds

14. Tricolor Dual-Spouted Vessel: Lizard and Birds

Another genre figure is a creature with a large crested head, bird-beaked nose, two legs, and a long serpentine body with distinctive loops. At least in some compositions (Fig. 13), this figure appears to represent the sun and the pathway of the sun (see chapter 7).

A distinct vessel form that seems to have made its debut between A.D. 200 and 400 is the dual-spouted jar (Fig. 14). The dual-spouted vessel marks the transition from early Tonosí to later Tonosí wares—Ichon's Montevideo Style, which we prefer to call Late Tonosí Style. Figures 14 and 15 demonstrate that, excepting the lizard handle, the form and decoration are clearly classic Tonosí Style attributes. The top of the lizard's head has a small penile aperture. As noted elsewhere in this publication, the lizard often has phallic connotations in the neotropical ethnographic literature. It appears that the earliest dual-spouted forms are those with lizard handles. They are contextually in association with graphic designs that reflect an early Tonosí Style. It may be that the later, attenuated, phalliform spouts of dual-spouted jars evolved as abstractions of these earlier lizard-form spouts. The larger spout connotes the female genitalia. The dimorphic sexual dualism associated with these forms is often graphically illustrated (Fig. 16, Cubitá Style). The double-spouted vessel form persisted well into the period of the Macaracas Style (A.D. 800–1000), after which it appears to have become increasingly rare and loses its sexual dimorphic symbolic intent.

Characteristic of Tonosí Style designs are parallel-line hatching, line ticking, use of dots, and large varieties of triangles arranged in bands or meandering patterns. Humanlike figures are usually geometricized and shown in profile. They are represented in groups, depicted dancing or sometimes carrying large objects (Fig. 17).

16. Tricolor Dual-Spouted Vessel: Female Genitalia

15. Tricolor Dual-Spouted Jar: Lizard and Birds

17. Tricolor Double Jar: Human Figures Bearing a Rectangular Object

18. Black-On-Red Bowl: Possibly Frogs or Lizards Joined in Opposing Fashion

19. Black-On-Red Bowl: Binary Geometrics in Negative and Positive Design

The bird is the most common realistic form depicted in the graphic art (Figs. 14, 15). Not uncommon are footed bowls that have been slightly modified to represent the form of a bird.

Another ware found in the Tonosí area is a type called Ciruelo black-on-red. Ciruelo black-on-red appears to be limited to one form: plain, round-bottomed bowls.

The designs on Ciruelo black-on-red are always found drawn in black and placed against the red slip of the interior bowl (Figs. 18, 19). Designs are effected using curvilinear and rectilinear geometrics, arranged in a complementary or oppositional dualistic manner (Figs. 18, 19). Life-forms such as birds, frogs, and lizards sometimes form the main element in the composition. The artistic intent in rendering such forms, however, is not the species itself. The artists often stress the underlying dualism and complementarity in the composition.

Also found in the Tonosí area during this period is a ceramic ware called Zahina Polychrome, excavated and identified by Ichon (1980:207). We are restricting the classification of Zahina Polychrome primarily to the black-and-white-on-red wares we feel constitute a cohesive style, as we have defined the term.

Ichon applies the term *Zahina Polychrome* to many wares that fall outside our more restricted definition for this style. The forms are generally bowls or jars with designs on the interior of bowls or on the outside of jars and on the lip of the vessel. A few figurines are known in this style. The designs are effected using a black-and-white-on-red scheme. The primary coloration of the design is executed in black, with a fine outline in white. The jars and vases are clearly related in form and decoration to the classic Tonosí Style (Fig. 22). The differences lie in the distinct Zahina color scheme and motifs found on the interior of bowls, which include star-form patterns, standing humanlike hieratic figures, and birds with wings outstretched (Fig. 22*a*).

A question of interest regarding the Tonosí painted-pottery styles is its origins. Did this style develop in situ in Panamá, or does it reflect new ideas and peoples entering the Central Region? Ichon (1980:197–99) initially felt that it reflected an incursion into Panamá of new peoples with new wares and ideas. Cooke (1972, 1976a, 1984a) feels that these wares reflect developments within Panamá itself and that the Tonosí Style polychromes were used as luxury wares by an elite within the Central Region (ibid.,1984a:288–91).

Tonosí Style pottery is found in the southern portion of the province of Coclé about A.D. 300–400. It occurs in the Tonosí Valley and on the Gulf of

20. Bichrome Bowl Decorated with a Composite Bird Form

21. Bichrome Bowl Decorated with a Lizard/Frog

22. Tricolor Double Jar: Shamanic Birds

22a. Tricolor Bowl: Bird with Wings Outstretched

Montijo between A.D. 200 and 500. We can infer from this that Tonosí Style polychromes were fairly widely distributed within the Central Region.

There is sufficient stylistic evidence to demonstrate that the Tonosí Style is not a radical departure from the Aristide Style, which includes three complementary types that share design elements (Girón, Cocobó, and Escotá), but rather that Tonosí reflects a possible evolution and elaboration of Aristide, applied in three colors with significant iconographic additions and a clearer demarcation of the design layout. Nonetheless, we should not preclude the possibility that between 500 B.C. and A.D. 400 new ideas may have been circulating in the Central Region of Panamá. The dissemination of ideas and even technologies do not necessitate migrations and diffusion of actual peoples. Certainly metallurgical technology entered Panamá from the outside (about A.D. 300–400), most likely from Colombia. It was adapted in large measure, however, to an already established Panamanian symbolic and iconographic inventory. The existing data would seem to indicate that metallurgy entered Panamá independent of any large migration of peoples. The same seems to be true of the new ceramic decorative styles that emerged between 500 B.C. and A.D. 400.

The Montijo Transitional Style A.D. 500–600

The Late Tonosí Style (Ichon's Montevideo Style) came to an end sometime around A.D. 500. It was replaced in certain areas by a new style that appears to be transitional and an antecedent to the true Conte Style. We have chosen to call this new style Montijo Transitional, after the Gulf of Montijo, as it appears to be found in abundance in and around Río de Jesús and northward. It was found at Sitio Conte in Grave 32 and referred to as foreign style B by Lothrop. The paste, some of the vessel forms, and design layouts are all distinct from true Conte Style. Many of the design elements and design motifs, however, are ancestral to those of Conte. It is possible that Montijo Transitional Style reflects a local style that developed in Veraguas and stylistically influenced the somewhat later true Conte Style found at Sitio Conte and over wide areas of the Central Region.

Typical forms are shouldered jars with short-to-moderate necks and slightly flaring rims, large slightly flattened, globular jars, and dual-spouted jars. The designs on the shouldered jars are distributed circumferentially along the shoulder of the vessel. Commonly there is a band above the main design (Figs. 23, 24, 25). Some have an additional circumferential band below the design (Fig. 26). The design yields distinct bilateral (Fig. 26), trilateral (Fig. 27), or quadrilateral (Fig. 24) patterns when viewed from above. Common motifs are encircling serpents, dragons, crocodilians, and mythic or cosmological creatures incorporating spirals in their bodies (Figs. 27, 26).

With Montijo Transitional, we see the introduction of certain elements that are to become elaborated and characteristic of the succeeding Conte Style: the outlining of designs in black (Figs. 23, 24, 26), the use of the color blue (Figs. 28, 29), the use of rectilinear geometric filler elements placed and articulated within the curvilinear contours of the bodies of certain life-forms (Figs. 57, 28), the emergence of the saurian as a key iconographic motif, and the use of the ϒC-scroll element (Fig. 57).

Certain of these traits, such as outlining designs in black, are evident in rudimentary form even in the Tonosí Style but become greatly elaborated in Montijo Transitional. The thin, parallel-line meanders of the Tonosí Style are avoided in Montijo in favor of wider, more uniform and spatially balanced linear expression. This evinces a more evolved, artistic mastery of the integration of line and form in effecting total composition. Also absent are hallmarks of the Tonosí Style: free-floating, parallel-lined, rectangular panels and concentric ovoids.

The Central Region A.D. 600–800

By A.D. 600 the entire Pacific lowland area of Central Panamá was marked by strong similarities in subsistence, art, and other attributes of culture. The archaeological evidence indicates relatively dense populations with well-established regional trade and communications networks. The record also reveals marked increases in the concentration of wealth, evidenced by impressive quantities of luxury goods accompanying elite burials.

There has been much speculation in the scholarly literature concerning the significance of the archaeological record. Most of the debate has centered around questions of rank, hierarchy, wealth, and power, and the form these elements assumed in Central Panamá from A.D. 600 to the Spanish Conquest.

New World cultures and civilizations evolved cultural values quite distinct from those of Europe and other parts of the Old World. In parts of Colombia, for example, gold was valued for its religio-esoteric significance. Among some groups in Panamá the iconography of the gold was what made it valuable. In societies where personal identity is subordinated to that of clan or other social unit, one must question the very meaning of a term like *chieftain*.

23. Tricolor Globular Jar: Serpent and Shelled Nautilus

24. Tricolor Jar Decorated with a Bilateral Serpent

25. Tricolor Jar with Sky Dragon Motif

27. Tricolor Globular Jar: Trilateral Spiral Design

26. Tricolor Globular Jar Decorated with Mythic Animal

Who, in such societies, is accorded status and on what basis? With respect to the cultures of A.D. 600–800, what can be noted is that certain individuals were accorded special burials, characterized by impressive quantities of grave offerings in the form of polychrome ceramics, hammered and cast goldwork, tumbaga, textiles, carved ivory, bone, stone, and a host of other goods. Were these individuals great chiefs, priests, or shamans?

The catalyst for all the debates was Sitio Conte, a site of impressive burials on the Río Grande, in the province of Coclé. Excavations at Sitio Conte were begun in 1931 under the direction of Samuel K. Lothrop of Harvard's Peabody Museum. Additional large-scale excavations were later conducted in 1940 by the University of Pennsylvania under the direction of J. Alden Mason.

The excavations uncovered a number of elite burials in which individuals had apparently been sacrificed to accompany the central figure to the grave. The main occupants of such graves were often bedecked from head to foot with gold apparel and jewelry, including helmets, breastplates, armguards, and other items. The graves also contained enormous quantities of polychrome ceramics and other luxury goods in addition to tools and weapons. Mason (1942:105) noted that some of the men buried at Sitio Conte were almost six feet tall. Such graves are

CENTRAL PANAMÁ: A CERAMIC ART HISTORY

28. Polychrome Dual-Spouted Figural Jar in the Form of a Bird

29a. Polychrome Shallow Bowl: Mythic Shamanic Creature

29. Polychrome Dual-Spouted Figural Jar in the Form of a Bird

29b. Shallow Polychrome Bowl: Composite Shamanic Creature Blending Saurian, Serpent, and Sawfish Characteristics

in stark contrast to the modest tombs of commoners, who were buried with ceramic vessels and little else.

Although Lothrop believed that Sitio Conte and the province of Coclé were the source of production and distribution for similar polychrome ceramics found at the site and all over the Central Region, this is no longer tenable. Researchers (Cooke, Linares et al.) have long argued, on the basis of empirical evidence, that these luxury goods were produced not only in Coclé but also in Veraguas and in provinces in the Azuero Peninsula. Distinct but related wares such as Joaquín Polychrome were being made as far south as the Tonosí Valley.

The Conte Style

The polychromes of the Central Region represent a veritable explosion of artistic creativity and virtuosity. Binary opposition and complementarity became a

GUARDIANS OF THE LIFE STREAM

30. Ring-Based Polychrome Bowl: Mythic Shaman Figure

hallmark of the new Conte Style, named after the famous site of that name. The blue color that was introduced in Montijo Transitional and possibly earlier, but used only sparingly, becomes a primary color and is predominantly employed as a contrast to red. The outlining of motifs with black also becomes standardized and characteristic of Conte designs.

Conte Style designs were applied to a large number of pottery forms, including ring-based shallow bowls or plates, flaring bowls, rectangular trays, spouted jars, dual-spouted jars, figural jars, and carafes. Among the more common forms is the ring-based shallow bowl. There are a number of different subtypes utilizing this form. A popular type is characterized by a red underside with the primary design placed on the inside of the bowl against a white ground (Figs. 30, 31, 32, 33, 34). The designs on this subtype are usually life-forms of a mythic, shamanic, or cosmological nature. They are not intended to represent specific species. Even in those cases where one can discern specific genera, such as a bird or crab, exaggeration of organs, added attributes, and other characteristics inform us that these are not ordinary members of such groups but rather icons used to impart knowledge relevant to the esotericism and beliefs of the artist's group.

Mary Helms, in her paper "Cosmological Chromatics: Color-Related Symbolism in the Ceramic Art of Ancient Panama" (1993:209–52), drew attention to several outstanding characteristics of Conte Style polychromes: the quality of serpentness in the formation of the bodies of life-forms; the possible use of the V element, Y element, or YC-scroll element as a kenning signifying the essence of serpentness; and the possible association of color symbolism with indigenous concepts of energy. We feel that the significance of the Y element lies not only in its association with the serpent as an icon signifying life but in the Indian's perception that the vital force is inherently dualistic, that is it is composed of male and female aspects. The fork in the Y element appears to be a reference to this underlying dualism.

We have long argued (Labbé, 1982, 1986, 1988, 1992) that the serpent was often used in precolumbian art over wide areas of Mesoamerica— and Central and South America—as an icon depicting the concept of vital force, essentially binary in nature, expressing both a "male" and a "female" aspect.

31. Tricolor Ring-Based Bowl: Composite Animal

32. Ring-Based Polychrome Bowl: Running Bird

33. Composite Creature: Animal - Human - Serpent

34. Ring-Based Bowl: Composite Creature Incorporating Human and Bird Characteristics

Underlying the use of the serpent as an icon for the life force is the belief that this energy is the animating principle in all life-forms, regardless of their external characteristics. "The serpent form is a primal vertebrate (and invertebrate) life-form, similar to the oral-intestinal tract of most animals, similar to the spinal cord, to the vegetal sprout, the vine, or the meandering branches of a tree. The serpent, as an essentially undifferentiated life-form, was the icon par excellence, used to represent the life force itself. With the inclusion of other iconographic characteristics, the serpent became a powerful instrument...of symbolic imagery, always connoting life and movement (a primary attribute of life), while also assuming other varied and sundry forms and guises." (ibid., 1982:8)

Helms echoes a similar observation: "Returning to serpent-like Y-elements or V-elements ...this mode of depiction or of design formation seems to associate animal forms with an inherent quality of serpentness, suggesting that creatures of all sorts...are basically or essentially composed of serpentness...ubiquitous in the dynamic fluidity of the basic physical form of many living things." (1993:229)

Neotropical groups dichotomize the qualities, forms, and other tangible characteristics of the world and cosmos into essentially male or female aspects. The YC- or Y-scroll pattern, as noted above, seems to have been used to imply a union of both male and female principles in any one form, a concept suggested by the bifurcation, or fork, in the Y. This unit is often used in purely geometric configurations to illustrate combinations of binary oppositions, as well as binary complementarities (Table B, *c-d*).

In Table B, detail *c*, the artist has created the design utilizing the Y scroll as a dominant design element in the composition. Note how two of the scrolls face inward, interfacing each other, while the lower two scrolls, forming the terminal points of the composition, face in opposition to each other. Note also that the composition is unified on a linear level. It is rendered as one continuous, unbroken line drawing. That the Y scroll is used to connote a life-sustaining vital force is implied by the use of this element in abstracting animal forms (Table B, *d*). In such compositions, the scroll itself is replaced by the head of an animal. The animal head often combines

CENTRAL PANAMÁ: A CERAMIC ART HISTORY

35. Polychrome Ring-Based Plate: Birds and Saurians

36. Ring-Based Tricolor Plate: Shamanic Transformation Theme

traits or characteristics found in a number of distinct species. In Table B, detail *d,* the head is characterized by antlers, a crocodilian-like mouth filled with teeth, and a birdlike head emanating from the eye. The composition thus combines water-, land-, and air-dwelling species in its conceptualization. The intent is not to denote a specific species, but rather to communicate something significant concerning the indigenous perception of the nature of life itself.

The Y element and YC-scroll element appear to be prehispanic Panamanian geometric renderings of ideas shared with other native groups to the north as well as to the south. In Aztec cosmology the life force is said to result from the union of two separate streams: the Cosmic Male principle called Ometecuhtli and the Cosmic Female principle called Omecihuatl. Their union results in the breath of life, Ehecatl (Lord of the Wind), an aspect of Quetzalcoatl (the Feathered Serpent-Precious Twin), who represents the embodiment of the Cosmic Male and Female principles. It is interesting to note that Ehecatl's emblem is the spiral, which represents manifestation, movement, the unfolding of life. Looked at in the light of Aztec cosmology, the fork in the YC scroll would represent the two streams of energy emanating from the Cosmic Male and Female

37. Polychrome Plate: Solar Motif with Four Saurian Panels

37a. Polychrome Shallow Bowl: Saurian-Headed Creatures at the Four Directions

principles. The scroll would represent the manifestation of their union as the life force. This simple geometric configuration appears to incorporate within itself some of the highest formulations of precolumbian thought. The early dates associated with this design element in Panamá would make it contemporary with the later phases of Teotihuacan Culture in México where Quetzalcoatl in his guise as Feathered Serpent was a preeminent icon.

Certain Conte Style design elements and motifs presage characteristics that become greatly elaborated in subsequent styles, such as Macaracas (c. A.D. 800–1000). Emanations from the bodies of fantastic creatures (Figs. 35, 36) and motifs such as the shaman-fish and the combative saurian (Fig. 37) become stock icons in later periods.

The pedestal-based bowl, commonly called *frutera*, which becomes a dominant vessel form during Macaracas, has its Conte Style antecedents. Similar but distinct vessels are found in the Tonosí Valley and rendered in a substyle called Joaquín Polychrome, a locally produced variant.

The pigments used to decorate Conte Style ceramics were obtained from inorganic substances—black from manganese; red, brown, and blue-violet from ochres, hydrated oxides of iron (Linares, 1977).

The Macaracas Style (A.D. 800–1000)

When Lothrop first excavated Sitio Conte, he divided the graves into early and late period burials. Lacking radiocarbon dating, he mistakenly estimated the age of the site to be significantly later in age than it actually was. Today it is known that the earliest tombs date from around A.D. 400–500 while the latest tombs date circa A.D. 700–900 and contain polychromes in the Macaracas Style. Sometime between A.D. 900 and 1100, the site was abandoned as a cemetery but continued to be occupied as a place of residence up to the Spanish Conquest.

Life continued much the same as it had previously, with minor modifications. Sites such as La Cañaza in the Tonosí Valley, Sitio Conte, Sitio Sierra, El Caño, and many others continued to be occupied. Sites such as Natá, El Hatillo, and Miraflores became significant centers of Central Panamanian culture. Burial practices remained essentially the same, except that in addition to primary and extended burials, urn burials in artificial mounds became more common.

The transition from the Conte Style (A.D. 600–800) to the Macaracas Style (A.D. 800–1000) is not always clear. The artistic dynamics that control the Macaracas Style, however, are evident. The relatively rare saurian of Conte Style matures and evolves into a

38. Polychrome Pedestaled Bowl: Standing Figure Emitting Stingray Spines

predominant iconographic motif, represented in a variety of poses, perspectives, and interactions. Particularly popular are the frontal (Fig. 38) and profile (Fig. 39) renditions of the anthropomorphic saurians. Macaracas places more emphasis on complementary and oppositional representations of figures. Paired representations (Figs. 40, 41, 42) are depicted facing or running in opposite directions, above or below each other, or are placed on opposite sides of a vessel. The compositions of Figures 41 and 42 contain a mediating panel of polychromatic zigzag elements. The associations of these design elements with lightning and fertility is firm for the geometric symbol tradition of the American Southwest and is strongly implied for many other groups over wide areas of the Americas. The concept behind the symbolism is that fertility and dynamism result from the interaction of male and female principles. Note

39. Polychrome Pedestaled Bowl: Shaman in Combat

41. Polychrome Pedestaled Bowl: Running Saurians

40. Polychrome Pedestaled Plate: Double Saurian with Serpentine Body

42. Polychrome Pedestaled Bowl: Birds

43. Polychrome Pedestaled Bowl: Stingray-Tailed Iguanas

that in Figure 41 the complementarity of the figures is indicated by positioning the saurians in opposite directions, while in Figure 42 the birds are color coded in complementary fashion. One bird has a red body with blue wings, while the other has a blue body with red wings. In Figure 43 two iguanids are juxtaposed yin-yang fashion. Their bodies are marked with a Y scroll terminating in a claw element. This evinces another trait characteristic of Macaracas: the abstracting of unique qualities of figures, particularly saurian figures, to suggest the whole, or perhaps a part as potential manifestation of the whole. The most common abstractions are claws and the heads of saurians or birds (Fig. 44).

Certain iconographic elements, such as stingray spines and animal emanations from the bodies of figures, are commonly used in association with saurians and other shamanic imagery (Fig. 38). Stingray spines were found in caches and as grave offerings at Sitio Conte. Although they have been interpreted by some as having been used as spearheads, we should not exclude other possible interpretations. Stingray spines were used in the Maya region and other parts of Mesoamerica as instruments of bloodletting in autrosacrificial rites involving the perforation of the penis or other bodily parts. Its associations are with the act of penetration and subsequent pain. In Panamá, they are found as an iconographic design element as early as the Conte Style. In the context of Macaracas Style art, the spines seem to emerge from every pore of the central figure's body. This may be an allusion to the penetrating power of a shaman's energy. In the symbolism of the northwest Amazon Desana Indians, the concept of penetration is closely related to shamanic manifestations of power and energy, particularly fertilizing energies. The shaman is said to project such power and penetrate into the inner being of people, sometimes to diagnose the cause of illness, sometimes to impregnate them with his power.

The Desana recognize a high grade of priestly shaman, which they call *kumú*. "...the kumú is a luminous personage who has an interior light, a brilliant flame that shines....The manifestation of this luminous energy is the penetrating glance." (G. Reichel-Dolmatoff, 1971:137) They explain the

CENTRAL PANAMÁ:
A CERAMIC ART HISTORY

44. Ring-Based Polychrome Jar with Neck and Flaring Rim: Transformed Shaman in Ritual Pose

45. Polychrome Carinated Jar: Standing Saurians

effects of this shamanic penetration as similar to the charge received from an electric eel or the shock felt when one strikes one's elbow against a hard object.

A hallmark of Macaracas compositions is the emphasis on motion and dynamism. The shamanic life-forms, in particular, are seen running, moving, emanating, pursuing, transforming. They are full of power, energy, and motility, and reference the dynamic nature of the shamanic universe.

As noted by Cooke (1985), Macaracas ceramics are generally better made than Conte vessels and the designs are more refined and sophisticated in their execution. Nonetheless, Conte often rivals Macaracas in terms of pure visual appeal. The primary colors are red, black, and blue/purple on cream-colored ground. Blue/purple is sparingly used, as compared with its use in Conte Style ceramics.

The pedestaled bowl or plate was a popular vessel form in Macaracas Style. Other forms included pedestaled jars, carafes, globular jars, carinated jars, large ollas, and figural jars, although the latter are less common than in previous periods. Gone or extremely rare are the double-spouted vessels of the Conte Style.

The carinated jar form (Fig. 123) anticipates similar carinated jars of the next period in Parita Style. The Parita Style forms, however, often incorporate a turtle's head and legs at the point of carination. The Macaracas form of this vessel also uses the saurian as a decorative motif (Figs. 45, 123), while saurians do not seem to have been used in the mature Parita Style, at least in the public and private collections examined by the writer.

A.D. 1000–1300

Life continued as usual. The basic pattern of subsistence had now been long established and was firmly rooted in Panamanian soil. Urn and mound burials continued to gain in frequency, as compared to other burial practices. By A.D. 1100 Sitio Conte seems to have been abandoned altogether, except perhaps for a few scattered households. The sites of El Hatillo and Natá maintained their significance throughout this period.

The Parita Style

The polychrome pottery of A.D. 1000–1300 in some respects continued a restricted repertoire of Macaracas vessel forms, motifs, and color schemes. When it was first studied, researchers (Ladd, 1964) had difficulty distinguishing Macaracas Style polychrome potsherds from those in the Parita Style. Ladd initially felt that the new wares were restricted to the province of Herrera, a point of view that has since been disproven. Additionally, the new pottery was felt to be contemporary with pottery that has now been shown to belong to the subsequent El Hatillo Style (A.D. 1300–1520).

An examination of Parita Style polychromes shows that it is distinct in many significant ways from Macaracas. The dynamic Macaracas saurian motif is supplanted by the hammerhead shark (Fig. 46), a life-form that was given expression in the previous period. Carinated jars incorporating a geometric circle-cross-X-pattern layout on the shoulder become more common. A stylized turtle is also incorporated along the carination in plastic or graphic design (Fig. 47).

A new vessel form (Fig. 48) makes its appearance. This vessel reflects a modification of the earlier pedestaled jar, becoming a figural jar in the form of a stingray. The stingray spine is always graphically emphasized in these compositions, so that there can be little doubt that the spine is an element of great iconographic importance. With Parita, graphic realism yields to a clear preference for abstraction and rectilinear and curvilinear geometrics. Figures 49 and 50 may be used to illustrate our point. In Figure 49 we are already confronted with the tendency toward abstraction. Note that the bird forms are highly stylized and abstract. By the time we get to the four abstract patterns on the shoulder of Figure 50, we cannot be sure what the geometric form suggests, although they are probably birds, judging from other intermediary depictions.

The pedestal bowl or plate form, which gained prominence in the Macaracas Style, is continued in Parita, but often in a proportionately taller, sleeker form. We have already seen that blue/purple paint was conservatively used in Macaracas. During A.D. 1000–1300 it was being used so sparingly that it is often unnoticed. Sometime during this period, or perhaps in the next, it is abandoned altogether. The reasons for this are unknown. As Cooke (1985:38) has suggested, the mineral source for this pigment may have dried up. On the other hand, it may have

46. Polychrome Pedestaled Bowl: Fish

47. Polychrome Carinated Jar in the Form of a Stylized Turtle

48. Tricolor Pedestaled Jar in the Form of a Stingray

49. Polychrome Pedestaled Bowl: Stylized Abstract Birds

50. Tricolor Carinated Jar with Solar Motif

been abandoned for conceptual reasons. Certainly far less emphasis is placed on dimorphic complementarity in the Parita Style than in Macaracas, where it looms almost obsessively. If gender-based dimorphic representation was no longer an esoteric artistic concern, then there would be no need to color balance the forms. This, of course, would raise intriguing questions with respect to the ideology of this period.

Parita designs are skillfully executed. The layouts are well balanced, the vessels competently made. It is intriguing to speculate why styles change from one period to the next. What impells a society to eschew certain motifs in favor of others, to move from realism to abstraction or from the baroque to more austere compositions? We will reserve our speculations, however, until we have examined the entire chronological range of polychromes from the Central Region.

A.D. 1300–1520

The culture of A.D. 1300–1500 is essentially that encountered by the Spanish conquistadors of the early sixteenth century. Much of what we know about this period has come down to us in the form of fragmentary, limited observations made by early Spanish chroniclers, conquistadors, explorers, and priests. Most of these observations are cursory, ethnocentric, and confusing. Nonetheless, when examined as a whole, against what we now know from archaeological and ethnographic research, a clearer picture of social and political organization emerges for this period than for any other. Social and political realities, however, take place against specific environmental backdrops.

Panamá is a long, narrow isthmus, stretching 470 miles from the Panamanian–Costa Rican border in the west to the Panamanian-Colombian border in the east. The widest point is a north-south line from the Caribbean coast, in the province of Colón in the north, to the tip of the Azuero Peninsula in the south. Even here, however, the land is scarcely more than 120 miles wide. For most of its length, the country is less than 70 miles wide, and at the canal it is only 40 miles in width. If one includes offshore islands, Panamá covers about 31,500 square miles, an area roughly the size of the state of Maine in New England.

The interior of the country is shaped by central mountain ranges, essentially volcanic in origin. The highest peaks (c. 11,000 feet) are found in the western region. In the Central Region, most of the mountains are modest in height. An exception is Cerro Cambutal (6,000 feet), a prominent feature of the southwest Azuero Peninsula. The highest elevation in the eastern region is Cerro Tacarcuna (6,150 feet), located near the Panamanian-Colombian border.

Panamá's varied topography is cut by numerous rivers and rivulets, most of which are modest in volume and extent, flowing north to the Atlantic and south to the Pacific from the central mountain ranges. In the Azuero Peninsula many rivers run east to west to the Gulf of Montijo, or west to east to the Gulf of Parita. Of the largest rivers of Panamá, only the Río Chagres drains to the Atlantic.

Climate and habitat not only vary from coast to coast but also change as one moves from the coast to the interior and as one progresses from lower to higher elevations. In general, the climate of the interior highlands varies from subtropical to temperate. The Pacific lowlands receive less than half the annual rainfall of the Caribbean lowlands, although this varies considerably from place to place. For example, the eastern sector of the Azuero Peninsula can be quite arid, but as Linares (1977) has noted, a mere thirty-two miles to the west, in eastern Veraguas Province, the climate can be as wet as on the Caribbean coast or the eastern province of Darien. The climate is marked by wet and dry seasons, which heavily influence the volume of water carried by Panamá's rivers, particularly in the central and western regions.

This topographically and climatologically varied land, marked by jungles, marshlands, mountains, and grasslands was home to a wide variety of fauna and flora typical of each habitat. The rich biota included felines, such as the jaguar, ocelot, margay, puma, and jaguarundi; monkeys; anteaters; tapirs; armadillos; 115 species of snakes, including coral snakes, pitvipers, and boa constrictors; crocodilians; turtles; lizards; frogs; deer; rodents; a wide variety of birds such as gulls, pelicans, cormorants, vultures, curassows, owls, toucans, macaws, parrots and parakeets, to name but a few. The prehistoric rivers, lakes, lagoons, mangrove swamps, shores and ocean waters were teeming with numerous fish, mollusks, crustaceans and aquatic mammals. Many of these, as we have seen, held iconographic significance in the art traditions of the prehistoric cultures. In prehistoric times as today, fauna, flora, and human activity constantly impacted one another.

By the sixteenth century, the Central Region of Panamá, like other parts of the country, was divided into a number of chiefdoms. Chiefdoms were typically characterized by a narrow strip of land along the coast, extending inland to the central ranges. Some chiefdoms, however, were landlocked. This arrangement gave each chiefdom access to a variety of environmental resources. Trade among chiefdoms was nonetheless vigorous, as was warfare.

Settlements were generally dispersed, with few nucleated settlements of any significant size. The larger centers may have been the seat of a chiefly family and associated retinue. The current state of ethnohistorical research for Panamá only allows generalizations for the Central Region, based on piecing together fragmentary data obtained from various parts of the country.

Chiefs were charged with the orderly distribution of food, the protection of territorial boundaries, the settling of disputes, the overseeing of trade, and the conducting of warfare. Chiefly dwellings were generally large in comparison with those of commoners. An impressive one, belonging to Comogre, a prestigious ruler of an eastern region chiefdom, measured 450 feet by 240 feet, that is, one and one-third the length of a football field and slightly less than a football field in width! Dwellings such as this, locally referred to as *bohios*, were made of huge timber beams. Some were even reinforced with stone walls. Other buildings in the chiefly compound might include a longhouse for warriors, storage facilities, and ceremonial structures of perishable materials.

According to Spanish accounts, storehouses, as well as markets, were teeming with food—maize, sweet manioc, sweet potato, and other root crops; peanuts and other nuts; green and red chili peppers; pineapples and a host of exotic fruits; turtles, crab, and fresh and dried fish; smoked venison, peccary and ground-feeding doves; maize beer and fermented drinks made from a variety of fruits.

The paramount chief of a chiefdom might have several subordinate chiefs under his jurisdiction. The subordinate chiefs might include members of his immediate family or lineage, or perhaps chiefs he had defeated in battle. Below the chiefly ranks were individuals who had attained an elite status by virtue of prowess or bravery. Next in rank were commoners. The lowest social strata was occupied by prisoners of war. These were marked on the face with specific designs that indicated their status. Sometimes one of their teeth would be knocked out as an additional emblem of their low estate. In essence, such individuals were bonded slaves who performed menial tasks or served as tradable commodities.

A powerful paramount chief could field thousands of warriors in battle. It appears that a prime goal of any attack against an enemy was to capture the enemy chieftain's compound. Such compounds were usually well defended and included bulwarks such as stone walls and, in some areas, columns of cactus. Occasionally, compounds were even surrounded by moats. The capture of a compound usually assured victory.

It was through valor in battle that male commoners could hope to rise in rank and be accorded privileges. Special recognition and status was also conferred on those who excelled in art or craft. Sixteenth-century Panamanian society had many different kinds of artisan specialists: potters, goldsmiths, weavers, knappers, net makers, crafters of weapons, pearl divers, healers, herbalists, diviners, dancers, singers, and feather workers, to name but a few.

Art was used in every dimension of life for magic, healing, body ornamentation, to decorate chiefly compounds and other buildings, to embellish items of dress, or to create objects of beauty for funerary purposes.

A paramount chief's special attire might include a diadem of gold and feathers, golden breastplates, armbands, wristlets, and anklets, in addition to other jewelry and finery in a variety of mediums. Paramount chiefs could have many wives, preferably women of rank. Only one wife, however, held full status, which conferred inheritance rights to her offspring. It was not unusual for high chiefs to take wives for the purpose of securing or maintaining political alliances.

The designs painted or tattooed on the bodies of chiefs were indicative of their status and power. When the son of a chief assumed power, he could either choose his own unique design or continue that of his father. The continuance of the father's design acknowledged the father's preeminence and dignity.

Travel in ancient Panamá was by foot or canoe. Chieftains were borne in litters by porters who were often former prisoners of war. Rivers were important arteries of transportation. Along the Pacific coast, travel was conducted in large seaworthy canoes of excellent construction.

It is tragic that so little was recorded concerning the indigenous religions. Observers only perceive what they are interested in seeing, a fact clearly evident even in our own times. The conquistadors and other early Spanish explorers were interested in wealth and power, and their recorded observations reflect these preoccupations.

The elite went to the grave with the same pomp and circumstance that they were accorded in life. Chieftains were buried in their gold and finery and were sometimes accompanied to the grave by subordinate wives and slaves, a practice that was archaeologically noted early on at sites like Sitio Conte. In parts of Panamá, the bodies of great chiefs were smoked and desiccated and hung in proper dress in special rooms in the chiefly compound, along with those of their predecessors, thereby establishing a visible line of succession that validated the power and authority of their living descendant and successor.

El Hatillo Style

The painted ceramics are different in many respects from those of previous periods. They continue the trend, observed for the Parita Style, of increased abstraction and use of geometrics in design. The designs, however, are usually sparser and less compacted. The vessel forms, though competently executed, are understated. The pedestal bowl, for example, which had great popularity and elegance in previous periods, is foreshortened and stemless (Fig. 51). The designs on these bowls are reduced in proportion to the amount of background color. The color scheme is usually red, black, and white. Often the base or lower portion of vessels are red, a custom running throughout all previous periods. Black becomes a dominant color in line drawing, although red is also used and is employed as infill. White is sometimes used as background color for black and red designs.

The relevance of binary opposition and complementarity is present, but not as evident as in previous periods. Also lacking are the bilateral, trilateral, and quadrilateral layouts. One must closely examine a motif, such as that found on Figure 51, to realize that the turtle is in large measure formed by two condorlike birds seen in profile and rendered in an abstract stylized manner. The technique used is reminiscent of that observed in early Ciruelo black-on-red wares (c. A.D. 100–400).

The juxtaposing of motifs is present, but it is done in a manner that cannot be traced to earlier styles. The crocodilian form of Figure 52, for example, has a stylized frog painted on its back, which can only be seen when the vessel is viewed from above.

El Hatillo Style undoubtedly evolved out of the Parita Style but discontinued many Parita Style vessel forms and motifs, stylistically moving into a starker,

51. Tricolor Footed Bowl: Turtle Motif

CENTRAL PANAMÁ: A CERAMIC ART HISTORY

52. Tricolor Vessel in the Form of a Crocodilian

53. Tricolor Figural Vessel
in the Form of a Horned Owl

more austere direction. We must caution, however, that our assessment of El Hatillo Style is conditioned by the relatively small number of specimens in this style recorded in the literature or noted in the public and private collections examined by the author. Ceramics in El Hatillo Style are apparently abundant at A.D. 1300–1520 period sites, many of which still await controlled, scientific excavation (Cooke, personal communication, 1994).

At Chitra, a site in the Veraguas foothills, about fifty miles from the coast, El Hatillo Style ceramics have been associated with a C-14 date of around A.D. 1650, which is later than previously thought for this style.

TABLE OF CHRONOLOGICAL PERIODS*

Period:		
I	**Paleoindian**	c.9000 B.C.
II	**Early Preceramic**	9000–5000 B.C.
III	**Late Preceramic**	5000–3000 B.C.
IVA	**Early Ceramic A**	3000–900 B.C.
	Monagrillo	3000–1100 B.C.
IVB	**Early Ceramic A**	3000–900 B.C.
	Sarigua/Guacamayo	1100–900 B.C.
VA	**Middle Ceramic A**	900–500 B.C.
	Bichrome and Trichrome Painting Introduced	
VB	**Middle Ceramic B**	500–100 B.C.
	La Mula Polychrome	
VC	**Middle Ceramic C**	100 B.C.–A.D. 300
	Aristide - Early Forms and Decorations	
VD	**Middle Ceramic D**	A.D. 300–500
	Tonosí	
VE	**Middle Ceramic E**	A.D. 500–600
	Montevideo, Cubitá	
VIA	**Late Ceramic A**	A.D. 600–800
	Conte	
VIB	**Late Ceramic B**	A.D. 800–1000
	Macaracas	
VIC	**Late Ceramic C**	A.D. 1000–1300
	Parita	
VID	**Late Ceramic D**	A.D. 1300–Spanish Conquest
	El Hatillo	
VIE	**Late Ceramic E**	Post Conquest

* After Ilean Isaza's, "Desarrollo estilístico de la cerámica Pintada del Panamá central con énfasis en el Período 500 A.C.–500 D.C." Master's thesis, Departamento de Arqueología, Universidad Autónoma de Guadalajara, 1994.

Note: There is still some uncertainty as to the chronological parameters of La Mula and Aristide. Cooke (personal communication 1994) feels that La Mula may date c. 100 B.C.–100 A.D. and that early Aristide types such as Girón, Escotá, and Cocobó likely date to A.D. 100–300. Cooke would also place Tonosí between A.D. 200 and 400. Isaza's Montevideo is our Late Tonosí. Our Montijo Transitional falls within Middle Ceramic E.

CHAPTER III

63. Polychrome Vessel with Deer's Head

CHAPTER III

THE CENTRAL REGION
Changes through Time:
An Art Historical Overview

The graphic art found on Central Region painted ceramics displays a cultural continuity extending from about 900 B.C. to the Spanish Conquest. It is a tradition, moreover, that is clearly marked by the expression of distinct shamanic themes, a point that will be explored in succeeding chapters, along with other thematic and symbolic interpretations. The focus on shamanic imagery is strongest in the Tonosí, Conte, and Macaracas styles. It is somewhat less evident in the intermediate style we are calling Montijo Transitional, and even less evident in the Parita and El Hatillo styles.

The diagnostic design elements for the Tonosí Style (Table 1, *a-f;* pg. 63) are rectilinear parallel-lined panels, concentric ovoids, hourglass-shaped elements, crosses, line ticking, and parallel-line meanders, the latter of which are often used as stylized serpents. It is possible, but by no means certain, that the rectilinear parallel-lined panels and concentric ovoids may be early abstract rectilinear and curvilinear geometric versions of the vulva motif found in Tonosí and Conte art. This seems to be inferred by the manner in which the female genitalia is indicated on the Tonosí Style hieratic personages (Figs. 12, 54), the manner in which it is rendered on the back of Conte and Macaracas crabs (Fig. 55), and contemporary neotropical ethnographic references to these configurations as vulvas.

In the subsequent Conte Style, the parallel-lined rectangular panels are dropped as free-floating

54. Polychrome Jar with Standing Hieratic Figure

55. Ring-Based Polychrome Bowl with Crab Motif

56. Polychrome Pedestaled Bowl: Shaman-In-Combat Theme

57. Polychrome Ring-Based Jar Decorated with Fantastic Creatures

elements, and rectilinear and curvilinear concentric ovoids are retained but usually restricted to the back of crabs and other crustaceans or distinctly used to indicate genitalia on figural vessels.

The hourglass-shaped element is usually found on the abdomen of hieratic, mythic, or anthropomorphic shaman effigies (Figs. 12, 54), or is used as a filler element. This design element is likely a reference to the union of male and female principles. In most Amerindian traditions the shaman is perceived as an intermediary. He unites sky and earth and balances cosmic forces. He is the guardian of fertility. The hourglass element unites two triangles, joined at the apices. In the geometric-symbol traditions of groups ranging from the American Southwest through the Amazon, the downward-pointing triangle represents the male, while the upward-pointing triangle represents the female. The union of the two implies fertility. In the Central Region of Panamá, in later stylistic periods, it is replaced by other binary, conjoined design elements (Table 3,*i,l,n,o,p;* pg. 65) that, interestingly, are also used to decorate the abdomen of anthropomorphic shaman effigies (Figs. 30, 56, 106). These elements seem to denote and connote the shaman's ability to mediate the biosphere and promote life. Naturally, such design elements may also have held additional meaning and significance, which is still to be uncovered by future research.

The simple cross element can have a different meaning and significance depending on its context. In the art of the Tonosí Style, it appears to have been used most often to represent a star (Fig. 13). This design element is used profusely in the Montijo Transitional Style in similar stellar contexts (Fig. 25), but it is not apparent as a star symbol thereafter in Central Region ceramic art. The use of the cross as a star symbol had wide distribution in the Americas, and the rationale behind its use is discussed in later chapters.

Line ticking—that is, the bordering of lines with dots, characteristic of both the Aristide and Tonosí styles—is retained as an artistic convention throughout the late Tonosí, Montijo Transitional, and Conte styles, but it is not characteristic thereafter.

The dominant figural motifs of the Tonosí Style are birds, long-legged birds with curved beaks, along with frogs, lizards, long-tailed lizards, mythic beings, theriomorphic and anthropomorphic constellations, and anthropomorphic hieratic figures. The long-legged bird motif is usually found in association with either the anthropomorphic long-tailed hieratic personage (Table 1,*i*; Figs. 12, 54) or the long-tailed lizard. In both cases, the long-legged birds are enveloped by loops in the tail of each figure. Other elements, such as concentric ovoids, are also often enveloped by these loops. The exact significance of this remains undetermined.

Tonosí Style design layouts are overwhelmingly bilateral. The designs are often restricted within panels that subdivide circumferential decorative bands (Fig. 13).

On the other hand, the Montijo Transitional Style emphasizes mythic animal forms, often in association with cross elements. This appears to be a reference to certain constellations. The bodies of these theriomorphic constellations are often serpentine and sinuous. Montijo Transitional motifs are quite different from those of Tonosí, as are many of the vessel forms. Both Tonosí and Montijo Transitional share the dual-spouted figural jar forms. Both

GUARDIANS OF THE LIFE STREAM

58. Polychrome Pedestaled Bowl: Standing Saurian Shaman-In-Combat Theme

prefer jar forms with relatively short necks. Montijo Transitional designs, however, are usually restricted to the shoulders or upper surface of the jar, while Tonosí designs often cover much of the vessel.

Montijo Transitional introduced or popularized certain characteristics that became common in later styles such as Conte and Macaracas. In Montijo Transitional the mouths of mythic animals, for example, are typically rendered as long snouts filled with rows of menacing teeth. The saurian is also apparently introduced for the first time (Fig. 57), but it nonetheless does not become a dominant motif until the Macaracas Style. Montijo Transitional also popularizes the use of filler elements, which tend to be sweeping free forms characterized by sharp-pointed edges (Table 1, *j–m*). The use and placement of filler elements are more akin to Conte and Macaracas than to any previous period or subsequent styles. The Montijo Transitional sharp-edged filler elements are likely the precursors of the Conte YC scroll (Table B, *2–4*, pg. 62). The Montijo Transitional elements, in turn, are modifications of a conceptually related Tonosí design element (Table B, *1*).

59. Polychrome Pedestaled Bowl: Mythic Creature

60. Mythic Shamanic Creature

The Conte Style retains the large concentric eye form (Table 1,*dd*) introduced in Tonosí, further elaborates and modifies the saurian figures that appeared in Montijo Transitional, and introduces a prolific repertoire of new design motifs. Table 2, detail *b* (Pg. 64), is probably the best candidate for precursor to the anthropomorphic saurian-in-profile figures that loom large in Macaracas Style art (Figs. 39,58). Note the anthropomorphic form in profile, the long snout filled with menacing teeth, the clawed appendages, and the double YC-scroll emblem at the chest. All of these are characteristic of the Macaracas saurian. Note the YC scroll attached to the snout or the emanations extending from the head of figure *k* in Table 2. terminating in bird heads. These are the prototypes of the animal emanations seen on the shamanic figures in Macaracas art (Table 4,*a, e, f;* pg. 65).

Clawed appendages, as opposed to the less dramatic paws seen in Tonosí art, are a prominent attribute of Conte shamanic animals and anthropomorphic figures. This continues up to the Parita Style. There are many variants of Conte Style claws (Table 1,*s,aa*).

The sinuous, serpentine, shamanic, or mythic creatures seen in Tonosí art (Fig. 13) are somewhat modified in Conte and found primarily on the interior of plates or shallow bowls. In Tonosí and Montijo Transitional art, they are invariably found on the exterior of various jar forms.

Conte artists tried various ways to impart a sense of motion and dynamism to their compositions. Early Tonosí Style compositions, although competently drawn, are generally rather static renderings. Progress was made in breaking through such limitations in the drawing of black-line, anthropomorphic stick figures (Fig. 17) that portray dance or forward movement in profile. In later Tonosí art, kinetic qualities are enhanced by angling the feet (Fig. 13). Montijo Transitional perfected the general trend begun in Tonosí: The feet are not only angled, they are given greater flexibility and articulation. Moreover, the torsos of the figures are also freed somewhat (Table 1,*o, p, q*). These developments were continued in Conte art (Table 2,*e,f*).

A trait characteristic of the Conte Style is the banding and segmenting of appendages such as arms,

61. Polychrome Pedestaled Bowl Decorated with a Scorpion

62. Polychrome Pedestaled Bowl: Shamanic Bats

legs, and tails (Table 2,*e, f, l*). This trait seems to have continued into early Macaracas, but it is not evident in other styles, where, if used, it is employed sparingly.

Figure 37 is transitional between the Conte Style and the more evolved Macaracas Style. The saurian head is clearly recognizable as the Macaracas saurian in profile, but it is drawn in a Conte Style manner. The figure's claws are the type seen in Table 1,*z* detail. The eye and head type are like those of Conte shamanic birdmen (Table 2,*d–f*). Only the snout is more Macaracas-like than Conte. The motif on Figure 86 is another case in point. The segmented body, claws, spurs, and YC-scroll elements are all typically Conte. The coral banding of the rim and the crowding of the design field, however, are hallmarks of the Macaracas Style. Examples such as these allow us to trace the evolution of Conte into Macaracas by comparing design elements and motifs componentially. The approach is viable for all periods and styles.

There is a clear transition from Conte to Macaracas. The differences, however, are noteworthy. Macaracas artists had full control over their mediums. Macaracas designs are fluid and dynamic, qualities captured by the brush stroke independent of any iconographic devices used in previous styles. Macaracas elevates the saurian head to a preeminent status. Relatively rare in Conte art, it becomes the overriding logo of Macaracas art. It may be attached to either an anthropomorphic or zoomorphic body or depicted disembodied.

The Conte habit of abstracting body parts, such as claws and heads, continues in Macaracas. In Conte such abstractions are usually connected to a YC-scroll element and rendered in black, although in later Conte disembodied saurian heads are sometimes polychrome. In Macaracas, the YC element is often highly stylized and difficult to discern. The scroll is often rectangular rather than circular.

The preferred Macaracas bird form is a burly, long-beaked bird with thick legs (Table 3,*u*). The most common fish looks somewhat like a hammerhead shark with large penetrating eyes (Table 3,*x*). This motif gains added prominence in the Parita Style.

Macaracas continues many Conte Style design elements while restricting or modifying some, such as the wedge-shaped Conte element (Table 3:*a*), and defining and emphasizing others, such as the large concentric eye form. Macaracas abdomen designs(Table 3,*l,p*) are very similar to those found in Conte art (Table 3,*f–i*). The Conte designs are ultimately linked to Tonosí prototypes (Table 1,*a*; Table B,*1*). Somewhat into the middle of its development, Macaracas graphic art becomes characterized by increasingly thinner, more refined lines, as compositions become more compact and baroque.

In the southern portion of the Azuero Peninsula, a substyle called Joaquín Polychrome overlaps both the Conte and Macaracas stylistic periods. Many of the designs and motifs appear to be crude mimics of the Conte Style. The earlier forms are bowls and jars. Trilateral and bilateral design layouts are common on the interior of the bowls. Birds, bats, and crabs are typical motifs. Later, Joaquín designs become more refined and better executed. A pedestal has been added to the basic bowl form to create the Joaquín version of the *frutera*.

A motif unique to Joaquín art is a scorpion incorporating a realistic vulva motif on its back (Fig. 61). This is reminiscent of the geometric vulva motifs seen on the backs of Conte and early Macaracas crabs. Popular motifs are mythic beasts, characterized by long serpentine bodies with legs (Fig. 59). Joaquín compositions are often imbued with a vibrancy imparted by complementary sets of matched curvilinear lines, which create a sense of radiating energy. The majority of designs with this quality are painted on the inner surface of the *fruteras*, or pedestaled bowls, the artist deftly using the natural contours of the bowl to enhance the effect (Fig. 61).

The finest Joaquín Polychromes are attractive in their own right and occasionally achieve a high degree of aesthetic impact equal to that which the finest Conte or Macaracas compositions solicit from an observer. The relationship among Joaquín, Conte, and Macaracas is still ill defined and difficult to discern, given the dearth of good absolute dates for the earliest Joaquín. At this point in time, it would appear that Joaquín was a provincial, local expression of the more widely distributed Conte or Macaracas styles, taking inspiration from them with respect to certain vessel forms and decorative motifs, while

62a. Polychrome Pedestaled Plate: Birds

applying these to particular local needs. Interestingly, although Joaquín is found in the southern region of the Azuero Peninsula, there is little either in terms of vessel forms, design elements, motifs, or compositions that links it to the previous Tonosí Style, which flourished in the same general area.

If Macaracas can be characterized as a style increasingly dedicated to baroque compositions, the subsequent Parita Style is a distinct movement away from such trends. Early Parita Style compositions continue the Macaracas penchant for refinement in the execution of line, but increasingly reduce the proportion of design to vessel surface. More significantly, the execution of the motifs becomes more abstract. Notably absent are the saurian-headed figures of Macaracas. Instead, Parita emphasizes certain fish forms (Fig. 46) and bird forms (Fig. 49). The latter become so abstract that they are indiscernible, unless one traces their evolution through time (Table 5,*j–n*; pg. 66).

Early Parita vessels are nonetheless clearly derived from Macaracas, but they reflect a more limited repertoire of motifs. Progressively over time, the coherency of certain motifs dissolves, as if the Parita artists were no longer clear about the meaning and original intent of some of their compositions (compare Table 5,*o* with Table 5,*p*).

Parita vessels are characterized by excellence in manufacture. The vessel walls are generally thinner than those of Macaracas and are characteristically well balanced and elegant. The carinated jar incorporating a turtle, conceptionally traceable to certain Conte prototypes, becomes relatively common in Parita. As explained in subsequent chapters, these vessels appear to be artistic models of the shamanic universe, in which the shoulder represents the Upper World, the carination and turtle the Middle World, and the bottom of the vessel the Lower World. The basic design layout seen on the shoulders of such vessels (the circle-cross-X pattern) is of great antiquity in the Americas and can be traced at least to the Conte Style (A.D. 600–800) within the Central Region of Panamá. As will be demonstrated in later chapters, this pattern is closely associated with the sun and its movement along the horizon.

Also characteristic of the Parita Style are vessel lugs in the form of small frogs. These are usually placed on the shoulder of jars in pairs, or singly on opposite sides of the vessel. As with other depictions of life-forms in Parita Style, they are sometimes so abstract as to be unrecognizable except by comparing a series of intermediate transitional forms, tracing them back to realistic renderings.

Early Parita color schemes differ from Macaracas in the paucity of purple used and in the increased importance of black in line drawing. In Macaracas, red and blue/purple were used to emphasize and accentuate both opposition and complementarity in design. Color coding is absent in Parita and motifs are generally not outlined. Given the importance of color coding in Conte and Macaracas, its absence in Parita is culturally significant.

Overall, Parita seems to be the beginning of a general trend toward deemphasizing shamanic themes in the graphic art of the Central Region. Whether this reflects a comparable diminution of shamanic influence in everyday culture cannot be determined at this time. A related question that remains unanswered is why the saurian, so closely associated with shamanic imagery in earlier styles, particularly in Macaracas, should be absent in Parita art. Parita does not reflect an evolution of Macaracas Style art as much as a revolution against it.

If later Parita art reflects a radical departure away from Macaracas, El Hatillo Style, which replaced it, shows little affinity to either Parita or Macaracas. We must caution that El Hatillo is at present still relatively scant in either scientifically excavated collections or unprovenienced public and private collections. The existing examples, however, reflect a ceramic technology and graphic art tradition by and large somewhat inferior in many respects to either Parita or Macaracas. Vessel walls are thicker and often coarser than Parita, while the graphic decoration is largely geometric and less dynamic. The compositions are adequately drawn but artistically more subdued, lacking some of the vitality of earlier compositions. The art leaves the investigator with the impression that the strong shamanic stamp characteristic of earlier styles has become but a faint whimper. With El Hatillo we no longer confront the visual reflections of a powerful inner vision. El Hatillo motifs are safe, almost saccharin. They fail to shake us at the core. The artistic gulf that separates Macaracas from El Hatillo raises intriguing questions, questions that cannot be answered for the moment.

In chapters 2 and 3 we have looked at the art of the Central Region chronologically and componentially. In the suceeding chapters we will examine the cultural backdrop that was the source of inspiration for this tradition.

64. Figural Vessel Incorporating a Bird

Table A
Design configuration of some dual-spouted vessels as seen from above, illustrating the vulva symbolism associated with this vessel form. Table A detail *1*, is also Figure 16; Table A detail *2*, is an unpublished, fluted Conte Style vessel; Table A detail *3*, is also Figure 115, a Conte Style figural vessel in the form of a bird.

Table B
Illustrated evolution of the YC scroll.
  Table B detail *1*- Tonosí Style design element found on the abdomen or chest of mythic and hieratic figures. The element appears to be the precursor of the YC scroll. Like the YC scroll, it is not only found on the abdomen of figures but is also used as a filler element.
  Table B, *2*: The Tonosí design element in Table B, detail 1 becomes the later Montijo Transitional element of Table B, detail *2*, which evolves into the element in Table B, detail *3*, a clear prototype of the fully evolved YC scroll found in Conte Style graphics.
  Table B, *a* : The YC-scroll design element.
  Table B, *b* : The YC-scroll design element repeated in a continuous uppercase, lowercase design band.
  Table B, *c* : Conte Style geometric composition based on stylized YC-scroll design elements.
  Table B, *d* : Conte Style composition illustrating the association of the YC scroll to life forms, in this case the head of a shamanic composite animal.
  Table B, *e*: Conte Style composition illustrating YC scrolls terminating in Table 1, detail *u*-type claw elements.
  Table B, *f* : Conte Style saurian motif incorporating modified YC-scroll elements in the mouth, at the eye, and as filler elements.

Table 1
Table 1, details *a–f*: Tonosí Style Design Elements
  a the hourglass element
  b the concentric ovoid or lozenge-shaped element
  c the rectangular parallel-lined panel element
  d the cross-shaped element
  e element illustrating line ticking
  f the parallel-lined meander and parallel-lined alternating chevrons, which seem to have evolved from serpentine prototypes
Table 1, details *g–i*: Tonosí Style Design Motifs
  g mythic figure
  h long-legged, long-beaked bird
  i standing hieratic figure with hourglass design elements on chest and abdomen and long tails enveloping long-legged birds
Table 1, details *j–n:* Montijo Transitional Style Design Filler Elements
Table 1, details *o–r:* Montijo Transitional Style Design Motifs
  o shamanic crocodilian or saurian
  p mythic or shamanic frog
  q mythic animal possibly representing a constellation
  r mythic serpent probably representing the Milky Way
Table 1, details *s–aa*: Conte Style Claw Element Variants
Table 1, details *bb–ff*: Conte Style Eye Element Variants
Table 1, details *gg–ii*: Conte Style Wing Element Variants

THE CENTRAL REGION CHANGES THROUGH TIME

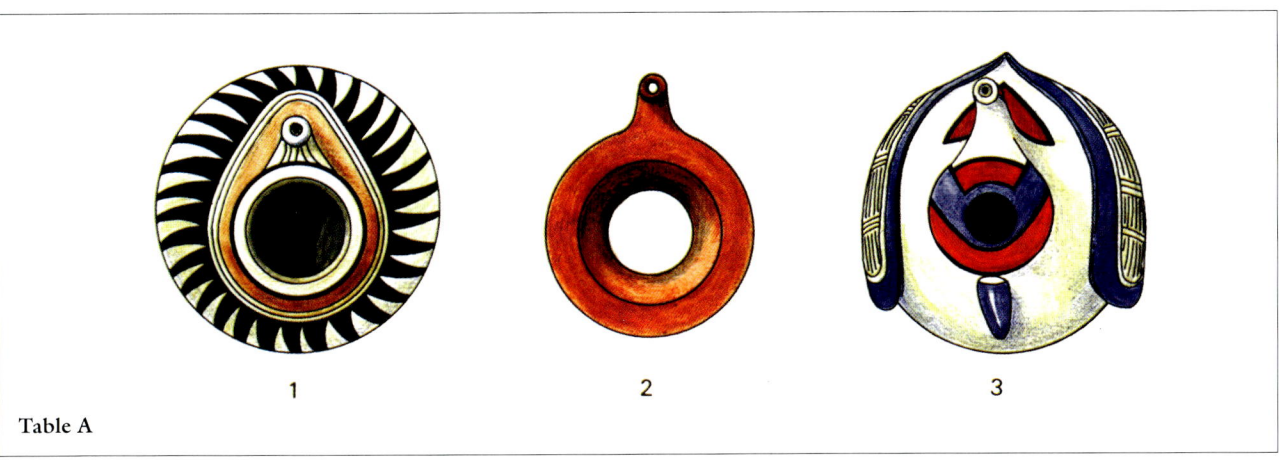

Table A

Table 2
Table 2, details *a–o:* Conte Style Design Motifs
- *a* hieratic or shamanic figure
- *b* anthropomorphic saurian shamanic figure
- *c* anthropomorphic shaman with regalia, probably a Panamanian version of the shaman as "the germinator"
- *d* shamanic bird-man
- *e–f* shamanic bird-man with serpentine tail
- *g* composite shamanic animal incorporating deer antlers, saurian mouth, and bird-shaped body with Table 1, detail *gg* type wing element.
- *h* composite shamanic animal incorporating saurian mouth and bird-shaped body with Table 1, detail *hh* type wing element.
- *i* shamanic bird
- *j* shamanic bird-man
- *k* shamanic creature with animal emanations (*tingunas*)
- *l* composite shamanic creature incorporating insect wings, segmented centipede-like body, human face, claws, and emanations from the head
- *m* crab motif incorporating the diamond-shaped vulva symbol on its back and the "vagina dentata" as its mouth
- *n* crab motif incorporating the "vagina dentata" as its mouth
- *o* crab motif with vulva connotations

Table 3
Table 3, details *a–e:* Conte Style Design Elements
- *a* wedge-shaped element
- *b* body-segmenting element;
- *d* diamond-shaped element connoting vulva
- *e* "vagina dentata" element

Table 3, details *f–i:* Conte Style Chest and Abdomen Designs
- *f–h* chest or abdomen designs based on the YC scroll

Table 3, details *j–k:* Macaracas Style Design Elements
- *j* stingray spine element
- *k* zigzag element with fertility and vital-force significance

Table 3, details *l–p:* Macaracas Style Chest and Abdomen Designs
Table 3, details *q–y:* Macaracas Style Design Motifs
- *q* running saurian
- *r* running saurian
- *s* fish-faced saurian with saurian and bird emanations
- *t* saurian head with abstracted body
- *u* shamanic bird with bulky body
- *v* shamanic humming bird; *w* shamanic iguana with "embryo" visible. "Embryo" consists of YC scroll terminating in type Table 1, detail *u*-type claw elements.;
- *x* shamanic fish with saurian/bird heads as eyes
- *y* embryonic saurian

Table 4
Table 4, details *a–c:* Macaracas Style Shamanic Transformation Frontal-Facing Figures
- *a* figure with saurian emanations (*tingunas*)
- *b* figure with saurian/bird-headed emanations (*tingunas*) and winglike arms
- *c* figure with stingray spines emanating from the head, winglike arms, and legs terminating in saurians

Table 4, details *d–f* Macaracas Style Anthropomorphic Saurian Figures Illustrating the Shaman-in-Combat Theme

Table 5
Table 5, details *a–e:* Parita Style Design Elements
Table 5, details *f–i:* Parita Style Design Motifs
- *f* stylized stingray
- *g* shamanic fish
- *h* abstract circle-cross motif
- *i* realistic circle-cross motif

Table 5, details *j–n:* Parita Style Bird Forms Illustrating the Progressive Transformation of Stylized Bird Forms (*j–k*) to Highly Abstract Forms (*l–n*)

Table 5, details *o–p* Comparison of Macaracas Style Bilateral Fish Face Motif (*o*) with a Parita Style Variant of the Same Motif (*p*)

Table 6
Table 6, details *a–d*: El Hatillo Style Design Elements
Table 6, details *e–f*: El Hatillo Style Design Motifs
- *e* frog
- *f* turtle incorporating two birds in profile

a

b

c

d

e

f

1

2

3

4

Table B

THE CENTRAL REGION
CHANGES THROUGH TIME

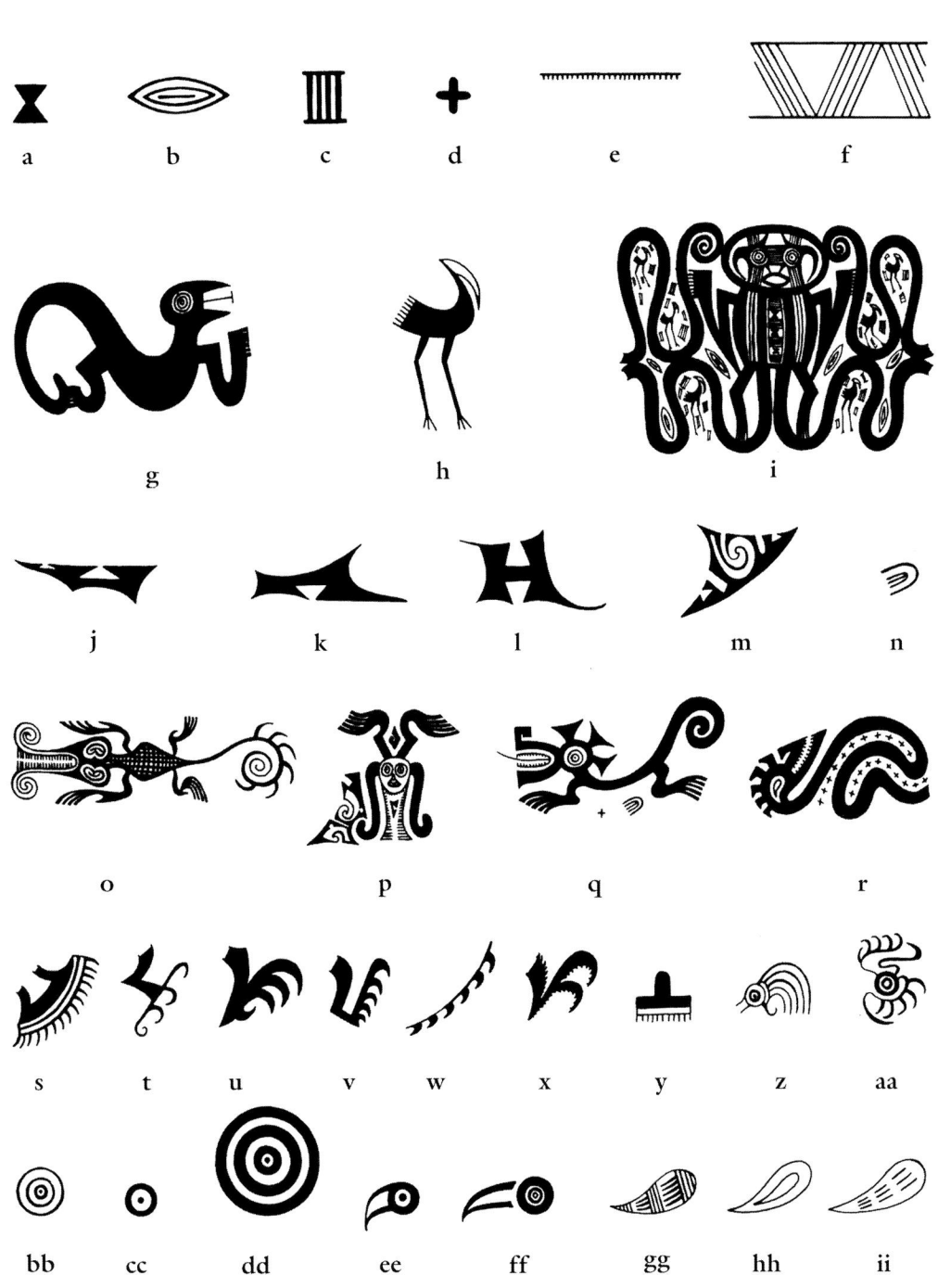

Table 1

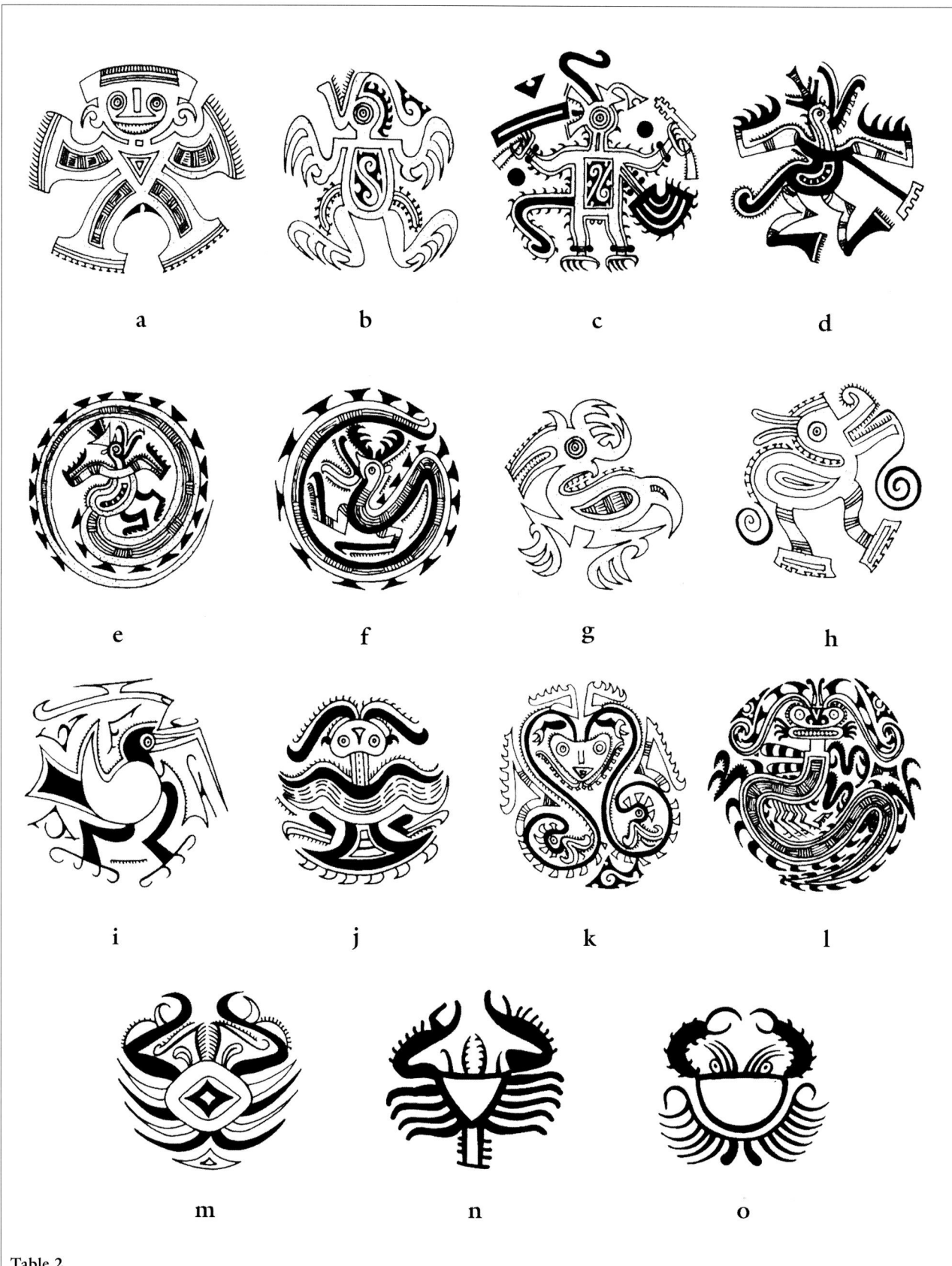

Table 2

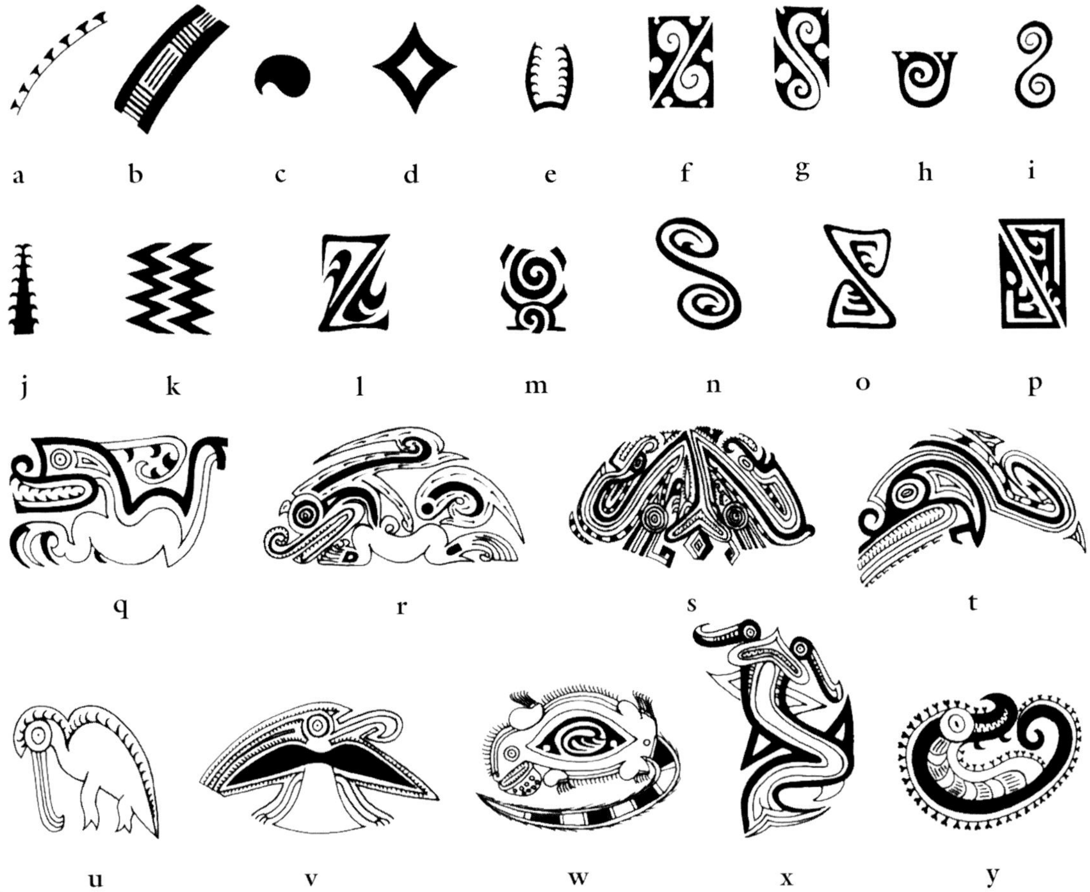

THE CENTRAL REGION
CHANGES THROUGH TIME

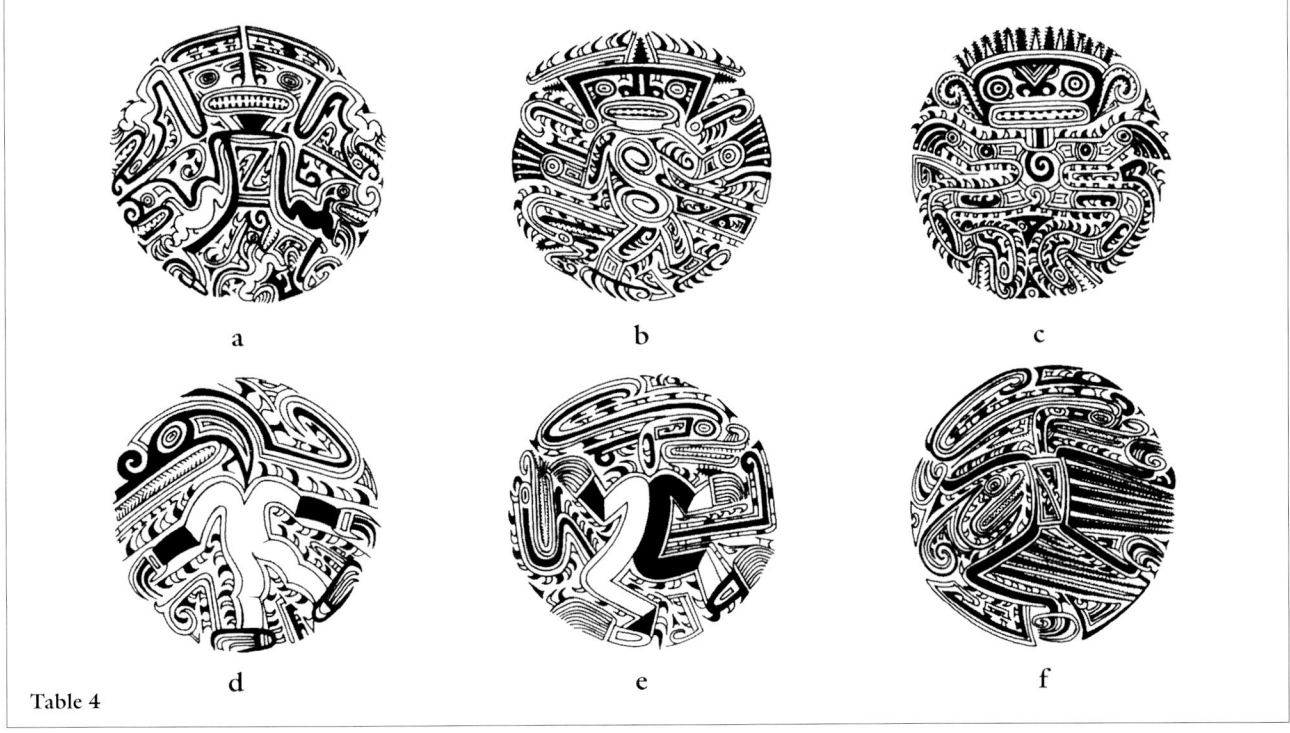

Table 3

Table 4

Table 5

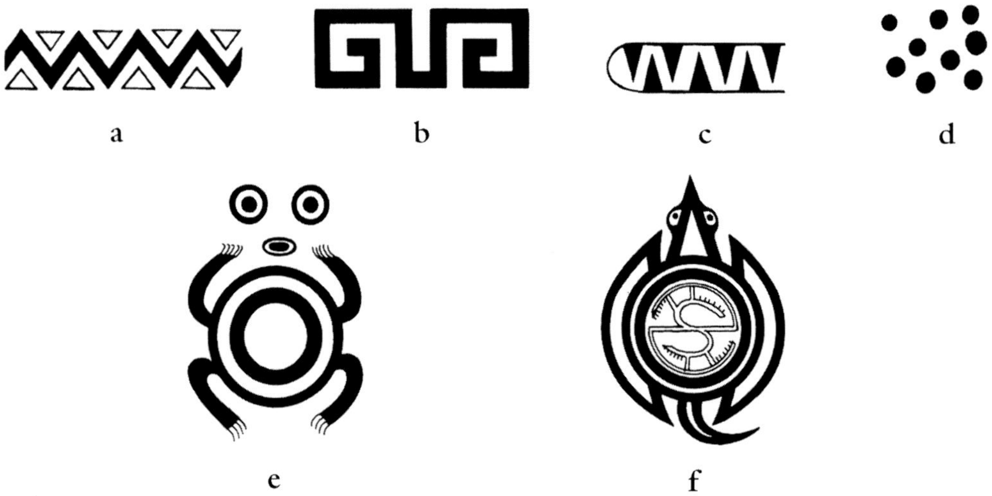

Table 6

CHAPTER IV

73. Tricolor Ring-Based Bowl: Mythic Figure

NEOTROPICAL AND NEW WORLD SHAMANISM

Although shamanic traditions differ from culture to culture with respect to particulars of ritual or manner in which knowledge and information are encoded, there remains a surprisingly consistent body of culturally shared perspectives.

Viewed globally, there seems to be greater similarity in shamanic traditions found within the same latitudes than with those equally distant longitudinally. Arctic shamanism, for example, is more consistent in attributes when viewed internally than it is with traditions found in tropical latitudes, regardless of their longitudinal location. This may reflect more of a necessity to respond in similar form to similar environmental challenges than the effect of diffusion per se, although diffusion undoubtedly plays a role within territorially contiguous regions.

Common to shamanic traditions everywhere is the perception that shamans have personal characteristics not shared by ordinary members of the group. The shaman is an intermediary between the visible and invisible realms of existence. The world perceived by the normal senses and their instruments of extension is believed to be but one of many coexisting and mutually dependent interactive realities. Each of these contains its own denizens, which may include numerous categories of spirits, gods, or disembodied human beings. Shamans are believed capable of interacting with some or many of the entities that populate other realms of existence. The shaman enjoins them to intercede on his behalf or that of his client or community. Most societies characterized by shamanism distinguish good shamans from bad shamans, those in service to their community from those who are self-possessed and self-serving—although the shaman's services may simply be for hire.

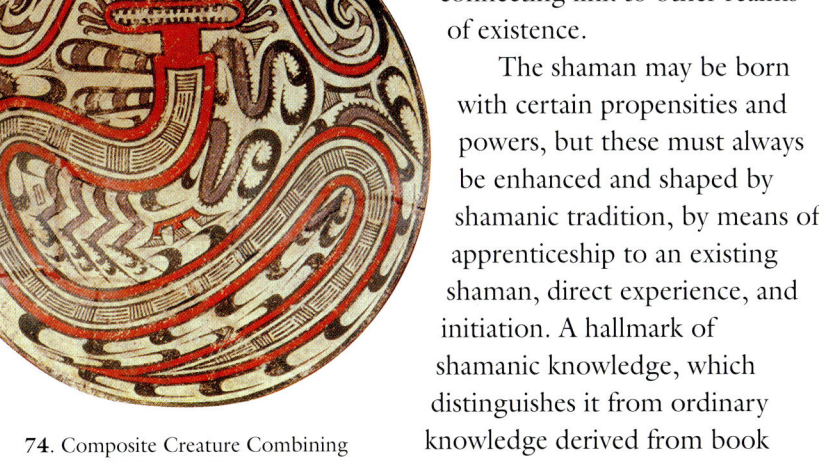

74. Composite Creature Combining Insect and Serpent Characteristics

The shaman may be the local healer, priest, psychologist, astronomer, chieftain, or psychopump, but regardless of role played, the shaman is first and foremost an intermediary, a connecting link to other realms of existence.

The shaman may be born with certain propensities and powers, but these must always be enhanced and shaped by shamanic tradition, by means of apprenticeship to an existing shaman, direct experience, and initiation. A hallmark of shamanic knowledge, which distinguishes it from ordinary knowledge derived from book learning, school, or other simple forms of mentation, is that it is acquired and confirmed by direct experience.

Shamanic experience usually begins by mapping and mastering the properties of the immediate, tangible, physical environment, acquiring an in-depth knowledge of physiographic features, plants, insects, animals, climate, and interrelationships among the above. Shamans are often keen empiricists with acute powers of observation.

The spirit realms, however, are the shaman's true domain. Mastery of the physical world is always keyed to gaining access to the other realms of existence.

GUARDIANS OF THE LIFE STREAM

75. Polychrome Ring-Based Bowl: Serpent-Feline Creatures

76. Polychrome Plate: Bats with Outstretched Wings

Every object, form, or creature found within the physical world is but a point of contact to the other realms. The portal to the "beyond," however, is the human psyche, which can be coerced and manipulated by training, exercise, diet, ritual, and other means into releasing its fixation and grip on the world of normal sensory perception to peer into and access other realities.

Also common to many traditions is the belief that the shaman can move about in one or more of his spirit forms and even shape shift—that is, alter the size and appearance of the spirit form. Unfortunately, the term *spirit* does not adequately translate the indigenous meaning. This shall be addressed later in our discussions.

Art plays a pivotal role in shamanism. Shamanic art is cultural power used to define and manipulate the shamanic cosmos. It reflects shamanic perspectives, points of reference, values, and beliefs, as these are encoded in line, form, symbol, motif, composition, myth, and cosmology.

One of the extraordinary legacies of Panamá's precolumbian past is its art, particularly its metal and ceramic art, which is rich in form and graphic imagery. If it can be demonstrated that the ethnographic present is a reflection of the archaeological past, then it should be possible to use the present to illuminate the past.

The general shamanic characteristics delineated above are also true with regard to neotropical and New World shamanism. New World shamanic traditions, however, have undergone their own internal evolution and development within the Americas. For the purposes of this study, we will consider the extant precolumbian shamanic traditions of the neotropical regions of northern South America, the upper Amazon, and lower Central America that provide particular significance to understanding ancient Panamá. Neighboring traditions, such as those of Mesoamerica and the Andean regions of South America, are also relevant, but only in specific contexts.

Neotropical shamanic traditions are typified by the use of a wide variety of psychotropic plants and other substances possessing mind-altering properties. One of the most widespread of the mind-and mood-altering plants was tobacco (*Nicotiana tabacum L.*), the effect of which varies according to the dosage used and the manner in which it is combined with other plants. Even taken by itself, tobacco can have a wide range of effects. It may act as a depressant, tranquilizer, stimulant, or hallucinogen depending on the variety or dosage taken (Emboden, 1979:35).

Tobacco was used in many different shamanic contexts, including divination, trance induction, purification rites, and healing rituals. Over much of the neotropical area, it was used in combination with ritual songs or power chants. In parts of northern South America, tobacco is ritually employed by groups such as the Warao of Venezuela in the form of large rolled cigars. Depictions of cigar-smoking ritualists are to be found in precolumbian art, including the art of the ancient Maya, and as far north as the Casas Grandes Culture of the northern Mexican state of Chihuahua, where the most common depictions are figural jars in the form of a seated male smoking a cigar. The backside of these figures is often in the form of a stylized frog, mouth wide open, looking skyward, presumably to call for rain. Naturally, it is impossible to confirm that these are depictions of *Nicotiana* cigars and not some other plant. It is known, however, that both *Nicotiana tabacum* and *Nicotiana rustica* were used by the Aztecs of México (Emboden, 1979:39). Dobkin de Ríos (1994:626), referencing Cooper (1984:49), records that tobacco was smoked by shamans in cigar form from the Caribbean islands down to Tierra del Fuego.

The ethnographic data on the use of any mind-altering substances in lower Central America is sketchy at best and extremely poor for Panamá in particular. Tobacco use, however, seems to have been widespread in the region and, as Cooke (1992b:186) has noted, tobacco smoking may have dominated Kuna shamanic practices. The Kuna, who inhabit the Archipelago de San Blás and adjacent lands on the mainland, are perhaps the best documented of Panamá's surviving indigenous peoples.

Another widespread mind-altering plant of the neotropics is *Banisteriopsis caapi*, known under a variety of indigenous names. The most common of these are *ayahuasca*, *yajé*, and *caapi*. *Ayahuasca* is the name most commonly used in the Peruvian Amazon, where it is also a favorite plant of mestizo *curanderos*,

77. Polychrome Ring-Based Bowl: Dancing Composite Figure

78. Tricolor Ring-Based Plate: Possibly a Swordfish

GUARDIANS OF THE LIFE STREAM

79. Polychrome Ring-Based Plate with Scorpion or Crab at the Center

81. Ring-Based Bowl: Fantastic Creatures with Tendrils Emanating from Their Mouths

80. Tricolor Ring-Based Bowl with Handprint at Center

82. Polychrome Ring-Based Plate: Shamanic Creature with Crab-Like Creatures

known as *ayahuasqueros*. *Yajé* is the favored term in the Colombian northwest Amazon. G. Reichel-Dolmatoff (1960:130–32) reported the use of this plant for both the Waunáan and Emberá in Colombia, both of whom are also found in the Darien region of Panamá. Its use is documented for indigenous groups in Perú, Ecuador, Brasil, and Colombia, and, by inference, in the adjacent parts of eastern Panamá.

Ayahuasca is a vine, a liana possessing powerful mind-altering chemicals. It is ingested in a number of ways, varying by group and region. The most common means of ingestion is as a brewed beverage, often containing a number of other plants that work synergistically. In parts of the northwest Amazon, it is sometimes taken as a snuff. Luna (1991:13), working in the Peruvian Amazon among mestizo healers whose practices are in large measure derived from Indian shamans of the Upper Amazon, reports the importance placed on special diets prior to taking *ayahuasca*. Diet and other practices are used to purify the body in preparation for the mind-altering experience.

Ayahuasca is used to attain visions, determine the cause and source of illness, contact spirit helpers, and, among some groups, to acquire and learn power songs used in healing and other shamanic enterprises. Not uncommonly, individuals have claimed to fly about in their spirit body, while under the influence of *ayahuasca*. This experience is akin to the theme known as shamanic flight, recorded not only in the ethnohistories and ethnographies but also seemingly depicted in the precolumbian art of Perú, Colombia, and Panamá.

Another plant, *Datura stramonium,* was used by groups in the eastern United States as part of initiation rites for young males coming of age. Similar rites were performed by groups in the western United States using *Datura inoxia*, a species also used in México. The use of datura for male puberty rites was probably widespread in precolumbian times. Some groups in the northwest Amazon until recently gave anal infusions of datura to boys during puberty ceremonies, using clysters to administer the drug (Emboden, 1979:118). In the forested regions of northern South America, *Datura candida* was used. In Colombia, it is recorded in use for the Paez shamans of the Tierradentro district for the early historic period (G. Reichel-Dolmatoff, 1975:54). In the Vaupes region of Colombia, it was employed as an additive to *yajé* (ibid. 40).

Roe (1982:125) reports the use of datura among the Shipibo, where it is associated with evil shamans who make a substance called *toé*. *Toé* is used to attain ecstatic states comprising fantastic dreams and visions. To make *toé*, small quantities of juice are squeezed from the stem of datura and placed in a small gourd. G. Reichel-Dolmatoff (1960:130–32) also reported the use of datura among the Waunáan and Emberá Indians of Colombia. As previously noted, both groups are also found in the eastern regions of Panamá bordering Colombia. Pharmacologically speaking, datura produces hallucinogenic and hypnotic effects.

One of the most widespread narcotic snuffs of the forested regions of Colombia, Venezuela, and Brasil was derived from the bean pods of a shrub or tree belonging to the species *Anadenanthera peregrina*.

Commonly called *yopo, vilva,* or *cahoba* by various groups, it was prepared in a variety of ways, one of which was to roast the seeds of the tree, grind them into powder, then snuff the powder using bird bones or other devices. It was used to create euphoric states, ward off hunger and fatigue, and create visionary effects, including the ability to see the world inverted (Emboden, 1979:110). G. Reichel-Dolmatoff (1975:9–47) has noted the use of *Anadenanthera peregrina* not only for groups in the tropical lowlands of South America and the Caribbean in antiquity but also for such highland groups in Colombia as the Muisca and others, including the Pijao of the upper Magdalena river.

In other parts of the Americas, a host of other hallucinogenic or mind-altering substances were used, among them the mescaline-bearing San Pedro Cactus (*Trichocereus pachanoi*) used in shamanic rituals from precolumbian times to today throughout the central Andes and coastal regions of Perú; the psilocybin-bearing mushroom (*Psylocybe sp.*) used in México, Central America, and Colombia.; amides of lysergic acid borne by the seeds of *Ribea corymbosa* and used by the Aztecs and by contemporary groups in Oaxaca, México. According to Reichel-Dolmatoff (1988:25), *Ipomea violacea*, a related species, is also used in Colombia. The mescaline-bearing peyote cactus (*Lophophora williamsii*) was used from precolumbian times to the present in western and northern México. Its use has spread in relatively recent historic times from groups such as the Huichol, Cora, and Tarahumara Indians of México northward across the southwestern United States and even into Canada.

Psychotropic plants are used to activate and enhance the power of the shaman, to allow the individual to go beyond the world of normal perception, and—through visions, dreams, or other means—establish communication with spirit beings who are believed capable of becoming teachers and/or allies. It is during these altered states that the shaman acquires the power to divine the nature of disease or illness, see into the future, travel in his spirit body, shape shift, and assume the characteristics of certain animals (such as the jaguar), or acquire the power songs that will enable him to effect cures, gain

83. Polychrome Dual-Spouted Figural Jar in the Form of a Standing Female Feline

84. Polychrome Dual-Spouted Figural Vessel in Form of a Feline

control over plants or animals, or even alter the weather.

According to Chaumeil (1983:33; Luna, 1991:13) the Yagua of the upper Amazon believe that the ingestion of psychotropic plants establishes contact with the spirits of the plants and serves as "the only path to knowledge." Among the Shipibo of Perú psychotropic plants are categorized as "shaman-makers" (Gebhart-Sayer, 1986:203; Luna, 991:13). Roe (1982:116) notes the belief among the Shipibo that archaeological potsherds sometimes are contaminated by residual energies from the souls of the deceased or even by spirits dwelling within the earth. Such potsherds can sometimes cause illness, especially to young children. "Shamans can attempt to cure such afflicted children by communicating directly, through the consumption of ayahuasca (rishi) a powerful hallucinogen, with the spirits of the ancestors embodied in the quënquësh (sherd)" (ibid.).

Considering the importance placed on mind-altering plants by a large number of neotropical Indians, the evidence for Panamá is somewhat paradoxical. *Banisteriopsis caapi* and datura were noted for the Waunáan and Emberá, but both groups may have migrated into Panamá within the historic period. Tobacco has been recorded for the Kuna, who have well-developed shamanic traditions and oral histories rich in lore pertaining to the exploits and powers of deceased shamans.

As we will seek to demonstrate in subsequent chapters, the precolumbian graphic art of the Central Region of Panamá is particularly rich in shamanic imagery. Why then is there an absence of references in the early Spanish chronicles, the ethnohistories, or ethnographies, to the use of powerful mind-altering substances by Panamanian groups?

The Spanish Conquest of Panamá was particularly brutal and thorough, undertaken by individuals with little interest in the customs of the indigenous peoples. Excepting Oviedo, there were no Sahaguns or Diego Duráns, as there were for Aztec México, to accurately record indigenous beliefs and customs before they were swept away by the forces of conversion and acculturation; or a Bishop Landa, who schizophrenically went about destroying the science and knowledge of the Yucatec Maya and then recorded what he could remember from all he had annihilated. By the time scientifically trained ethnographers came upon the scene in Panamá, many of the seven surviving groups—Emberá, Waunáan, Kuna, Buglé, Ngöbé, Teribe, and Bribri—had already undergone significant acculturation or had become self-protective and reluctant to discuss such matters with outsiders.

The possibility remains, however, that mind-altering substances really didn't play a significant role in Panamanian shamanism. One of Luna's Peruvian informants (1991:18) indicated that if one knew the *ícaro* (power song) of a particular plant one did not need to use the plant itself. This could certainly be the case among the Kuna, who place great emphasis on the intrinsic efficacy of power songs.

In his 1932 study of Kuna healers and diviners, Erland Nordenskiöld reported that the *néle*, a Kuna term for a certain class of diviners, was born with particular innate psychic and clairvoyant abilities. The *néle* works in tandem with a healer called an *absogédi*. The *absogédi* chants and thereby enables the spirit of the *néle* to communicate with the animal familiars or spirit helpers. If a *néle* has not been assisted by an *absogédi*, the diagnosis of the cause of an illness may turn out to be erroneous.

Néles are also believed capable of finding human spirits who have temporarily become disassociated from the body and have become "lost." It is significant that the *néle*'s powers are activated and enhanced by the power song of the *absogédi*. No mention is made of the use of a psychotropic plant for this purpose (Nordenskiöld, 1932). A powerful *néle* is said to be able to see what is occurring at a great distance from his person. He can even discern the cause of illness in an individual he hasn't seen. If a patient stands before him he can peer within his body with his penetrating vision and determine the cause of illness or loss of spirit.

One should not imagine, however, that shamans are only healers or visionaries. They also function as ritualists and officiates at ceremonies, marking significant stages in the lifeway, such as birth, puberty, marriage, and death. They are often shaman-chiefs

85. Polychrome Figural Jar in the Form of a Feline

holding great status within their group. They also sometimes act as arbiters in social disputes.

Among some groups, the shaman is the keeper of time, an astronomer who observes the movement of the sun, moon, planets, or stars. A prime function of the highest grade of shaman, however, is to assure fertility and fecundity. Among the Kogi Indians of the Sierra Nevada de Santa Marta, a class of shaman-priests, called *mamas*, refer to themselves as the guardians of fertility. In this capacity, the shaman mediates the bio-forces of the world, maintaining harmony and balance between species and between males and females, thereby assuring the replenishment of life-forms that inhabit the waters, land, and sky. In order to do this, the shaman must have a keen understanding of the nature of nature. His vision must be cosmic in perspective and pragmatic and efficacious in practice.

CHAPTER V

90. Tricolor Jar: Mythic Lizard

CHAPTER V

MAPPING AND STRUCTURING THE SHAMANIC UNIVERSE

Shamanic experience does not occur in a vacuum. It is guided by tradition. Personal experience is used to ascertain and validate culturally prescribed perceptions concerning the nature of existence. The individual's experiential observations are guided by underlying models and are consequently reclassified in accordance with the categories generated by these models. In order to understand the shaman's perceptual and conceptual world, one needs to carefully observe how knowledge and data are organized, classified, and graphically illustrated in shamanic art. This will facilitate the discerning of underlying laws and patterns, which will enable us to infer the inherent paradigms and models employed.

The shamanic universe is multilayered and multidimensional. It may be modeled on many forms, depending on culture and geographic region. It is usually characterized by three major divisions or worlds—the upper world, the middle world, and the underworld. On the exotic level, the middle world refers to the surface of the earth, while the upper world refers to the sky, including the sun, moon, and stars, as visible from the earth, or middle world. The underworld, on the exotic level, includes the depths of water, earth, and material substance. It is the region of in and down. It should be noted that sky elements metaphorically move through the upper world and descend into the underworld, rising at the eastern horizon at one time of day or year and setting at the western horizon at another time of day or year. As these movements are predictable and cyclical, they formed the basis for shamanic astronomical time reckoning.

On the esoteric level, the upper world is the dimension of beneficent spirits, supernaturals, certain deities, and higher consciousness. The middle world is the field of normal perception and ordinary consciousness, but it is also a point of focus and contact for beings and forces emanating from both the upper and lower worlds. The underworld is mainly a dimension of darkness, danger, and malevolent forces and entities.

Both the upper and lower worlds are usually stratified or layered. There may be nine, eleven, or other numbers of levels of the upper world and equal or unequal numbers of layers in the underworld. The world tree, or axis mundi, passes through the center of all worlds and serves as the connecting link and passageway through all levels. The center is the point of emergence, the point of manifestation, from the underworld to the middle world and from the upper world to the middle world.

Shamanic geometry is characterized by reference to seven points—the center, the four cardinal directions, the zenith, and the nadir. The four directions are metaphorically and actually determined by the movement of the sun and stars across the zenith and along the horizon: the sun by day and stars by night. How these are used varies from group to group, but recurring imagery and patterns are common.

The movement of the sun was often used as a sort of directional mandala to serve both practical and didactic ends. The east is the place of the rising sun, a place of emergence, manifestation, birth, morning, spring. The south is associated with growth, becoming, maturity, midday, the sun at the zenith, summer. West is associated with waning and declining energies, descent, dying, the setting sun, autumn. North is dormancy, gestation, a place of transformation, the sun at the nadir, winter. In those regions typified by a rainy and a dry season, the position of certain constellations in the heavens, and their ascent and descent at the horizon at night or seasonally, served similar functions. In many cases both models were used.

91. Carinated Jar: Bat with Animal Emanations as Wings

Aspects of the solar mandala are reflected in widely dispersed cultures within the Americas, such as the Hopi Indians of northern Arizona, the Aztecs and Mixtecs of México, and the Macusi and Warao of South America.

In contemporary Hopi myth, the sun is sometimes personified as Masau'u, who reflects the sun at the zenith as well as the sun in the underworld. In myth he plays various roles. He is the spark of life, the Lord of Fire, a comely youth. His alter ego, however, reflects other qualities. He is skeleton man, the Lord of Death and the Underworld, the consort of Huruing Wuhti.

Huruing Wuhti is the feminine complement of Masau'u. She is a personification of gravity-mass, the matrix of creation. Her name means Hard Beings Woman. She brings form into being. In myth she is said to reside at the center of all things, to draw material substance to herself and make it hard. She dwells within, in the underworld, in the place of in and down, in the west.

The relationship of Huruing Wuhti to Masau'u is mythic metaphor used to illustrate the relationship of gravity, a predominant feminine force, to energy, a male force symbolized by the sun. Masau'u as comely youth, the Lord of Fire, represents manifesting energy, the hot sun of the zenith, the sun of the south, of the mandala. Masau'u as skeleton man represents the sun descending toward the western horizon, waning in heat and strength, about to be defleshed and absorbed by Huruing Wuhti, who waits below in the west, in the underworld.

From the American Southwest to South America, however, bones symbolize semen. They represent potential new life. The belief that humans and animals can be resurrected from their bones is found in shamanic traditions over much of the world (Eliade, 1964:160–64). It is in this sense that Masau'u is the consort of Huruing Wuhti. The descent of the sun at the western horizon symbolized an act of fertilization, procreation. This imagery is found as far south as the Peruvian Amazon.

On a more profound esoteric level, the union of Masau'u and Huruing Wuhti represents the union of energy and matter. Energy, however, can be released from matter by means of friction, symbolized by intercourse. Intercourse is the friction that generates heat and gives birth to the spark of life, just as the fertilizing action of Masau'u as skeleton man ultimately gives birth to Masau'u as spark of fire, represented by the sun emerging from the womb of the earth at the eastern horizon.

The same imagery is retained in the directional mandala of the Nahuatl-speaking peoples of México. Among the Aztecs, the sun of the east was Xipe Totec, Our Lord the Flayed One, who represented the sprout breaking the "hymen" of the seed, emerging as new life. Huitzilopoctli, the mature warrior, represented the sun of the south and zenith. Quetzalcoatl, who in myth descends to the underworld to retrieve the bones of primordial man, represents the sun in the west. Mictlantecuhtli, the skeletonized Lord of the Underworld, represents the sun of the north (Labbé, 1982; 1986).

With respect to South America, Roe (1982:248) notes, "The sun rises resplendidly yellow, the bringer of light and warmth (Whitten, 1976: 44, on the Canelos Quichua). The young, vigorous, and very hot ascending sun is wrapped in a great number of new white cushmas to protect his carriers from his heat (Weiss, 1975:374, on the River Campa). He arrives at the zenith of his mature glory. Then he descends, exhausted, to the west and the mountains, where he will begin the cycle all over again, dying and entering the subaquatic underworld to light it with his feeble light and gain strength (by growing younger) for the next day (Whitten, 1976:35, on the Canelos Quichua)."

The Canelos and Campa narrative, however, is missing a key component of the Southwestern imagery—namely, the devouring, consuming, transformative, feminine force of Huruing Wuhti. This is to be found not far afield among the Macusi (Roth, 1915:135; Roe, 1982:248–49). According to the Macusi, a devouring feminine force, in the form of a dragon, awaits at the zenith and western horizon. She is also said to consume fire.

In a Warao myth recorded by Barral (1960:62; Roe, 1982:249), the sun's consort waits for him in the sky at the zenith. From there, using her feminine charms and running in front of him, she lures him to the western horizon, where, awaiting him with open mouth, she swallows him.

It is germane to our investigation of Panama's precolumbian ceramic art to understand the basic structural models generated by the native astronomies and cosmologies of the New World, as these are widely reflected in both precolumbian and ethnographic art. It would seem reasonable to expect that depictions of pertinent astronomical elements, such as sun, stars, and constellations, might also have been depicted in ancient Panamanian art.

Archaeoastronomy is a relatively recent discipline, but one nonetheless that has yielded key insights into the methodologies and applications of astronomy by New World peoples. From 1982 through 1983, this writer participated in an archaeological project organized by two California institutions, the Bowers Museum of Cultural Art and the Santa Barbara Museum of Natural History. The project goals were to identify and examine California Indian archaeoastronomical sites, related art, and artifacts. Numerous sites were examined. Some were confirmed solstice and/or equinox sites, some simply potential archaeoastronomical sites. This research resulted in an exhibit in 1983 titled Skywatchers of Ancient California, which subsequently toured California museums and observatories over the following two years. Essentially, it was determined that the methods of solstice observation employed by California Indians were similar to those employed in the American Southwest and northern México. We can infer that they probably had wide distribution in the Americas, particularly in the temperate latitudes.

Over the last fifteen years, New World archaeoastronomy has developed into a serious discipline that has generated new insights and understanding of how New World sciences were intimately interwoven within the cultural fabric of indigenous mythologies and cosmologies. Agricultural societies, in general, require a reliable annual calendar in order to determine the most propitious time to plant and harvest crops. Naturally, this is more critical in those societies in which agriculture plays a significant role in the subsistence base. In many native groups the annual cycle of public rituals and ceremonials is correlated to the yearly calendar cycle, which is usually keyed to specific combinations of solar, lunar, and stellar events.

The observation of the heavens was normally entrusted to specialists—initiated shamans or priests—as precision and accuracy were critical to the survival of the group. In the more temperate latitudes, at least, annual calendars were determined by observing the movement of the sun on the eastern horizon. Early on, it was observed that the sun rises at a slightly different place each day on the eastern horizon and, that over the course of a year, moves from a set point south on the horizon to a set point north and then back again.

The farthest point south on the eastern horizon reached by the sun marks the winter solstice in temperate latitudes and occurs around December 21–22. The term *solstice* derives from the Latin *sol*, sun, and *sistere*, to stand still, for this is the time when the sun stops its northward or, alternatively, its southward trek and appears to stand still, that is, it appears to rise on the same point for about two days, before reversing its direction and continuing on its journey. These phenomena had great relevance to precolumbian peoples.

The farthest point reached on the northward trek, on the eastern horizon, marks the summer

89. Ring-Based Polychrome Bowl: Shamanic Sawfish

solstice in temperate latitudes (about June 21–22). A point midway along its north-south trek marks off the autumnal equinox. The vernal equinox (about March 21) is the midpoint reached by the sun during its south-north journey.

There were, and even are today, different ways of observing and marking off the solstices and equinoxes. One technique, direct observation, involved simply watching the movement of the sun on the eastern horizon from a predetermined, stable, observational point and noting correlated geographical features on the horizon as solstice and equinox markers. Such features might be mountain peaks or notches between mountains where the sun rises on these special days. These features inevitably became part of the sacred landscape.

Indirect observation usually entailed the interaction of sun and a designated artwork, such as a graphic solar motif or concentric circles painted (pictograph) or inscribed (petroglyph) on rock surfaces. In indirect observation, a shaft of light from the rising solsticial or equinoctial sun strikes the motif and thereby heralds the event. Not uncommonly, such motifs were placed on rock surfaces in diminutive caves, with the mouth of the cave, as well as the motif, facing the eastern horizon.

92. Polychrome Jar with Geometric Decoration

In parts of Mesoamerica, solar observations were supplemented by and correlated with observations of the planet Venus and particular stars, such as Aldebaran, a red star of the first magnitude in the eye of the bull in the constellation Taurus.

Venus was of great importance to Mesoamerican astronomers. Several pages in the Dresden Codex, as well as in the Grolier Codex, are devoted to this celestial entity. The Maya divided the 584-day (average) synodical period of Venus into 236 days of visibility as morning star, followed by a 90-day period of invisibility during superior conjunction. This was followed by 250 days of visibility as evening star, ending with 8 days of invisibility during inferior conjunction (Labbé, 1982:17). There was a set relationship between the Venus cycle and the solar calendar. Five Venus cycles of 584 days equaled 8 solar years of 365 days.

Among the Mexicans, year counts were calculated in multiples of 4 and multiples of 13. The 52(4 x 13)-year cycle was particularly important. A 12-day adjustment to the solar calendar was made immediately following a 52-year cycle. Interestingly this accounts for an extra day every four years with the adjustment made at the beginning of the thirteenth day. At midnight of the twelfth day, as the star Aldebaran passed at the zenith, new fires were kindled, thereby inaugurating a new "century." (We read, however, in Chapter Nine, Book VII of the Florentine Codex, that the completion of two 52-year periods was held in particular reverence: "...at which time the two (52 year) cycles might proceed to attain 104 years. It was then called 'one Old Age'" when twice they made the round, when twice the binding of the years had come together." It is interesting to note that 52 years of 365 days equals 32.5 Venus cycles, a fractional number. Fractions were not used in Mesoamerican numeration. One hundred and four solar years (52 x 2), however, equals 65 Venus cycles, which is also equivalent to 146 cycles of the Aztec's sacred ceremonial calendar, the 260-day Tonalpohualli.

Our brief digression into some of the astronomical observations made by the Aztecs and Maya simply underscores the depth, complexity, and sophistication of New World astronomy. More germane to our

86. Polychrome Pedestaled Bowl:
Needle-Nosed Serpentiform Creature with Legs

study of Panamá is the role played by astronomy in the New World tropics. Among the Barasana of the northwest Amazon, the sun, sky, moon, and stars are said to have been some of the first beings created in the universe. The Barasana picture the movement of the sun and stars as a joint journey across the upper world sky continued in the underworld below. This journey begins as an east-to-west movement in the upper world and continues in a west-to-east movement in the underworld. On many Conte Style vessels employing the circle-cross-X design layout, the east-west axis of the composition often has saurians at each of the four directions. In this composition, that placed at one end of the axis is upright, the other upside-down, possibly representing the west-to-east movement in the underworld. The stars simply follow the star path of the sun. Star paths are sometimes pictured as snakes or, more specifically, as an anaconda. Stars and constellations are named after mythic personages or named and illustrated as specific species, such as snake, scorpion, caterpillar, ant, armadillo. They may also be named after artifacts such as an adze, a fish rack, or a corpse bundle.

The position of stars and constellations in the night sky are used by the Barasana to determine the beginning of the wet and dry seasons, as well as to regulate the ritual and agricultural calendars. "The stars, in their nightly passages, also repeat their annual movement from east to west and each year they are said to return to the east as flocks of migratory birds whose passage corresponds to the heliacal setting of particular constellations. The Pleiades return as bobolinks (Dolichonyx orizivorous), Orion's belt and sword as unidentified small black seed-eating birds, and other constellations as egrets (Leucophoyx thula)." (Hugh-Jones, 1982:185)

Star Thing (the Pleiades) is also called Woman Shaman in her aspect as First Shaman and creatress, or Star Woman. "Star Thing is a woman, the Star Woman whose eight stars are eight strips of wood like those used to set fire to the dry wood of a cleared swidden site or chagra. Each strip is marked with alternating bands of red and black: the red is the fire of a burning chagra that lights up the eastern sky and brings the dry season as the black is the charcoal that remains after the fire is out and is the dark, overcast sky of the rainy season. Star Woman, the Pleiades, thus controls the seasons and agriculture." (ibid.:189)

Just as Star Thing (the Pleiades) is particularly associated with the dry season, the constellation known as Caterpillar Jaguar, associated with the wet season, is sometimes pictured as a jaguar with a serpent tail or as a serpent with slight or no jaguar characteristics. Interestingly, in Panamanian Guaymi tales the great snake is associated with celestial-terrestrial conjunction, in terms of activities signaling rain and the proper time to plant (Gonzalez and Gonzalez, 1989:119–20; Helms, 1993:218).

Among the Desana of the northwest Amazon the constellation Orion is shamanically pictured as the Master of Animals, while the Milky Way is imaged as two huge snakes in his pathway. Orion is, however, also used as a backdrop on which to project a multitude of shamanic images that at the same time stand apart and yet on deeper levels of mythic imagery are related to one another. "Orion is Man: Man the Progenitor, the Hero, the Hunter, the Sinner and, finally, the Victim. But every year he rises anew and, when people see him resurrected in the sky, shamans remind them of everything this constellation stands for. In some images, Orion is a rack upon

MAPPING AND STRUCTURING THE SHAMANIC UNIVERSE

which the adulterer has been put. In other images Orion is a tapir hide stretched out to dry between stakes; or a potstand or a fish trap. Orion's belt is the severed penis of the incestuous youth, or the castrated father; in another image, the belt is the adze used to extract starch from split palm trunks, a phallic instrument that is the main attribute of the Master of Animals." (G. Reichel-Dolmatoff, 1982:173–74)

The observation of the heavens served as the basis for the structure of the shamanic cosmic model. The zenithal point in the sky, whether referenced as the zenith of the sun or stars, is the point defining the top of a layer of the axis mundi, or world tree. A line drawn from this point exactly perpendicular to the earth marks the center of the middle world. This seems to be the rational basis for the fact that all native groups claim that their homeland is the center of the world. An imaginary line extending from the center of the middle world downward through the underworld and opposite the zenith is the nadir. The movement of the sun defines the four directions. The pathway of the sun, however, when traced from east to south to west to north to east, yields an ellipse (Fig. 125), as the sun is in the south when it has reached zenith and in the north, in the underworld, when it has reached nadir. The zenith and nadir, as defined by the stars, determines the axis mundi, which passes through and unites the upper, middle, and lower worlds.

Among the Kogi Indians of the Sierra Nevada de Santa Marta in northern Colombia, the structure of the universe is metaphorically represented in imagery as a gigantic spindle whorl. The spindle symbolizes the axis mundi. The large whorl at the center represents the middle world. Each successively smaller whorl above represents a layer of the upper world, while successively smaller whorls below represent those of the underworld. This cosmic model is mirrored in the shape and function of the conical temples found in Kogi villages: "A small hole in the conical temple roof admits a ray of sun or moonlight that, in the case of the sun, traces the outline of solstices and equinoxes in the dark interior... Kogi villages, ceremonial centers, isolated temples, shrines, and other structures, are always sited according to astronomical principles" (G. Reichel-Dolmatoff, 1982:177). In Central America, Kogi language and other aspects of culture such as architecture show the greatest affinity to the Bribri and Cabécar of modern Costa Rica (Cooke, personal communication, 1994).

Far to the north of the Tukano and Kogi, in the American Plains, we find similar astronomical patterns of culture among the otherwise culturally very different Skidi Pawnee. Sky elements such as Venus,

87-88. Polychrome Jar with Sawfish and Mythic Creature

93. Polychrome Figural Jar: Feline with Saurian Decoration

sun, moon, and stars are perceived as living beings. They play dominant roles in Skidi myth, cosmology, and art, and the Skidi home reflects and models the astronomical world: "The simple dwelling is full of beauty to him who knows its meaning. There is no part of it that is not symbolic. The entrance must always face the rising sun; the round domed roof is a symbol of the sky, and each post represents a star which tells the Pawnee of some divine being" (Murie, quoted in Chamberlain, 1982:155).

Another way that Skidi astronomy reflects cultural patterns far to the south is in the manner that male and female divisions of the sky reflect a preponderant male-female classification of phenomena, forms, structures, and functions in general. The sky was divided into eastern and western quadrants. As among the Hopi, Aztec, and many South American groups, the eastern sky was considered a male provenance, while the west was the domain of the female principle. We need only recall the Huruing Wuhti-west-female v. Masau'u-east-male or the South American Dragon-west-female v. Sun-east-male dichotomies to illustrate our point.

"She, (Venus as Evening Star) along with Moon and other female deities, was stationed in the west, while the great male star (Venus as Morning Star) governed his fellows, including Sun, in the east...the general westward migration of the heavenly bodies to unite the male principle of the east with the female principle of the west seems to be intimately related in Skidi thought to male-female attraction and thus to the very origin of human life" (Chamberlain, 1982:58).

We have given, in these pages, but a brief outline of precolumbian astronomical practice and lore. Enough has been exposed, however, to illustrate the following:

- Astronomical observation was sophisticated and seems to have been practiced in all regions.

- Observation of the sun, moon, stars, constellations, or combinations of the above was not only used to develop calendars but, equally important, was employed in delineating and mapping sacred space.

- Sun, moon, planets, stars, and constellations were perceived as living beings and were used as characters in mythic and cosmic themes and dramas.

- It is not uncommon to find similar, if not identical astronomically derived, cultural metaphors used by groups separated by great distance and seemingly quite distinct with respect to language, dress, environment, and other exotic aspects of culture.

As will be illustrated in succeeding chapters, all aspects of the shamanic universe covered in previous chapters are clearly reflected in New World art. Our exercise to this point has been to lay the foundation for an interpretative framework within which to reference the precolumbian art of Panamá.

In the following chapter we will examine how precolumbian and New World peoples classify their universe and order their knowledge. We will present a model that will seek to explain why elements of the indigenous world are classified the way they are. Later we will attempt to demonstrate how this has inspired and conditioned certain traits, patterns, and relationships inherent in some of the artistic traditions found over large areas of the Americas.

CHAPTER VI

94. Polychrome Globular Figural Jar in the Form of a Shamanic Bird

CHAPTER VI

PARADIGMS AND MODELS:
A Key to Understanding the Inherent Dualism of the Shamanic Cosmos

One of the most notable characteristics of American indigenous thought is the emphasis placed on duality. Whether we examine the art and mythology of the Caribbean Taino; tropical forest Carib, Tukanoan, or Quechuan; mountain or forest Chibchan; fertile valley or arid desert Uto-Aztecan, the single most outstanding concept is that of duality.

Duality permeates every nook and cranny of the indigenous conceptual universe. In precolumbian art it is reflected in form, line, design element, motif, composition, and layout. In the ethnographies, it is inherent in the native classificatory systems and characterizes the structure of the various indigenous mythologies and cosmologies. In daily living, it is manifested in the division of labor, the layout of a household, or the naming of features of the geophysical and astronomical worlds. Darkness is contrasted with light. Up is contrasted with down. East complements west, as male complements female. This emphasis on duality pervades the graphic art of the Central Region of Panamá, particularly from Late Tonosí Style times through Macaracas Style times.

The New World systems are neither strictly linear, static, exclusive, nor absolute. They tend, rather, to be fluid and polymorphous, dynamic and relativistic. This is particularly true in the neotropics, where it is not uncommon for the same entity to be referenced as both male and female or good and bad depending on position, time, and context. To the uninitiated, the various classificatory systems observed in the ethnographies appear to be arbitrary and somewhat chaotic. Nothing could be further from the truth. And although we can speak of numerous cultural classificatory systems, on closer analysis there appears to be one common paradigm from which they all derive. It is this underlying paradigm that we will seek to expose in this chapter.

In Mesoamerica, the fundamental principles that governed the dualistic dichotomizing of the world were called Ometecuhtli-Omecihuatl in Nahuatl, the language of the Aztecs. Although Ometecuhtli-Omecihuatl is commonly translated as "Two Lord-Two Lady," the writer (Labbé:1982, 1986a,b, 1988) has long argued that such translations are puerile and inadequately convey their significance. *Ome* can mean both "two" or imply duality. *Tecuhtli* literally means "lord," but is simply a male honorific. In the same manner, *cihuatl* literally means "lady," but is a female honorific. Ometecuhtli-Omecihuatl is also jointly referred to as Ometeotl. Although *teotl* was commonly translated as "god" in earlier writings, as Townsend (1979) has shown, it is more accurately translated as "sacred energy." A more precise signification of Ometecuhtli-Omecihuatl would be "Oh Great Dual-Natured Masculine Principle–Oh Great Dual-Natured Feminine Principle." *Ometeotl* then is rendered "Oh Great Dual-Natured Sacred Energy."

In Nahuatl myth the universe is manifest when Ometecuhtli and Omecihuatl unite, or come together. This union constitutes the beginning. From their union several things come into being simultaneously. Their union manifests as Quetzalcoatl, in his aspect as Ehecatl, or "Lord of the Wind," "the Breath of Life." Concurrent with this emanation is the manifestation of motion, time, and directional space.

As the Breath of Life, Quetzalcoatl embodies the unified streams of both the sacred masculine principle and the sacred feminine principle. It is for this reason that he is referred to as the Precious Twin. Quetzalcoatl literally means "feathered serpent" or "precious twin." This exemplifies a common play on imagery in Nahuatl. *Quetzal* refers to the brightly colored plumage of the quetzal bird and hence connotes anything beautiful or of great value. In

95. Polychrome Jar with Mythic, Shamanic, or Cosmological Creature

Nahuatl, *coatl* literally means serpent, but it also means twin, which may be an indication of the antiquity of the symbology associated with the serpent, used as an icon to refer to the dual-natured life force (Labbé, 1982, 1986a,b, 1988, 1992). The forked tongue of the serpent was an ideal expression of the union of two principles in one form. This association has great antiquity in the Americas.

Translated as "feathered serpent," Quetzalcoatl refers to the pictograph depicting a serpent with feathers placed above the head, variants of which are to be found from the American Southwest to Costa Rica and beyond. As precious twin, Quetzalcoatl is an esoteric reference to the myth in which he emanates as the Breath of Life, following the union of the cosmic male and female principles in Ometecuhtli-Omecihuatl.

Quetzalcoatl, therefore, is an esoteric principle, an avatar of the cosmic duality, manifesting as life in the material universe. In more popular lore, he becomes a character in various religio-historical dramas, often with little relevance to the deeper esoteric significance. In the art of Mesoamerica, he is represented as a feathered serpent or emblemized by the spiral or interlocking spirals that refer to his aspect as the Lord of the Wind, the Breath of Life—as movement, motion, and manifestation. His astronomical reference is to the planet Venus, which symbolized his dual nature, since Venus is both evening star and morning star, female as well as male, dark as well as light. It therefore embodied the full range of dualistic associations in the Mesoamerican Nahuatl mind. This dichotomy was personified in religious myth as Quetzalcoatl vs. his alter ego Xolotl, who assumed the dark, sinister role of antagonist, while Quetzalcoatl played that of the hero-protagonist.

Another avatar of the Cosmic Duality was Huehueteotl-Xiuhtecuhtli. As with other Nahuatl terms, Hueheteotl has been somewhat trivialized in translation. He is commonly referred to as "the Old, Old God." A more insightful rendition might read, "Most Ancient of Sacred Energies" or "The Primordial Sacred Energy." Xiuhtecuhtli literally means "Lord of Fire" and informs us that fire not only referred to the epi-electron phenomenon we experience as flame but on a deeper level symbolized the inner essence, the undifferentiated energy of life hidden in all things.

The direct relationship of fire to the Cosmic Duality is not only graphically rendered in precolumbian art (Labbé, 1982:19–24), it is illustrated in the colorful imagery embedded in a Nahuatl poem found in the Florentine Codex (Book VI, folio 71,V). In translation, it is usually rendered:

> "Mother of the gods, father of the gods, the old god, spread out on the navel of the earth, within the circle of turquoise, He who dwells in the waters, the color of the blue bird, He who dwells in the clouds, The old god, He who inhabits the shadows of the land of the dead, the Lord of fire and of time."

In accordance with the rhythm and nature of precolumbian thought, the metaphors inherent in this poem are keyed to exotic as well as esoteric imagery. The reference is to the exotic imagery of the Cosmic Duality, manifesting as the movement of the sun along the horizon. At dawn, the sun figuratively emerges on the eastern horizon from the womb and bowels of the earth mother. Then, growing ever stronger, it ascends to the zenith in the southern sky, where it reaches its peak of physicality, heat, power, and maturity. These are masculine quadrants of the sky. The west and north constitute the female quadrants, the quadrants where the feminine forces exert their influence. The sun begins its descent from the zenith to the western horizon, continually diminishing in strength and intensity. It is here that it descends into the gaping mouth of the underworld. The reference to fire and time in the poem is a reference to the movement of the sun on the horizon, marking off the four directions as well as marking off time and the calendar.

The reference to turquoise is a reference to the fact that turquoise symbolized fire among the Aztecs and other Nahuatl-speaking peoples, as it does among the Pueblos of the American Southwest. Turquoise is a hard blue to blue-green stone and, as such, was closely associated in the Hopi mind with Huruing Wuhti, Hard Beings Woman, whom, as we have previously seen, personified the power and force of gravity-mass and its role in forming and shaping matter. Turquoise symbolized fire trapped in matter, hidden in the matrix of material substance. Matter is the issue that emerges from the matrix, that is, the womb of the cosmic mother principle. Turquoise, therefore, symbolizes the entrapment of Masau'u (the Lord of Fire) within the matrix-womb of Huruing Wuhti (gravity-mass as a feminine force of nature), who dwells down and within the underworld. Masau'u, the Lord of Fire, therefore is trapped in the underworld of matter in the embrace of gravity or Hard Beings Woman. Masau'u is simply a Pueblo version of the Mesoamerican Xiuhtecuhtli.

The writer suggests the following as a translation of the above-noted Nahuatl poem:

> "Oh Great Dual-Natured Masculine Principle, Oh Great Dual-Natured Feminine Principle, the Most Ancient of Sacred Energies, the Primordial Energy! Ye who is to be found even in the watery depths, the color of the bluebird. Ye who is to be found even in the clouds. The Most Ancient of Energies, which is to be found even in darkness, such as that of the underworld, the land of the dead. Ye who is both Lord of Fire and of time!"

As the essence of the material universe, Ometeotl is symbolized by the element of fire. In this aspect, the avatar Xiuhtecuchtli is represented as a seated old man with wrinkled face and an open mouth with only two teeth, indicative of his dual nature. An interesting rendition of Xiuhtecuhtli from El Salvador graphically illustrates Xiuhtecuhtli's dual nature by rendering the avatar as two separate figures, exact mirror images of each other. The seated posture, wrinkled face, and mouth with two teeth, however, are retained as essential icons. The arms and legs of each figure are bent and positioned exactly opposite to each other and are configured in the form of a stylized "swastika," a common symbol associated with both the sun and fire. The vertical pole of the symbol is the male stick that is twirled in the process of fire making. The horizontal pole is the stationary female stick from which the spark will be generated. The crampons, or arms, of the symbol indicate motion and the direction of spin. As such, it was used to indicate both solar and earth motion. Accordingly, it was also closely related to fire and associated with the sun. It is found in stylized form in the ancient art of Panamá, usually incorporating animal or bird icons as the crampons (Fig. 96).

As essence taking on living form, Ometeotl assumes the guise of the avatar Quetzalcoatl and is symbolized by the feathered serpent, a serpent with a head at each end of its body, a serpent with one body but two heads, two entwined serpents, or two serpents in profile with both heads joined to give the appearance of the single head of a creature such as a frog or toad. The bifid tongue of the serpent becomes a secondary icon used to emphasize the inherent duality conjured by Ometeotl. Double-headed serpents, serpentine life-forms, bifid tongues, and the conjoining of two forms in profile to create a single form are also characteristic of the art of the Central Region of Panamá. Binary emanations emerging from the mouths of serpents or saurians are common in goldwork as well as ceramics. The serpent or saurian head with binary emanations emerging from the mouth was a common form of gold or tumbaga lip ornament, a labret, among the Tairona of Colombia. The Tairona examples all seem to date from about A.D. 1000–1600. Similar Panamanian imagery dates to as early as A.D. 700, apparently predating the Tairona use of this icon.

In the art of western México, Ometeotl's association with fire and duality, and the related icon of the serpent, is graphically rendered in the form of a figural incensario (Labbé,1982:20, Figs. 23,24). In a common rendering, the composition consists of two standing, aged figures with joined bodies positioned back to back. The top of their heads is opened and serves as a receptacle-brazier. Above them is a bowed superstructure with two entwined serpents, serving as a handle.

Enshrined within the conceptualization of Ometeotl, the Cosmic Duality, is the perception that all things contain within themselves both male and female principles and that all relationships involve various expressions of interacting sets, pairs, or dyads. These may take many forms: complementarity, opposition, homogeneity, or heterogeneity.

The dimorphic, binary thought of Mesoamerica is also mirrored in the cosmologies of South America. As León-Portilla (1978) has said of the Mexican system:

"There was always a need for an active masculine aspect and a passive or conceiving feminine counterpart...Generation and conception were moments inseparably unified in the dual divinity (*Ometeotl*)."

This is very similar to a homologous Desana concept:

"So the energy of procreation-creation is a masculine power that fertilizes a feminine element that is the world. Of course, the biosphere has both masculine and feminine aspects, but seen in its totality, as a field of creation, it has primarily a feminine character over which the Sun exercises its power" (G. Reichel-Dolmatoff, 1971:42–43).

Behind the sexual dimorphic classification scheme is the perception that the interaction of male and female principles governs the dynamism and order of the world. Male forms of energy invest, impregnate, extend, and move outward. Female forces receive and transform male energies, converting them into new forms.

Accordingly, the Desana classify the color yellow as containing within itself the fertilizing energy of the sun and therefore elements of the male principle. Yellow-colored honey, semen and semen-colored saliva, yellowish or milky-white semen-colored quartz crystals, yellow squirrels, the macaw, manioc starch (cream colored), cotton (cream colored), and other elements of like color are similarly classified. Color symbolism then becomes a means of identifying whether an element partakes of either the male or the female principle. It should be noted that the seminal symbolism of the quartz crystal exists among other groups within Colombia, for example, the Kogi Indians of northern Colombia (G. Reichel-Dolmatoff, 1951). Far to the north in Mesoamerica, the association of semen and saliva is graphically rendered in a Quiche Maya story recorded in the Popul Vuh.

The story occurs in the underworld, a dimension associated with the female principle. A young girl is walking about when suddenly she is beckoned by a call coming from above. The call is uttered by a skull located in the branches of an underworld tree. The

96. Polychrome Jar with Egg-Laying Bird

The uterus is described in Desana metaphor as the place where one cooks, or transforms energy. The *boga*, in this respect, is a uterus, seen as a vehicle of transformation and creation, an essentially female principle (that is, it contains and transforms), but the *boga* itself results from the action of a complementary male principle called *tulari*. *Tulari* causes *boga*; it makes *boga* function. "Thus, Tulari is masculine energy, and boga is feminine energy. The two together - tulari boga and uhuri boga - are fertilization and fecundity; they are the great current that circulates." (G. Reichel-Dolmatoff, *Amazonian Cosmos,* 1971:54–55). With respect to *tulari*, *boga* is form, but form that gives expression to *tulari*, in much the same way that an electrical appliance gives expression to the electricity that circulates through it.

In the indigenous mind, form itself can possess and express symbolic significance. Vertical elements, in general, but especially tubular vertical elements, are often perceived as male or phallic. Inverted U-shaped forms are generally female or uterine, connoting protection and sometimes transformation. Turtle shells, armadillo shells, and house roofs are often employed as uterine symbols. Cavities or open receptacles and containers depict a female capacity. Among the Desana, we are told that:

"As the *recipient* of masculine semen, the female finds diverse symbolic expression. Her *receptivity* is compared with the gesture of soliciting or joining her hands before her breasts in the form of a *concave receptacle*" (ibid.61, emphasis added).

In general, concavity has female significance and connotations. Caves, mouths, and similar concavities are felt to be female forms. Relevant to the above description of Desana symbolism is the use of words like *recipient, receptivity,* and *concavity* on the part of the ethnographer to translate the Desana symbolic intent.

"Symbolically the hearth represents the uterus... the vessels and the plates represent the Creation. The hearth is thus an instrument of cosmic transformation, a crucible" (ibid. p. 109).

Sexual dimorphic symbolism is used to portray the dynamic interaction of cosmic and terrestrial forces. Centrifugal force, an outward movement, is

skull instructs the girl to extend her hand palm up. It proceeds to spit into the hand and, with great insight, instructs her concerning life and death, how one transcends the other, though they are inseparably part of a single process. The spittle, of course, represents semen. The skull then informs the girl that the strength and comeliness of a great lord or noble is not lost with the dissolution of the body for it is passed (via the semen in her hand) from generation to generation.

In indigenous thought, bones and skeletons are associated with the male principle. In one of the mythic legends of Mesoamerica, the culture-hero-avatar Quetzalcoatl descends to the underworld in order to retrieve the bones of a previous manifestation of mankind. He bleeds his penis, allowing the flowing blood to fall upon the bones. The red blood, a female principle, imparts flesh to the bones and thereby animates them.

Among the Desana Indians of the northwest Amazon, the interaction of the male and female principles takes place within a circuit of energy called the *boga*. The energy that flows within the *boga* is composed not only of male and female principles, but also of benevolent and malevolent aspects. That which promotes health, harmony, life, and well-being is benevolent while that which promotes sickness, disease, disharmony, and death is malevolent.

an expression of the male principle. Centripetal force, a drawing inward (gravity), is an expression of the female principle.

The female principle, however, does more than just receive; it also transforms what is received. The Sun Father may impregnate the Earth Mother with his rays, his fire-serpents, his semen, but it is the Earth Mother who receives and absorbs this energy and converts it into the biosphere. The seed gestates within the earth, but the earth converts it into a sprout. We may observe that there are two female and two male cycles. The first female action is to receive, the second is to conceive and transform. The first male action is to emerge and move outward; the second, to mature and decay. Male descending into female is an act of fertility, the emergence from the female womb is an act of fecundity.

The receiving of the male also entails a taking, a diminishing. This process, as stated earlier, was graphically illustrated in the American Southwest, as well as in South America, by mythologizing the movement of the sun (Huruing Wuhti v. Masau'u and Dragon Lady—of South American myth—v. the Sun). The appearance of the sun in the east and its ascent to the zenith in the south represents the two phases of the male action. The descent of the sun from the zenith to the western horizon and its continuation to the nadir of the underworld in the north represents the dominance of the primary and secondary functions of the female principle, namely to receive the male principle and transform it. As Roe (1982) has noted, many South American groups view the consummation of the sexual act, during which the male's virile member is transformed into a flaccid female form, as a metaphor for the copulation of the sun with the female force of the underworld, which diminishes his strength and defleshes him, so to speak.

In his seminal volume on Desana Tukanoan symbolism and cosmology, Reichel-Dolmatoff (1971:98–103) lists various elements of significance

97. Globular Polychrome Jar: Running Saurians

to Desana culture and notes how they were classified and associated in the Desana mind:

> The sun is a primary male, fertilizing element associated with the following male elements: phallus, semen, heat, light, the color white, yellow, the jaguar, tinnamou, macaw, squirrel, and bee. It is also closely associated with other male elements, such as lightning and quartz crystals. Lightning in turn is closely associated with fertility, quartz crystals, and the jaguar. Fire is associated with the sun, heat, coitus, and food (food engenders heat). Interestingly, firewood represents concentrated, accumulated, or condensed male energy. Rain is a male symbol. Earth, water, houses, cavities, and caves are associated with the female. The rainbow is perceived as a kind of cosmic vagina. Deer, because of their strong sexual-attractive nature, are perceived as a female principle. The armadillo is an essentially uterine emblem, as is the turtle. The bat symbolizes the vagina, particularly those bats that suck blood, which associates the bat with menstruation. Another reason may be that the bat lives in caves and operates by night, both of which are characteristically female.
>
> The forest is primarily a male principle because it is wild and untamed, whereas the *maloca*, or dwelling and garden, is a female domain. Although the anaconda is usually a uterine, maternal symbol associated with the color black, the boa constrictor is a male element opposed in myth to the anaconda.
>
> The owl is a guardian of graves and cemeteries. It is also active at night. It symbolizes death. The hummingbird, which has a long beak and flits about from place to place, represents the penis.
>
> The Milky Way is considered a star path. It is also considered a place of origin for illness. Stars may be either male or female since they are perceived to be living beings.
>
> Some animals, such as the anteater, can have ambivalent denotations depending on the context. The size of its penis associates it with virility. It is noted that, when cornered, the anteater will attempt to castrate its antagonist. The tongue of the anteater, however, symbolizes impotence.

> In the Desana mind, oversized penises are associated with menacing lewdness, an undisciplined, instinctual condition. For this reason, the coati is considered a model animal, for it has a small penis.

According to Weiss (1975:356; Roe, 1982:153) the Campa associate the frog with females and female forms of excessive sexuality. It is said that the frog may devour the fire. This symbolizes the female dragon of the underworld who consumes the sun, but it also refers to nymphomania, which exhausts and extinguishes the sexual fire of the diminished male partner.

Among the Aguaruna Jívaro of the Alto Río Mayo in Perú, the following gender-based symbolic oppositions prevail: Warfare, hunting, the forest, woodworking, and above-ground crops such as maize, plantain, and tobacco are classified as male elements, while childbearing, gardening, swidden, and below-ground crops such as manioc and sweet potato are considered female (M. Brown, 1986:127). This implies that those things that are out, up, or away are male, while those that are in, within, down, or near are female.

Roe (1982:170—71) makes note of associations of this kind collected by other researchers: Men are considered dry, while women are considered wet (Arcand, 1974, on the Cuiva); men are associated with the east, women with the west (Hugh-Jones, 1974:213, on the Barasana).

One could multiply the ethnographic references greatly, but those cited serve our purpose. The Desana record is particularly significant because of the large number of references derived from a single ethnicity. Suffice it to say that the above citations are not unique, but rather reflect a common pattern with wide distribution in the Americas.

Some researchers have thought that "the opposing lists of terms derive from the sex act itself" (Roe, 1982:170). If this were true, the attributions would quickly become arbitrary, as the sex act governs limited functions and structures and could not possibly account for the consistency and comprehensiveness of attributions viewed cross-culturally.

The sexual dimorphic characteristics of the system more likely evolved as a heuristic mechanism, that is, to stimulate interest and memory retention. Sexual dimorphism is a vehicle of conveyance, not the underlying model used to generate a rationale as to why things should be classified as either male or female.

Does such a model exist? We would have to assume that it does, in order to account for the consistency and pervasive distribution of the classifications. What is the nature of the model? It could be inferred from the database that it would have to predict the attribution or classification of structures as well as its functions. It is the thesis of this chapter that such a model does indeed exist, that it is to be found in the existing database, and that it served as the closest thing to a "unified field theory" that was available in precolumbian America.

The Model

As we have seen, the Nahuatl-speaking peoples of Mesoamerica had codified their understanding of the nature of duality in the form of the Cosmic Duality, or Ometecuhtli-Omecihuatl. Ometecuhtli is the male principle in the dyad, Omecihuatl, the female. In the Nahuatl system, we are exposed to a large number of elements that are classified as male or attributed as female. The so called Aztec pantheon expresses numerous male-and-female paired "deities." We are not, however, fundamentally informed as to what precisely constitutes the nature of the male or female principle. This, however, is revealed in the Hopi database.

The female principle is revealed to be gravity-mass, in the form of Huruing Wuhti. The male principle is identified as energy in the form of Masau'u, the Lord of Fire. Huruing Wuhti is said to stand at the center of all things, drawing material substance to herself and thereby making it hard, hence her name. In Hopi myth, these functions are communicated metaphorically and allegorically. It is said that in the very beginning Huruing Wuhti dwelled at a kind of cosmic center, or nucleus, in the underworld that gathered matter around its reef (Tyler, 1981:82; Labbé, 1986b).

In determining who or what Huruing Wuhti is, one must note the qualities that are associated with her in myth and allegory. She is female, a feminine force, dwelling in darkness, down in the underworld, where she attracts and draws in. Things are made hard by her action. She cohabits with Masau'u, the Lord of Fire. In other Hopi myths, she is said to have formed the world. Masau'u is Lord of Fire, the spark of life, energy in modern parlance. The relationship of these two forces governs phenomena. It also forms the implicit basis of a model that yields insight into the nature of indigenous classifications. Like any good model, it should assist us in explaining our empirical observations of the database and allow us to predict how things will be classified given similar variables. The model can also assist us in translating underlying esoteric concepts implicit, though not necessarily explicit, in the indigenous world view.

The relationship between gravity-mass (the female principle) and energy (the male principle) generates and determines both structure and function in phenomena. It is our postulate that this relationship formed the basis for gender-based (male-female) classifications found in many, if not most, New World cultures. If the model is valid, one should be able to independently classify the natural world, according to the dictates of the model, into male and female categories and yield classifications that reflect those found in the indigenous database. A comparison of the following model-based classifications with classifications found in the ethnographic database demonstrates that this is precisely what happens.

Gravity controls two directions, in and down, while energy also controls two directions, up and out. In the natural world, down is a direction created by a dominant center of gravity and up is a direction opposed to that same center. In this sense, there is no absolute up, it is always defined in relationship to such a center. To move in opposition to such a center, energy is required.

Gravity dominates two states of matter in the physical world—earth and water—while energy governs air and fire. We would therefore classify the first pair as female elements and the second pair as male elements. Energy (male) expresses itself in straight-line vectors, while gravity (female) bends these to form curvilinear lines. Rectilinear, therefore, is male; curvilinear, female. Gravity contracts, it is centripetal. Energy expands, it is centrifugal. Things that contract or draw in are female; things that move out and expand are male. Things that decrease energy exemplify the female principle. Phenomena that increase energy exemplify the male principle. Thus it would follow that cold is female, while hot is male. As the female principle dominates the male principle, energy condenses and is reduced to gas, liquid, and solid, successively. As the male principle dominates the female principle, solid is induced to liquid, gas, and energy, successively.

Gravity generates darkness (female); energy generates light (male). The right amount of gravity-mass, however, results in a reflex action, giving birth to its opposite. This is precisely what happens in the physical universe. When a material body reaches critical mass, that body has the potential of becoming a star, in which case, gravity-mass gives birth to light. It is illuminating to note that in English the word *gravity* is related to the word *gravid*, which means to be heavy with pregnancy. Both terms are derived from the Latin word *gravis*, which means to be heavy, loaded. Applying our model to the human body should yield the following classifications. The mouth —a cavity, a hollow, a place of darkness, a place where things enter and are taken down—would be female, as would the vagina. The penis, on the other hand, since it expands, grows, and ascends, would be male. Its detumescence, being contractual, would be perceived as a female process and condition.

All of the senses, since they are receptors, structurally similar to cavities and holes, are female, while sensory phenomena such as light and sound, forms of energy, would be male. The movement of sound and light to the organs of perception would be described as a fertilizing action. The eyes and ears would be structurally described as wombs, organs of transformation.

Ingestion or eating, a consuming, devouring act, would be female, as would digestion. The mouth, stomach, and intestines would be female structures. Following digestion, there is a movement of nutrients out of the intestines to the blood. This implies a male process. The blood, in turn, is received by a multitude of cells constituting the body. The movement of blood to cell expresses a male fertilizing action. The transformation of these nutrients into flesh, bone, and hair by cells represents a female process.

The phenomenal cycle of water also evinces the inherent processes and dichotomies of the model. The ocean, the great sea, is the mother. The sun, a male element, fertilizes the ocean with its light and heat. Light and heat engender the birth of water molecules, which invisibly emerge from the ocean (the mother) and ascend (a male process) skyward. There they condense (a female action) and form clouds, a womblike form, from which raindrops, like seeds (male forms), emerge and descend to fertilize the earth. The downward impulse of the male, which is a reaction to the attractive power of gravity (female) represents a fertilizing action, which ultimately results in transformation and in a reciprocal upward impulse —fecundity, an emergence, a manifestation.

For the woman, sex takes the form of an allurement, an attraction, while for the man, it is a form of hunt or pursuit. The man chases the object of desire; the woman captures it in her net, her web, her matrix. Beauty in any gender is a female force, for it attracts, draws toward itself. Beauty desires admiration, it attracts pursuit, while strength seeks to impress through expression.

That which is near is the domain of the female principle; that which is far, the male principle. Gathering and consolidating are female activities, while going out, such as hunting and exploring, are male activities. The female form has a lower center of gravity, hence greater width at the hips. Males have centers of gravity that, relatively speaking, shift upward, hence the greater width at the shoulders.

A tree, like everything else in the universe, incorporates both male and female structures and processes within one and the same entity. Relative to the earth, the roots are above, hence the roots are male structures. The branches and leaves are in relationship with the sky (male), hence they are below or female. The roots draw the female elements of earth and water upward. The leaves (womblike structures) draw from the sky carbon dioxide (air) and sunlight (fire), two male elements.

As an entity, the tree is the result of complex relationships and interrelationships. There is, in fact, no tree apart from these relationships. There is no shape or form to the tree apart from gravity, wind, and sun; no color apart from sunlight; no scent apart from earth, wind, and water.

In the real world, these dichotomies and relationships exist in innumerable gross and subtle combinations. To understand why the Indian classifies one thing as male and the other as female, one must clearly discern the underlying relationships that are being observed and portrayed. One must also determine whether the classification is a reference to structure, function, or process.

We must always allow for the element of arbitrariness in classification. Whether red will be classified as female and blue as male may in fact be arbitrary, or at least relative. We cannot assume that the model is operative in all cases and circumstances, as this would necessitate that only individuals who at least implicitly understood the model were responsible for generating classifications, even those that have resulted from acculturation to Western civilization.

With respect to color, the model would predict that red and black would tend to be perceived as female and white and blue as male. Relative to black, however, red would be perceived as male. Black and white are easy to understand. One is associated with darkness, the underworld, caves, wombs, gravity, and other female-related forms and functions. White, correlatively, is associated with brightness, sunlight, and other male attributes. Red might be viewed as female by association with menstrual blood, but on a purely empirical level, since red is a longer wavelength and at the lower frequency end of the color spectrum, it should be classified as female. Blue is of shorter wavelength and higher frequency, hence it should be classified as male. Interestingly, we say infra(below, female)-red and ultra(above, beyond, male)-violet. There does not appear, however, to be any avenues, other than experiential intuition, that could inform the native classifier of this fact. With respect to black relative to red, one would expect red to be classified as male, since black reflects an absence of color and is so clearly associated with female categories. It is fascinating, therefore, to see how closely actual indigenous color symbolism conforms to the predictions postulated by the model.

Roe (1982:186–88), studying the South American database, made the following observations, "When red is opposed to black, there is no ambiguity; red is always male and black is always female....but when white or yellow are opposed to red, red takes second place to the crucial light-dark contrast and is often linked with women, as is the case, via its connection with their blood."

98. Figural Pendant in the Form of a Feline with Foot in Mouth

PARADIGMS AND MODELS

99. Figural Pendant: Shaman Undergoing Transformation

100. Figural Pendant: Shaman Undergoing Empowerment

101a. Figural Pendant: Frog with Saurian Emanations
101b. Figural Pendant in the Form of a Shamanic Frog
101c. Figural Pendant in the Form of a Crocodilian

102a. Figural Pendant Rattle: Joined Shamanic Zoomorphs
102b. Figural Pendant: Shamanic Zoomorph

PARADIGMS AND MODELS

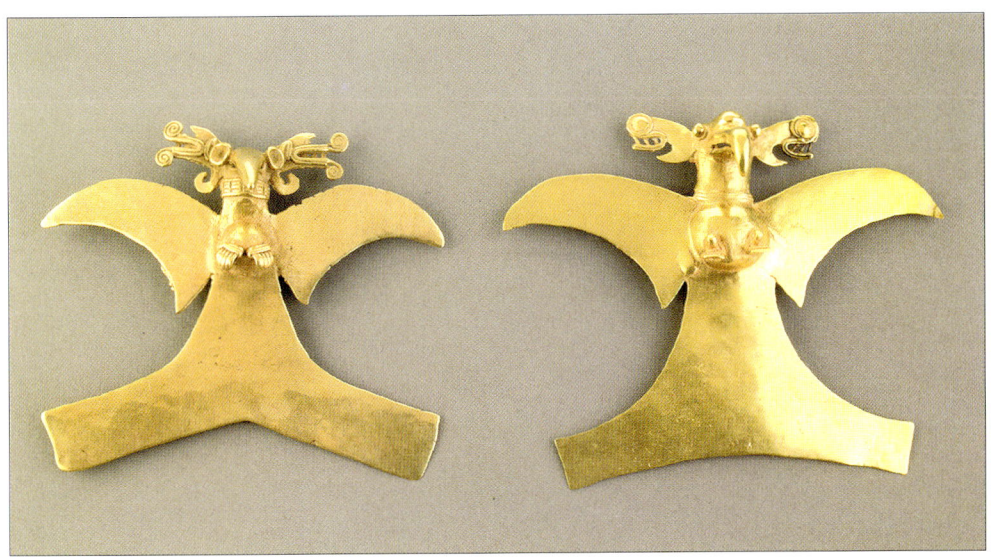

103a. Figural Pendant in the Form of a Shamanic Eagle
103b. Figural Pendant in the Form of a Shamanic Eagle

104. Shamanic Frog Figural Pendant

GUARDIANS OF THE LIFE STREAM

105. Figural Pendant in the Form of a Shamanic Hieratic Saurian

CHAPTER VII

106. Polychrome Pedestaled Plate:
Shamanic Transformation Theme

CHAPTER VII

CONTEXT AND MEANING IN THE ART OF CENTRAL PANAMÁ

The preceding chapters serve as a framework and context against which the precolumbian art of Panamá can be viewed. In the present chapter, we will look at the actual database comprising the painted ceramics of the Central Region of Panamá to determine if we can identify elements or compositions that reflect cultural concepts and perspectives encountered in our previous discussions.

The Central Region includes areas comprising the provinces of Veraguas, Los Santos, Herrera, Coclé, parts of Colón, and Panamá, including large stretches of the coast of the Bay of Panamá. Our time frames are the periods embraced by 900 B.C. and A.D. 1520, which encompass the development, evolution, and ultimate demise of the painted ceramic tradition of the Central Region.

It has been demonstrated by a large number of researchers that precolumbian art is overwhelmingly cognitive in nature. G. Reichel-Dolmatoff (1988:11–16) noted, "One thing is very clear to me: archaeology cannot be separated from ethnology....by recognizing this relationship between ritual objects and shamanic ideology, I was able to gain an understanding of their deeper significance."

David J. Wilson (1992:38), addressing problems in Andean archaeology, but in a manner applicable to all areas of the Americas, observed that, "apparent parallels in myth and ideology connect prehispanic and traditional modern groups across broad geographic areas and through several thousand years of cultural development in South America." The cognitive dimension of precolumbian art may lie in its symbology; its reference to myth, history, or cosmology; its use in defining status or validation of power or authority; or simply in the perceived ritual power or efficacy of its design.

Shamanic Imagery in the Ceramic Art of the Central Region of Panamá

One of the problems confronting the student of Panamanian ceramic art is how to approach the voluminous database. Literally thousands upon thousands of painted ceramics have been uncovered through scientific excavation, as well as through uncontrolled digs by amateurs, treasure seekers, and looters alike.

Given the shamanic nature of neotropical indigenous cultures, it would seem reasonable to postulate that the prehistoric cultures would also be marked with a strong shamanic stamp. The question arises, therefore, as to whether shamanism is reflected in the ceramic art.

We should begin our inquiry by seeing if perhaps we can discern any imagery that directly represents the shaman. In order to identify such a figure, we will need criteria that can be used to identify him as such.

The shaman, it should be recalled, is first and foremost an intermediary between the world of men and the world of spirits. The spirit world is accessed by going into a trance or altered state of consciousness. Once he has entered this state, he can shape shift, undergo transformation, and access the power and counsel of spirit familiars. The shaman, capable of flying in his spirit body, may then engage in combat with other shamans or malevolent spirits.

Reichel-Dolmatoff (1988), studying a large body of iconography associated with the prehispanic goldwork of Colombia, identified a number of artworks that he felt reflected certain themes, such as shamanic transformation and shamanic flight. He concluded that the theme of shamanic flight was a major portrayal in precolumbian Colombian goldwork. He felt that representations of bird-men, combining various human and avian attributes in association with other icons, were the best candidates. He noted that many of the shaman-in-flight figures were accompanied by animals, which he identified as the shaman's animal familiars. He divided these into several categories: animals that help the shaman to fly, those that assist in diagnosing disease, those that function as messengers, and those that serve as executioners.

This writer's own work on prehispanic Colombian ceramics (Labbé, 1986, 1988) had been driven by a similar perception that precolumbian iconography was keyed to concepts and practices that in certain cases were still current in extant ethnographic groups. The writer's investigations of the ceramic record supports Reichel-Dolmatoff's findings in the goldwork.

An examination, by this writer, of Peruvian coastal ceramics and textiles in the collections of the Bowers Museum of Cultural Art revealed the following basic shamanic themes: shaman in trance or meditation; shaman transformed, accompanied by auxiliaries, shamanic flight; and shamanic combat (Labbé, 1993).

In the Peruvian coastal context, the shaman in trance or meditation theme was associated mainly with ceramic sculpture in the round, depicting a seated figure, usually with a bulge indicated in the cheek to represent coca chewing. The eyes are large and vacant and glance upward and outward into space.

The second theme—shaman transformed, accompanied by auxiliaries— consists of a standing anthropomorphic figure shown frontally. This figure usually has emanations in animal form extending from each side of the top of the head. Similar emanations are often seen at the waist, as well as the feet. In some cases, the animal familiars do not emanate from the central figure's body but rather flank the central figure in profile. There is a consistency through time in the essential icons associated with this theme, as found in the art of Chavín, as well as that of Paracas, Chancay, and Chimú, bridging two thousand years of Peruvian coastal prehistory. The same basic complex of icons are present in Colombian examples studied by Reichel-Dolmatoff (1988:141–42). The shaman in flight theme, in the Peruvian context, usually takes the form of an anthropomorphic figure with wings.

On the south coast this theme is closely associated with trophy heads, often with blood streaming forth in the form of serpents. In Colombia, the theme is best represented by birds with human heads or other proportions, blending avian and human characteristics.

The theme of shamanic combat in coastal Perú is most closely associated with the theme of shamanic flight. Common are winged warrior figures brandishing weapons—knives, spears, or clubs. The figures are usually shown in profile, in contrast to the transformation figures, which are shown frontally, accompanied by animal auxiliaries.

In the Central Region of Panamá, the shamanic transformation theme and that of shamanic combat seem clearly represented. These themes are most evident in the art of the Macaracas Style, which dates from A.D. 800 to 1100. The transformation theme (Fig. 106) consists of an anthropomorphic figure shown frontally. In Figure 106, animal emanations, in the form of running saurians, emerge bilaterally from the top of the head and from the arms, while an additional saurian is visible between the central figure's legs. Each saurian is characterized by a crest above the head, a long crocodilian-like mouth full of menacing teeth, and huge claws at the feet. The artist has also skillfully contrasted parts of the body in blue and in red. The use of red and blue is not arbitrary. Red-bodied saurians have heads in blue, while blue-bodied saurians have red heads. This basic dimorphism in the use of red and blue is characteristic of several periods. Blue or blue/purple was added to the Central Region's ceramic color repertoire of red, black, and white sometime between A.D. 400 and 500. After A.D. 1100, the use of blue or purple became exceedingly rare and was employed only in extremely small quantities, disappearing altogether sometime before the Spanish Conquest (Cooke, 1985:36–38).

With respect to the animal emanations issuing from the central figure's body, we should note that Luna's (1991:33) mestizo Peruvian shaman informant, Pablo Amaringo, used the term *tinguna* to refer to electromagnetic emanations "which may adopt any form–for instance that of animals or people" and which can be controlled by means of shamanic song. The same author notes that "according

107. Polychrome Pedestaled Bowl: Shamanic Transformation Theme

109. Polychrome Pedestaled Bowl: Shamanic Transformation Theme

to Barbara Freedman (personal communication) *tingunas* are, in Lamista shamanism, figures related to protections: they can be plants or animals or even spirit helpers of vegetalistas (a category of mestizo shaman-healer whose power derives from their knowledge and mastery of plants)."

In Figure 107, the arms of the central figure terminate in the form of feathered wings, a condition also suggested in other examples. In Figure 38 the emanations from the body take the form of deadly, barbed stingray spines.

If the frontal poses effectively portray the shaman as energized, transformed, and ready for combat, then the anthropomorphic standing saurian figures imaged in profile (Figs. 56, 111) portray the shaman in hot pursuit, already engaged in shamanic combat.

That we are indeed still confronted with the personage of the shaman seems apparent. The head of our standing profile figure is identical in configuration to that of the saurian emanations seen in the frontal figures. The profile figures appear to be portrayals of complete transformation. That this is a human shaman—and not some other shamanic personage such as the Master of Animals or the Master of Fish—is supported by the essential anthro-

110. Polychrome Pedestaled Bowl: Shamanic Transformation Theme

111. Polychrome Spouted Jar: Shaman-In-Combat Theme

pomorphic nature of the figure's form, particularly by the bipedal, upright posture.

The Master of Animals and the Master of Fish are personages found among many neotropical groups, and the concept is found even among Nahuatl-speaking groups in México. They control the fertility and distribution of the spirits of species within their respective domains. Often they are themselves portrayed as great shamans. A major function of human shamans is to mediate the bioforces of the three worlds (upper, middle, and lower) in order to assure fertility and the replenishment of species in the middle world, the world of living humanity.

A personage akin to the Master of Fish may be the subject of Figure 112. That a shamanic being is intended is suggested by the large concentric eyes, which are also bird heads in profile, and by the fact that this creature is no ordinary creature but one with two heads. The elongated down-turned mouth seems to be Central Region artistic convention used to indicate a fishlike face seen frontally (Fig. 113). Billfish can be seen flanking both heads, much in the manner of the animal familiars depicted flanking human shamans.

Although vessels like Figure 113 represent a fish when viewed frontally, they are often polymorphic.

Other examples may incorporate features such as a fish face when viewed from one perspective, while many other forms and images are also incorporated into the composition. Polymorphous qualities are characteristic of Central Region polychromes. In Figure 113, for example, the eyes are shaped like bird heads with elongated beaks. These, in turn, are connected via an undulating serpent body to saurian heads. Implied in such compositions are concepts central to New World shamanic ideology—that there is fundamentally but one life-giving energy, dualistic in nature, having both male and female aspects, and that form is a mask that can be changed at will by individuals such as shamans, who can shape shift and assume a variety of forms in their spirit bodies.

A large number of motifs found in the Conte Style (A.D. 600–800) consist of a particular animal form such as a bird or other creature, sometimes realistic, other times fantastic, but always with emanations extending from some part of the body. It is reasonable to assume that these creatures represent particular manifestations of shamanic power, but not necessarily that of human shamans. In Figure 35, an example of this genre, the artist contrasts the upper wings, which are blue, with the lower wings, which are red. The same contrasting scheme is used for the bird's beak. Dimorphic color symbolism seems to be implied. Over much of precolumbian America, dots are used to represent seeds, potential points of emergence for new life. They are also used to represent raindrops, which are viewed as seeds falling from the sky, fertilizing the earth beneath. Dots therefore connote fertility, which in the indigenous mind always results from the union of male and female principles. If color symbolism is operative in this composition, our model would predict that the lower red wings would be considered the female dyad and the blue wings the male component. The union of the two would result in a fertilizing action, here represented by the dots.

Another compositional category consists of figures that incorporate characteristics associated with a number of different species but which are not found together in any species existing in the natural world. These composite creatures are particularly common motifs in the Conte Style (A.D. 600–800). This

112. Tricolor Ring-Based Bowl:
Double-Headed Mythic Fish and Swordfish

113. Polychrome Jar: Split Image Fish/Saurian/Bird

114. Tricolor Ring-Based Bowl. Composite Animal: Deer, Bird, and Other Animals

genre is usually found on the inner surface of ring-based shallow bowls or plates. In Figure 114, for example, we are confronted with a creature that has the antlers of a deer, the body of a bird, raptorial clawed feet, and a long snout full of menacing teeth. Note that a bird's beak forms the animal's tail. Birds and deer are animals associated with shamanism over much of the world. The trapezoid design elements bordering the body appear to be artistic conventions used to indicate motion. These should be distinguished from the somewhat similarly shaped hooked elements used to represent a claw or spur.

The cognitive intent in these motifs is somewhat more difficult to discern, but it appears to be related to the concept that form is but appearance, that there is an inner essence, energy, or vital force common to all forms of life. In many neotropical mythologies it is stated that animals in previous creations once had the ability to change form, even occasionally assuming human form. In the present creation, however, only shamanic creatures have such power. It is also commonly believed that there are shamans within many different species. Human shamans, when traveling in the aquatic or other realms, are said to sometimes encounter animal shamans.

The composite creatures of the Central Region may be related to such concepts, or they may simply be representations of shamans who incorporate within themselves the characteristics of the various species represented. In any case, such motifs pertain to the complex of ideas associated with shamanism.

Form as Symbolism

The above-noted compositions differ markedly from depictions of realistic animals (Figs. 29, 115, 116, 117). Seemingly invariably, in the ceramic art of the Central Region these take the form of spouted figural vessels. These can be divided into double-spouted forms and single-spouted forms. In the double-spouted variety, a dimorphic symbolism seems to be implied in both the shape and articulation of the spouts. Our model would predict that the tall, cylindrical, attenuated spout is phallic in intent, while the wider, funnel-shaped spout expresses an essentially female form, vaginal in intent and configuration. Luna (1991:22) notes, for example, that in

115. Polychrome Dual-Spouted Figural Jar in the Form of a Bird

116. Tricolor Spouted Figural Jar in the Form of a Deer

117. Polychrome Figural Jar in the Form of a Crocodilian

the Peruvian Amazon morphological criteria are used to differentiate male and female plant species regardless of the fact that any species contains both male and female plants: "If a plant species has two varieties, one of them with thorns, this one is considered male. If the leaves of one variety are thin and long, and the others round, the first is considered male and the second female." In his study of Desana Indian symbolism, Reichel-Dolmatoff (1985:32) states, "Funnel-shaped elements, such as those present in some traps or in small cups made from twisted leaves, are always interpreted as female organs." On the other hand, he notes that long, slender traps are always classified as male. The dimorphic symbolism inherent in these spouts is particularly evident when viewed from above. From this perspective, funnel-shaped spouts more often than not are fairly realistic representations of female genitalia, replete with clitoris (see Table A, chapter 3). We will examine this at greater length later in our discussion.

118. Polychrome Dual-Spouted Figural Jar in the Form of a Crab

If dimorphic symbolism is implied, then fertility is intended. It is not unreasonable to suggest that vessels such as these were associated with concepts involving the replenishment of species. The shaman is the guardian of fertility and the sentinel of the biosphere. He is responsible for assuring the fecundity of species. The species represented, by these vessels are limited. They are also, in a sense, generic. No particular species of bird, for example, appears to be intended, simply the quality of birdness, perhaps as a representative of species that fly and dwell in the air. Figure 118, a crab, may simply represent another ecological niche in the native biosphere.

Certainly we should distinguish the dual-spouted genre from the single-spouted animal figures. Species replenishment may still be intended, but we lack any supporting criteria on which to base such an interpretation. It is true that in the context of American Southwest geometric symbolism, the checkered pattern decorating the body of the crocodilian (Fig. 117) has fertility connotations, however, we have no collaborative ethnographic support for such an interpretation in the neotropics. Nonetheless, these patterns are not uncommon in the art of the Central Region, and when they occur, it is not unusual to alternate the color of the square or diamond, thereby implying dimorphic symbolism.

Vulva Symbolism

Vulva symbolism is prevalent in a limited number of associated forms and implied in a number of others. In the graphic art, it is most closely associated with crab motifs, and sometimes with scorpions. In its abstract geometric form, it appears to be a principal decorative element associated with the base of the common form known colloquially as the *frutera*. It also appears as a preeminent motif associated with dual-spouted figural jars.

Among the Desana Indians of the northwest Amazon, it is said that the mouth of a crab when on land opens and looks just like a "vagina dentata," that is, a vagina with teeth (Reichel-Dolmatoff, 1985:35). Diamond-shaped outlines are also directly associated with the vulva by the same group (ibid.36).

The interior bowl of Figure 61 depicts a scorpion incorporating a very realistic image of a vulva forming the back of the creature. The scorpion's stinger has been modified to look like the clitoris. The scorpion's mouth is exaggerated and may also possess vulva symbolism. Compositions often unite multiple vulva motifs. Mouth, back, and hind parts may all reflect strong vulva symbolism, in association with the crab. The diamond pattern on the crab's back is often essentially curvilinear, but in other specimens it is rectilinear. It appears that the precolumbian artists of the Central Region of Panamá are reflecting concepts shared with modern-day Desana Indians of the northwest Amazon.

As expressed in the South American database, the vulva is viewed in both a positive and a negative manner. The negative perspective is reflected in the various myths surrounding the so called vagina dentata, that is, the devouring, menacing vagina with teeth.

If the basic diamond or rhomboid are geometric representations of the vulva, then the same motif found on the base of *fruteras* may possess a similar significance. This might also be a clue as to the significance of triangular-shaped cutouts often found on the base of these vessels, particularly those in the Macaracas Style (A.D. 800–1100) Certainly these cutouts have ceremonial or ritual significance, as they were made after the vessel had already been hardened by firing. If they were simply arbitrary, for added decor, they would have been carved while the clay was still relatively soft. They are always associated with the base of the *frutera* vessel form, and the cut is always in the form of a wedge or triangle.

It is tempting to hypothetically link the cutting out of clay, in a part of a vessel that is commonly decorated with vaginal imagery, with the possible practice of clitorectomy. Clitorectomy, the excising of the clitoris, was indeed practiced in the neotropics and is still practiced by some groups such as the Shipibo (Roe, 1982:102–7). The clear depiction, however, of intact clitorises in the graphic and plastic art of the Azuero Peninsula, at least from A.D. 100 to 800, would at least argue for the fact that if the practice did exist it was not universal in the Central Region. There is simply insufficient data at this time to test such a hypothesis.

One can argue more forcefully and credibly, however, that there was artistic intent in depicting a vagina and clitoris in the dual, dimorphic spouted vessels and figural jars. This is supported by the graphic realism with which the genitalia are portrayed (Fig. 16), by the consistency in the iconography, by confirmation from existing South American neotropical ethnographies, and by reference to our model.

In all of the dual-spouted forms, the phalliform spout is positioned behind the funnel-shaped spout and is connected to this spout. It is this connection and the remaining extension of the phalliform spout that gives the appearance of the clitoris (see Table A, chapter 3). Any banded decoration at the base of the female funnel-shaped spout is always open, never closed at the back. This canon was scrupulously adhered to in all specimens examined. Occasionally, the phalliform spout is modeled in the shape of a lizard, an animal closely linked with phallic symbolism in neotropical cultures. In such cases, there is little more than a large pin hole at the top of the lizard's head, again reinforcing the penile associations of this form. Graphic realism in vulva symbolism appears to be strongest in the Tonosí and Conte styles, that is, from A.D. 100 to 800. If our interpretations of the diamond and rhomboid designs are correct, then after A.D. 800 vulva symbolism was increasingly, if not exclusively, rendered in geometric form. The vulva motif evident in the composition of the scorpion on Figure 61 is an exception to the general trend, as this is a Joaquín Polychrome in an early Macaracas Style.

Geometric Designs

Many of the designs found on Central Region painted ceramics incorporate geometrics in the total composition. Usually the designs comprise human, animal, or fantastic life-forms in combination with geometric designs. In a few examples, only geometric designs are used. Typically, the geometric designs have been looked upon by most researchers as having little more than aesthetic significance. In all cases, however, where ethnographic information has been solicited on geometric forms or design, we are informed that various geometric designs are highly symbolic, or that they reflect a tradition in which symbolism once prevailed but the symbolic significance has either been forgotten or is no longer known.

119. "Nipple-Spouted" Bottle with Geometric Design

This writer's own research on the geometric design elements of the American Southwest, embracing a large number of Puebloan groups, has shown that not only were these design elements imbued with powerful symbolism but, moreover, they were keyed to two distinct levels of meaning, one exotic and destined for the layman, the other esoteric, the provenance of shaman-priests. It was also shown that this geometric tradition was common to other areas of the Americas, and that in those areas where ethnographic information on the cognitive content of these designs is available, they are in conformity with interpretations given by Southwest Indian informants. This research culminated in a monograph titled *Art, Myth, and Cognition: An Exploration of the Esoteric Content of Southwest Indian Geometric Art* (Labbé), which has been available to scholars in microfiche and manuscript form since 1986.

It is beyond the scope of this chapter to review the geometric tradition in depth. It is the opinion of this researcher, however, that the geometric designs found on central Panamanian painted ceramics are cognitive in intent and that they were used essentially in the same manner as similar symbols found over wide areas of the Americas. The writer is not stating that every geometric design element had exactly the same exotic meaning or significance cross-culturally, but rather that, on an esoteric level, the geometric shapes and configurations reflect basic perceptions concerning the nature of relationship in the physical and biological worlds.

Our approach to the database has been empirical and essentially combines inductive and deductive models, in that order. We have observed that the precolumbian cognitive model is essentially binary. The Indian classifies his world in accordance with this model, which emphasizes the dynamic fertilizing nature of male-female interactions. We have also noted that the cognitive model will predict that rectilinear forms will be viewed as male, while curvilinear forms will be viewed as female. The model also predicts that protrusions, extensions, and convex forms will be classified as male; concavities, holes, and depressions as female. Color is more problematic but retains symbolic significance in extant ethnographic groups. In those cases where data is available, black is essentially a female color, while white and yellow are male colors. If the color scheme is binary and one is contrasted with the other, however, then in a black-and-red context black is female and red is male. With respect to Panamanian painted ceramics, where the color blue or purple is used, we are hypothesizing that blue/purple is the male dyad.

The shamanic universe, we have noted, is structured and divided into upper, middle, and lower worlds. The ethnographic literature informs us that the lower world is viewed as a domain dominated by female processes and is a mirror image of the upper world. We indicated that this view derived from using the movement of the sun and stars as a model. Hence, the sun, stars, and other entities are upright in the sky, but in their passage westward, as they fall from view at the western horizon and enter the underworld, their trek continues, but in an easterly direction in an upside-down position. We should also expect that color symbolism is reversed in underworld depictions.

One of the most common patterns found in geometric art is the juxtaposition of contrasting sets of alternating upward- and downward-pointing triangles. Patterns such as this are invariably interpreted as the interaction of male and female dyads

120. Polychrome Ring-Based Bowl: Square and Rosette Design

121. "Nipple-Spouted" Bottle with Geometric Design

122. Tricolor Ring-Based Bowl: Abstract Eye Motif

with strong fertility connotations (Fewkes, 1898:258; Reichel Dolmatoff, 1985:32). The design found on some vessels is composed almost entirely of such elements, contrasting black and white triangles arranged in bands. In Figure 119 red and blue triangular chevrons arranged in horizontal bands are contrasted with one another against a white ground. In the Southwest geometric tradition, this pattern is used to represent water but still retains the fertility connotations associated with the intersecting triangle motif (Waters, 1963:77–78; Labbé, 1986b:69).

Figure 120, a ring-based plate, is decorated with geometrics solely on the underside, while the upper side is painted red. Our model would suggest that since the design is found on the underside of the vessel, structurally this side would be viewed as the female or underworld side of the composition. It is interesting that the motif at the center of the composition is one commonly found on prehistoric American Southwest Anasazi painted ceramics, particularly the Kayenta branch of this tradition. The form is that of a stylized swastika, which in Southwest traditions is associated with fire and the movement of the sun (Waters, 1963:138–39; Labbé, 1986b:76–80). Note that in our Panamanian example the crampons are bent, indicating a left-to-right clockwise motion. The sun in the daylight sky moves counterclockwise from east to west, but in the underworld, it would move west to east in a clockwise direction. Our model would also predict that the daylight sun is essentially imbued with strong masculine energies, which dissipate and wane between the zenith and the western horizon. Vis-à-vis the daylight sun, however, the underworld night sun has been transformed into a feminine mirror image of its daylight self. Therefore, it is not unexpected that in the underworld our essential blue-red color contrasts would be reversed. Note also how the rectilinear projecting elements in the composition interact with the curvilinear forms, again emphasizing male-female dichotomies. Whatever specific meaning or artistic intent this composition may have held for the society for which it was created, on a general level it is in perfect conformity with the canons of the model.

The beautiful composition evinced in Figure 121 combines complementary as well as oppositional configurations incorporating the popular YC-scroll design element, both of which were noted in Lothrop's study of Coclé ceramics excavated at Sitio Conte. Note how the artist has contrasted red and blue claws in alternating fashion, while sets of paired opposites are juxtaposed to create sets of paired complementary designs. The main import of this composition is the emphasis on duality, as it expresses itself in varying combinations.

In Figure 122, alternating circular bands of red and blue are arranged concentrically against a white ground. This motif is possibly an abstraction of the eye design element. Although there are a number of ways Central Region artists illustrated eyes, the forms most commonly used to depict shamanic eyes were concentric circles, the circle and the dot, and the long-beaked, bird-head-in-profile eye element.

Motifs with Possible Solar or Astronomical Significance

A decorative scheme commonly used on carinated jars is the circle-cross-X pattern. It is most often used to decorate the shoulder of carinated vessels (Figs. 47, 123, 124), but is also found in other forms (Fig. 37). The circle-cross-X decorative pattern was widespread and is found in the prehistoric art of groups in

123. Polychrome Carinated Jar:
Solar Pattern with Saurian Decorative Panels

124. Polychrome Carinated Jar
in the Form of a Stylized Turtle

California, the American Southwest, México, Central America, and South America. Typically, this motif is used to decorate the shoulder of vessels that also incorporate a turtle as a dominant element. It is still being made in this form by contemporary Pueblo Indian ceramists, as well as by indigenous groups in Brasil.

The prehistoric Panamanian examples are usually large carinated jars that have been slightly modified either by modeling or painted design to show the head, legs, and tail of a turtle. In the American Southwest Indian context, it is a genre showing the relationship of the movement of the sun along the horizon and the earth. (For the use of the circle-and-cross motif to represent the sun, see Mallery, 1972:694; Fewkes, 1973:156–58; Labbé, 1986b:74–75.) The turtle is widely used as a symbol of the earth. It should be noted that the circle-cross-X is incorporated in the basic layout of the famed Aztec calendar stone. In North America, the earth is often referred to as "turtle island." Roe (1982) and Reichel-Dolmatoff (1971) have emphasized the female, uterine, vaginal connotations associated with the turtle.

Our interpretation of the combined turtle and circle-cross-X imagery as signifying a cosmological representation of upper, middle, and lower worlds and the movement of the sun along the horizon is, of course, hypothetical for the ancient Panamanian context, but it nonetheless deserves closer scrutiny. In our model, the carination represents the horizon. The circle-and-cross, represents the sun. The turtle represents the earth and the lower vessel represents the underworld. The spout, itself, may represent the axis mundi. It is interesting to note that in Figure 124 care has been taken to distinguish the arms of the cross. In some specimens, a short rectangular mark is opposed along the same axis by a long rectangular mark. In Figure 124, one of the arms of the cross is greatly reduced in size as compared to the other arms of the cross. We would expect that this marks the east-west pole of the cross, indicating the rising and setting of the sun at the eastern and western horizons, respectively. The rationale behind the circle-and-cross motif is that the circle can represent the disc of the sun as well as the horizon, while the cross is related to symbology referencing stars, fire, and the four directions. Since the sun is a heavenly body related in fact and myth with the stars and the earth as well as with a complex of myths relating to fire, the symbol is rich in relevant associated imagery. The symbol, therefore, would not only represent the sun but also the four directions and other correlative imagery. The most common geometric symbols used to represent stars in the Americas were the simple cross and the circle and dot. The use of the simple cross as a symbol for a star is noted for the Skidi Pawnee (Chamberlain, 1982), for the Hopi (Colton 1959:18), Southwest Indians and North American Indians in general (Mallery, 1972:697). It is strongly implied as a symbol for a star in the art of the Shipibo and Conibo of Perú.

The use of the circle and dot as a symbol for a star is noted for the Chumash of California (Hudson and Underhay, 1978; Labbé, Hudson, and Moser, 1983) and the Aztecs of México (Aveni, 1980), among others. The deer-tibia whistles containing star maps consisting of circles and dots arranged in the form of constellations (Labbé, Hudson, and Moser, 1983) are very similar to homologous artifacts found in Ecuador. In the Chumash example, small circular shells with the center drilled out were affixed to a deer tibia bone in patterns suggesting constellations. A notch at the top of the bone may have been used to sight the stars. In the Ecuadorian examples, the circles and dots are incised into the bone and arranged in patterns, again suggesting constellations. Carved notches are also prominent in the Ecuadorian examples.

An interpretation of the composition on Figure 125 is problematic. As with Figures 47, 123, and 124, a turtle is incorporated as part of the overall composition. Figure 125 is also carinated. This would suggest that the composition might be related to solar movement and its relationship to the earth. Only two arms of the cross, however, are indicated in red. A valid hypothetical interpretation of this composition in conformity with our structural model would be the following: the red bands represent the east-west pole. The red discs represent the sun, while the dotted circles represent stars. A common South American metaphor for the Milky Way is the image of stars caught in a net, which in this composition is

125. Polychrome Carinated Figural Jar: Turtle

126. Polychrome Pedestaled Plate: Solar Shamans

represented by the black-outlined white bands. One half of the composition may delineate the east-west movement of the sun during the day; the other half, the west-to-east movement of the sun in the underworld at night. Note that this solar pathway forms an ellipse, as described in the ethnographies. Given the complex of associated iconography, such an interpretation, although of necessity hypothetical, is not without merit.

In South Amerindian mythology, the Milky Way is often portrayed as a river. As Roe (1982:136) has noted, it is the celestial analog to the underworld river of death. Both streams are closely associated with illness among many groups. The sinous flowing form of the celestial Milky Way is also often compared to a serpent or anaconda (Tastevin, 1925:182, on the Tupi; Roe, 1982:173; Reichel-Dolmatoff, 1982:178; Hugh-Jones, 1982:185–86).

The design on the shoulder of Figure 25 would seem to closely conform to the iconographic criteria associated with the representation of the celestial Milky Way. The predominant form is a gigantic serpent. The serpent's body clearly marks off the four cardinal directions when the vessel is viewed from above. Numerous cross elements border the contour of the serpentine body along its course. These most likely represent background stars associated with the Milky Way. Again, although our interpretation must remain hypothetical, it is given credibility by the cohesion and consistency of the iconographic elements, when compared to the ethnographic references and associations.

On the other hand, the imagery depicted on Figure 13, although also serpentine in essence and associated with cross elements, is different and distinct from Figure 25. In Figure 13 the creature has a birdlike head with unusual cresting, legs, and serpentine body. Note the large concentric eye and the fact that the crest covers not only the head but the beak as well. Moreover, the cross elements are grouped in distinct patterns. Over wide areas of the Americas, a disc with a serrated corona is used as a solar symbol. The crested figure appears to be a personification of the sun as First Shaman, an association made by the Desana, Kogi, and many other South American groups. The large concentric eye dominates the head and clearly identifies the creature as shamanic or supernatural. The pattern represented by the cross elements suggests a specific constellation of significance to indigenous astronomy. It would appear that the serpentine body of the creature represents a "star path" (see Hugh-Jones, 1982:186–87, for the serpent used as star paths by the Barasana). The design on this vessel is bilateral, found in mirror-image form on each side of the vessel. Our interpretation of this motif is as follows: The constellation represented is one used by the native group to signal the advent of two events, possibly the heralding of the dry and wet seasons. Our reasoning is this: If the serpent's body is a star path and the subject of the composition is the sun, then the body represents the path taken by the sun in a daily or yearly cycle. If this is correct, then the loops in the body show the relative position of the sun with respect to the cross elements forming the constellation. Note that each loop of the body alternately shows the sun as either above or below the constellation. We could interpret this as signifying that when the sun is visible at the zenith, the constellation is in the underworld at the nadir, and when the sun is invisible, the constellation is in the night sky at the zenith.

Similar patterns of alternating upper and lower worlds seem to be implied in the design of other vessels. In some cases, the cross elements are in association with a human figure. Instead of a clear serpentine star path, the pathway appears to be represented in geometric form as a band of parallel lines in black with a red border. Articulated bands envelop the purported constellation within triangular panels. The human figure is alternately placed upright or upside down, in the same manner that the loops of the serpent's body in Figure 13 were either above or below the constellation.

In Figure 26, cross elements can be seen below a large shamanic mythic figure characterized by a large concentric eye and long slender body that terminates in a monkey-like tail. As in Figure 13, the layout is bilateral. Although this composition would seem to fall within the category of motifs with solar or astronomical intent, the supporting criteria is not as strong as in the preceding examples.

Figure 126 has strong solar connotations. It is characterized by four rectangular panels and four circular panels with swirling motifs. Two of the rectangular panels are decorated with a bird-beaked serpentine creature, while two have bird-beaked, standing anthropomorphic figures. The head of each standing figure is decorated with the circle-and-cross, motif, a solar symbol. Additionally, each figure has a crescent-shaped discoid element in yellowish-red adjacent and to the left of the body. This may represent a solar disc being eclipsed or a scene depicting a ritual associated with the sun. In any event, the quadrilateral layout (possibly marking off the four directions), the solar disc used for the head, and the devices in the circles, which in the American Southwest geometric tradition are motion symbols with strong associations with the sun, conjoin to suggest the overriding solar significance of the composition on a general level.

Postscript

Our investigation of art and prehistory in the Central Region of Panamá has revealed a rich, cohesive tradition that must be ranked among the most expressive and dynamic yet found in prehispanic America. Thanks to the patient persistence of numerous investigators from diverse disciplines, this long neglected chapter in New World prehistory is finally taking form. Much work remains, however, before the gaps in our understanding can be filled.

Undoubtedly, as additional information is secured, chronological schemes and interpretations will have to be adjusted accordingly. Our purpose has been to record what is known to date and to offer insight into the cognitive world of these precolumbian artists and the societies they served.

GUARDIANS OF THE LIFE STREAM

Various Perspectives of the Basic Pedestaled Bowl Form:
Interior Bowl, Underside and Upright

GLOSSARY

Acculturation: The adopting of another group's culture by someone who was born into a different culture.

Anthropomorphic: Having humanlike form or characteristics.

Apices: Plural of apex, a tip, point, or summit.

Baroque: Characterized by compact, extravagant decoration concentrating and intensifying the proportion of line to space.

Bifid: Divided into two sides by means of a median cleft.

Bilateral: Characterized by having two sides.

Billfish: Any number of fish, such as marlin or gar, characterized by long slender jaws.

Canon: A body of laws, rules, principles, or criteria governing a field of art.

Circumferential: Characterized by extending around or encircling the body of a vessel.

Clyster: Enema.

Cognitive: Inherent meaning based on the process of knowing; as used in the text, the meaning behind the form and imagery in art.

Cosmology: Study of the origin, structure, and nature of the universe.

Crampon: A hooked crutch; as used in the text, perpendicular lines extending from the ends of a cross, forming a "swastika."

Crosshatching: The practice of hatching, or shading, by means of two or more intersecting or parallel lines.

Dimorphic: Characterized by two distinct forms.

Dyad: A pair or set of two.

Esoteric: Pertaining to knowledge or understanding that is restricted to elite groups, such as shamans and priests.

Ethnocultural: Pertaining to the culture of a specific ethnic group. Ethnocultural art is art that is specific to certain groups and used for the internal purposes of that group.

Ethnography: The gathering and recording of information on human cultures.

Fecundity: State of being fruitful in bringing forth progeny.

Genre: A recognizable class or style of art composition that is found repeatedly within an art tradition and is typtified by a particular form, content, or technique.

Heuristic: Serving to aid or assist in learning.

Hieratic: Of or pertaining to priestly characteristics.

Homologous: Characterized by similarity in form, structure, or other attributes.

Iconography: Refers to the images and symbolism associated with a work of art.

Meanders: Pattern characterized by irregular bends, curves, or winding.

Metaphor: Broadly speaking, it is figurative language in which a word or image denoting one thing is used to suggest a similarity with something else that it does not literally denote.

Nadir: The point opposite the zenith in the celestial sphere; the lowest point.

Neotropical: Of or pertaining to biogeographic tropical regions of North and South America, including the West Indies.

Paradigm: An underlying example or model; an outstanding, clear archetype. As used in the text, an underlying model that serves as the rationale for cultural patterns.

Phalliform: Shaped like a phallus or penis.

Piedmont: Area or region at the base of mountains.

Plastically: Characterized by modeling.

Polymorphous: Characterized by the ability to change or assume different forms.

Punctate: Characterized by dots or points.

Quadrilateral: Characterized by having four sides.

Saurian: Having lizard or dinosaurlike characteristics. In Panamanian art, a stock icon characterized by a lizard or crocodilian head and/or body.

Scarified: Characterized by scratches or small cuts, or irregular incisions.

Shaft-and-Chamber Tombs: A grave characterized by a vertical shaft leading to a hollow, or chamber, at the base. The bodies are placed in the chamber along with grave offerings. Shaft-and-chamber tombs are found from west Mexico through South America, mainly in the western reaches of the continents. Shafts vary in depth from relatively shallow shafts of six feet to deep shafts, such as some found in southern Colombia, which measure more than one hundred feet in depth.

Theriomorphic: Shaped like a beast or animal.

Trilateral: Characterized by having three sides.

Zenith: The highest point reached in the heavens by the sun or stars.

PHOTO LISTINGS

4 POLYCHROME JAR WITH SPLIT-IMAGE (FRONTAL AND LATERAL) SAURIANS
Macaracas Style. Central Region, Panamá.
c. A.D. 800–1000. Fired Clay, Paint.
16" h. x 18 1/3" w.
The basic design layout is bilateral, with frontal-facing, split-image figures on opposite sides of the vessel, while the remaining two sides are decorated with juxtaposed pairs of serpentine saurians with complementary body coloration. The neck and rim of this vessel appear to have been intentionally cut away in antiquity, perhaps as part of a burial ritual.
Anonymous Collection, Carmel.

5 POLYCHROME OLLA WITH BILATERALLY SPACED SAURIAN HEADS AT THE NECK
Macaracas Style. Central Region, Panamá.
c. A.D. 800–1000. Fired Clay, Paint.
25.5" d. x 19 3/4" h.
The neck of the vessel is missing, possibly intentionally cut away in antiquity as part of a burial rite. The decoration consists of YC scrolls used as the body of a creature with the head of a saurian. Note the tendrils emanating from the saurian's mouth, indicative of its shamanic nature.
Thomas Collection.

6 POLYCHROME OLLA DECORATED WITH LARGE SHAMANIC EGG-LAYING BIRDS
Macaracas Style. Central Region, Panamá.
c. A.D. 800–1000. Fired Clay, Paint.
21.5 " d. x 17" h.
The shamanic nature of the birds is indicated by the stylized YC scroll terminating in a claw decorating the body of each bird. The birds are spaced equidistant from one another along the neck of the vessel. The neck is missing, probably intentionally cut away in antiquity as part of a burial rite.
Anonymous Collection, Los Angeles.

7 POLYCHROME FIGURAL JAR WITH DUAL HANDLES
Macaracas Style. Central Region, Panamá.
c. A.D. 800–1000. Fired Clay, Paint.
The face blends anthropomorphic and birdlike characteristics. The body of the vessel is decorated with Y-scroll elements terminating in claw elements.
Anonymous Collection, New York.

10 BICHROME JAR: MYTHIC THEME INCORPORATING A SERPENT, BIRDS, AND BEETLE
La Mula Style. Central Region, Panamá.
c. 500–100 B.C. Fired Clay, Paint.
13 1/2" h. x 13 3/4" w.
Anonymous Collection, San Francisco.

11 BICHROME JAR DECORATED WITH THREE BIRDS
Unidentified Black-on-Red. Central Region, Panamá.
c. A.D. 100–200. Fired Clay, Paint.
12 3/4" h. x 14 1/2" d.
The design layout is trilateral and comprises three birds with outstretched wings positioned end to end. Vultures may be the intended avian species. The dating of this specimen is problematic but based on componential analysis of design elements and vessel form it stylistically falls between the La Mula and Tonosí styles.
Anonymous Collection, San Francisco.

12 TRICOLOR GLOBULAR JAR OR OLLA: MYTHIC FIGURE WITH BIRDS
Tonosí Style. Central Region, Panamá. Azuero Peninsula.
c. A.D. 200–400. Fired Clay, Paint.
13" h. x 16 3/4" w.
The central figure is a mythic being, characterized by two huge serpentine tails. The figure's chest is decorated with black vertical triangles paired with white horizontal triangles. This pattern appears to represent interacting male-female dyads, with strong fertility connotations.

The dualism in the composition is given further emphasis. An identical figure stands opposite this figure on the other side of the vessel. Both figures are joined together at the tails. As in other related compositions, the undulations of the tail enclose the figure of a bird. Also familiar are the parallel-lined rectangular panels and the ovoid, lozenge-shaped elements. The neck and rim of vessels such as this appear to have been intentionally cut away or broken off in many specimens.
Anonymous Collection, San Francisco.

13 SHORT-NECK TRICOLOR JAR WITH PANELED DESIGN: COMPOSITE CREATURE COMBINING BIRD AND SERPENT WITH POSSIBLE ASTRONOMICAL SIGNIFICANCE
Tonosí Style. Central Region, Panamá.
c. A.D. 400. Fired Clay, Paint.

131. Tricolor Jar: Geometrics and Faces

c. 10 1/2" d.
The creature's head has a beak and is birdlike. The spiked crest, however, is suspicious, as it extends even over the beak. The cross elements in the background likely represent stars, specifically some constellation of significance to the artist's group. Note that the same pattern of crosses is repeated and enveloped by alternating up or down coils of the creature's body. The cross was widely used as a symbol for stars in the Americas. The bird's head may represent the sun, the serpentine body the seasonal movement of the sun, using the constellation as a marker for the seasons. Although this interpretation is purely hypothetical, it is not without interpretive basis given South American and Central American Indian astronomical lore. Constellations were widely used in South America to herald the dry and rainy seasons.
Courtesy of Museo Antropológico Reina Torres de Araúz.

14 TRICOLOR DUAL-SPOUTED VESSEL: LIZARD AND BIRDS
Late Tonosí Style (Ichon's Montevideo). Central Region, Panamá.
c. A.D. 400–500. Fired Clay, Paint.
13" h. x 12" w.
A lizard with front legs on rim looks over the large central spout. The lizard's tail is long, serpentine, with many undulations. Placed within the space created by each loop or undulation of the tail is a large bird with a long red beak. Cross elements, possibly representing stars, can be seen in the background, along with rectangular panels and concentric lozenge-shaped forms. The composition suggests a theme taken from indigenous myth or cosmology having celestial or sky connotations. The concentric lozenge-shaped elements are of two kinds, those with red centers and those with a single black line at the center. The top of the lizard's head is perforated, confirming the lizard as a spout. As is common with the dual-spouted vessel form, female genitalia are suggested, when the vessel is viewed from above.
Thomas Collection.

15 TRICOLOR DUAL-SPOUTED JAR: LIZARD AND BIRDS
Late Tonosí Style (Ichon's Montevideo). Central Region, Panamá.
c. A.D. 400–500. Fired Clay, Paint.
9 1/4" h. x 10 1/2" w.
This composition constitutes a thematic genre incorporating a large lizard with serpentine tail and birds placed within the curves of the tail. Cross-shaped elements, possibly representing stars, and parallel-lined rectangular panels of unknown significance form part of the general background. In this example as well as others, the birds alternate with vulva-shaped concentric ovoids. Vulva-phallic symbolism is also connotated and possibly denoted by the shape and juxtaposition of the dual spouts, one phalliform, one suggesting the female genitalia. Note the open-ended bands at the rim, neck, and shoulder, with the phalliform lizard placed in front of the opening. In the American Southwest geometric tradition and elsewhere, such forms have been interpreted as womb symbols. The cross elements in the background suggest that this theme also has cosmic or celestial significance. A small hole extending to the inside of the jar is visible at the top of the lizard's head, lending further corroboration that the lizard is phallic in intent, as this would serve as a penile aperture and is too small to have effectively served as a normal spout. Additionally, within the context of the American Southwest geometric symbol tradition, both the design on the rim and around the neck would have fertility connotations. The white elements would be male elements while the black and hachured elements would be female.
Thomas Collection.

16 TRICOLOR DUAL-SPOUTED VESSEL: FEMALE GENITALIA
Cubitá Style. Central Region, Panamá.
c. A.D. 500–600. Fired Clay, Paint.
6 1/2" h. x 8 1/8" d.
The dominant motif in this vessel is that of the female genitalia, replete with pubic hair. The spout serves as the clitoris. This specimen reinforces the perception that female genitalia are an intended motif in all of the dimorphic dual-spouted vessels from Central Panamá. The female organ of generation was the portal for new life, a place of emergence, growth, and transformation and, as such, a sacred enclosure, sacred space.
Thomas Collection.

17 TRICOLOR DOUBLE JAR: HUMAN FIGURES BEARING A RECTANGULAR OBJECT
Tonosí Style. Central Region, Panamá.

c. A.D. 200–400. Fired Clay, Paint.
9 3/4" h. x 12 1/4" w.
It is difficult to discern the exact scenario intended in this composition. The design is bilateral and is repeated not only on each side of the vessel but is also in an upper and lower circumferential band. Each scenario is identical with respect to the number and placement of the six bearers. These are absent in the lower frieze. Also, the cage, box, or other object being borne by the upper frieze bearers has added decor atop the object in the lower frieze.
Anonymous Collection, Texas.

18 BLACK-ON-RED BOWL: POSSIBLY FROGS OR LIZARDS JOINED IN OPPOSING FASHION
Ciruelo Black-on-Red, Cubitá Group. Central Region, Panamá.
c. A.D. 500–600. Fired Clay, Paint.
c. 12" d.
Each set of paired design elements is used to compose a basic component of the frog's body. Note that the legs of the frogs are formed by using a design element associated with the concept of unity among other Amerindian groups. That this may be the intent here seems to be supported by 1) the elements are not true legs, but seem to be emphasized in and of themselves as a unit, and 2) the dualistic rendering of the frog in which one points up and the other down, is in conformity with the use of this symbol elsewhere as an element that unites paired opposites, such as heaven and earth, male and female, and positive and negative energies.
Courtesy of Museo Antropológico Reina Torres de Araúz.

19 BLACK-ON-RED BOWL: BINARY GEOMETRICS IN NEGATIVE AND POSITIVE DESIGN
Ciruelo Black-on-Red, Cubitá Group. Central Region, Panamá.
c. A.D. 500–600. Fired Clay.
c. 12" d.
The artist has skillfully employed the interplay of positive black line design and negative red ground design to create interlocking sets of paired forms.
Courtesy of Museo Antropológico Reina Torres de Araúz.

20 BICHROME BOWL DECORATED WITH A COMPOSITE BIRD FORM
Ciruelo Black-on-Red, Cubitá Group. Central Region, Panamá.
c. A.D. 500–600. Fired Clay, Black Paint.
8 1/2" h. x 24 1/8" d.
The intended form is most likely that of a bird. The artist, however, appears to be playing on dimorphic symbolism. The upper portion of the bird is formed by a single band with an eye indicated at one end and streamers, possibly representing a foot or perhaps tail feathers, at the opposite end. The lower part of the bird is also formed by a single band, also incorporating an eye at one end and similar streamers at the opposite end. The head of the bird is composed of the two individual bands. The body of the bird consists of an ovoid form decorated with a net pattern. Note the intentional splitting of the two bands at both the beak and the tail end. The bird is flanked by decorative panels embellished with horizontal and vertical bands containing lines of black dots. Within the context of the Southwest and other geometric symbol traditions, dots represent seeds or potential new life. Note, bowl 21 was reputedly found inside this larger bowl. The bilateralism evident in design suggests male/female dichotomies and, hence, fertility—the net pattern that results from the crossing of weft and warp or male and female elements—unites the two principles within itself.
Thomas Collection.

21 BICHROME BOWL DECORATED WITH A LIZARD/FROG
Ciruelo Black-on-Red, Cubitá Group. Central Region, Panamá.
c. A.D. 500–600. Fired Clay, White Paint.
7" h. x 20 1/8" d.
The design is restricted to the interior of the bowl. A large lizard with a froglike head dominates the central design field. The artist has carefully divided the basically white animal with a median strip of background red, which runs the length of the body. The head of the animal extends within a confined space created by a set of two white lines. The lizard/frog is flanked by decorative panels, each comprising a horizontal band containing rows of dots and vertical bands with rows of dots. The artistic emphasis in this composition is on bilateralism. Although the design is rendered in white, this may simply be due to the chemical breakdown of the original black paint.
Thomas Collection.

22 TRICOLOR DOUBLE JAR: SHAMANIC BIRDS
Zahina Polychrome. Central Region, Panamá.
c. A.D. 200–400. Fired Clay, Paint.
13" h. x 14" d.
The design is bilateral. The designs on the upper vessel is mirrored in that of the lower vessel. Beginning with the upper vessel, observe a hieratic figure with arms upraised in negative design. This figure may represent the shaman in his role as mediator between upper, middle, and lower worlds. Note his upside-down reflection in the lower vessel. Note how this figure is flanked by two large birds, heads in profile, also mirrored in the composition below. Birds in profile are common icons associated with the shaman-in-transformation theme of which this composition appears to be a variant.
Anonymous Collection, Texas.

22a TRICOLOR BOWL: BIRD WITH OUTSTRETCHED WINGS
Zahina Polychrome. Central Region Panamá.
c. A.D. 200–400. Fired Clay, Paint.
2 1/4" h. x 8 3/4" d.
Anonymous Collection, New York.

23 TRICOLOR GLOBULAR JAR: SERPENT AND SHELLED NAUTILUS
Early Montijo Transitional Style. Central Region, Panamá. Prob. Veraguas Province.
c. A.D. 500. Fired Clay, Paint.
12 1/3" h. x 14" d.
The artist has skillfully drawn the serpent so that there are exactly five upward-pointing loops. The serpent itself is bilateral, formed by two black bands, joined only at the neck and tail. A band of red with black dots runs the length of the body and emerges from the serpent's mouth as a bifid tongue. The red band is separated from the black bands by two white bands, created as negative design by the ground. Five nautili, curiously shaped at one end like a human hand with five digits, decorate the space between the upward loops of the serpent's body. A smaller, sixth nautilus with an immature spiral is couched between the head and tail of the serpent.
Anonymous Collection, Los Angeles.

24 TRICOLOR JAR DECORATED WITH A BILATERAL SERPENT
Early Montijo Transitional Style. Central Region, Panamá. Veraguas Province.
c. A.D. 500. Fired Clay, Paint.
12 1/8" h. x 13 3/4" l.
The primary motif comprises a bilaterally divided serpent, with a central black-dotted band outlined in red. The serpent's body is created by uniting two serpents in profile. In appearance they suggest the horned "avantyu", a mythic horned serpent of the American Southwest Pueblos associated with water and the underworld. The artist has intentionally left the two halves of the composite head unconnected to emphasize that the new form is a by-product of two distinct forms, undoubtedly male and female aspects. The dotted band suggests a band of eggs or seeds, hence the association of this mythic creature with fertility. Dots are commonly used in the Americas to represent seeds, raindrops (figuratively imaged as seeds falling from the sky to fertilize the earth mother). On an esoteric level, the dot is any point of emergence, that is the emergence of new life. When viewed from above, the coils of the serpent create a quatrefoil design layout.
Anonymous Collection, Los Angeles.

25 TRICOLOR JAR WITH SKY DRAGON MOTIF
Montijo Transitional Style. Central Region, Panamá. Veraguas Province.
c. A.D. 500–600. Fired Clay, Paint.
12 1/4" h. x 14 1/2" d.
The primary design consists of a saurian-headed serpent whose body encircles the shoulder of the vessel. The head, coils, and folds in the serpent's body mark off the cardinal directions and give the design an overall quadrilateral layout. The numerous cross-shaped elements may represent stars. This would suggest that the serpent is celestial or cosmological in intent. In several widely dispersed Indian cultures the image of a

127. Tricolor Double Jar: Frogs in Negative Design

serpent encircling the heavens is used to represent the MilkyWay. The large number of stars in this composition would suggest such an interpretation for this composition.
Anonymous Collection, Los Angeles.

26 TRICOLOR GLOBULAR JAR DECORATED WITH MYTHIC ANIMAL
Montijo Transitional Style. Central Region, Panamá. Prob. Veraguas Province.
c. A.D. 500–600. Fired Clay, Paint.
12" h. x 13 1/2" d.
The design field consists of a band encircling the vessel. The design consists of two stylized animal forms characterized by long tails curved inward to form spirals. Small cross elements can be seen under the animal's body. One faces the other's tail, while on the other side a spiral-base geometric separates the head from the other's tail. The small cross elements may represent stars, while the animal form may be a mythic sky personage or constellation of significance to the indigenous cosmology.
Anonymous Collection, Los Angeles.

27 TRICOLOR GLOBULAR JAR: TRILATERAL SPIRAL DESIGN
Montijo Transitional Style. Central Region, Panamá.
c. A.D. 500–600. Fired Clay, Paint.
12" h. x 12 3/4" w.
The artist has skillfully used positive and negative space in executing this composition. The contours of the continuous design in red yields a complementary design in white, using the background as a color element. The red and white spirals result as an illusion created by the undulations of the red band. The resulting white design yields two interlocking yin-yang-like curvilinear forms suggesting dualistic complementarity. This patterning is repeated throughout the design utilizing both curvilinear and rectilinear elements. Note that in every instance

the red is used to create female "womb" or "socketlike" forms, while the white forms always interpenetrate the red forms. The design layout yields a double trefoil pattern, consisting of three curvilinear spirals and three rectilinear irregular triangular forms with circular quatreifoil rosettes at the center. The inherent blending of male and female forms is implicit in the composition.
Anonymous Collection, San Francisco.

28 POLYCHROME DUAL-SPOUTED FIGURAL JAR IN THE FORM OF A BIRD
Montijo Transitional Style. Central Region, Panamá.
c. A.D. 500–600. Fired Clay, Paint.
7 1/2" h. x 12" w.
The bird is characterized by a long red beak. The wings are outstretched and decorated with a composite creature, incorporating a serpentine body, a monkeylike tail, birdlike head, saurian mouth, and two saurian or crocodilian legs. The tail of the bird is decorated with a stylized bat.
Anonymous Collection, Los Angeles.

29 POLYCHROME DUAL-SPOUTED FIGURAL JAR IN THE FORM OF A BIRD
Montijo Transitional Style. Central Region, Panamá.
c. A.D. 500–600. Fired Clay, Paint.
7 1/4" h. x 7 1/2" w.
As in most dual-spouted specimens, the phalliform spout is always connected to the top of the larger central spout. Also, in most examples, an inverted U-shaped area is indicated at the back of the head and faces the phalliform spout.
Anonymous Collection, Los Angeles.

29a POLYCHROME SHALLOW BOWL: MYTHIC SHAMANIC CREATURE
Early Conte Style. Central Region, Panamá.
c. A.D. 600–700. Fired Clay, Paint.
This composition incorporates design elements from the earlier Montijo Transitional Style defined in this publication, such as the YC scroll, as well as the precursor to the Y element developed in the Tonosí Style which can be seen at the posterior of the creature just beneath the tail.
Courtesy of Robert T. Coffland and Mary Hunt Kahlenberg.

29b SHALLOW POLYCHROME BOWL: COMPOSITE SHAMANIC CREATURE BLENDING SAURIAN, SERPENT, AND SAWFISH CHARACTERISTICS
Conte Style. Central Region, Panamá.
c. A.D. 600–800. Fired Clay, Paint.
Note the creature has two heads, one at each end of the body.
Courtesy of Robert T. Coffland and Mary Hunt Kahlenberg.

30 RING-BASED POLYCHROME BOWL: MYTHIC SHAMANIC FIGURE
Conte Style. Central Region, Panamá.
c. A.D. 600–800. Fired Clay, Paint.
2 3/4" h. x 13" d.
The shamanic nature of this figure is indicated by the large concentric eye, the bilateral YC-scroll element, at the chest and the anthropomorphic form with clawed hands and feet. The representation may be that of the shaman in his role as "the germinator." One of the functions of the shaman is to assure fertility and viability of the biosphere. Note the rattles at the wrists and anklets. Also note the long serpentine phallus and how the artist has lined the inner legs of the figure with hairlines, possibly to illustrate a vulva. Compare this with the illustrations of the "vagina dentata" motifs associated with crabs in Conte art. The long, rectangular implement held to the mouth may be a tubular flute, an instrument associated with spring vegetation renewal rites among some Amerindian groups. The crossed object in the left hand appears to be a staff or scepter, similar to those used by the Tairona of the Sierra Nevada de Santa Marta in Colombia.
Anonymous Collection, Texas.

31 TRICOLOR RING-BASED BOWL: COMPOSITE ANIMAL
Conte Style. Central Region, Panamá.
c. A.D. 600–800. Fired Clay, Paint.
2 1/8" h. x 10 1/8" h.
The design is restricted to the interior of the bowl. The central motif is a composite animal form with an animal head, bird's body, and two clawed feet. Two volutes or scrolls can be seen front and aft, one emerging from the mouth, the other seemingly serving as the tail.
Anonymous Collection, San Francisco.

32 RING-BASED POLYCHROME BOWL: RUNNING BIRD
Conte Style. Central Region, Panamá.
c. A.D. 600–800. Fired Clay, Paint.
3 1/2" h. x 10 1/4" d.
The design is restricted to the interior of the bowl and consists of a running bird with filler elements in the background.
Anonymous Collection, San Francisco.

33 COMPOSITE CREATURE: ANIMAL - HUMAN - SERPENT
Conte Style. Central Region, Panamá. Coclé Province type.
c. A.D. 600–800. Fired Clay, Paint.
c. 10" d.
Composite creature of mythic or cosmological significance with long serpentine body, human posture, and animal head. Note the clawed hands and feet indicating a combative nature and the stylized T elements bordering the serpentine body.
Courtesy of Museo Antropológico Reina Torres de Araúz.

34 RING-BASED BOWL: COMPOSITE CREATURE INCORPORATING HUMAN AND BIRD CHARACTERISTICS
Conte Style. Central Region, Panamá.
c. A.D. 600–800. Fired Clay, Paint.
c. 7" d.
The artist has combined a human head—with long tendrils emanating from each side of the mouth—with the body of a bird. Two clawed feet can be seen below the wings. Claw elements border the birdtail. This composition is likely a rendering of the shaman-in-flight theme. In some South American Indian cultures (for example, the Warao) the shaman is said to be able to extend long fibers of vital force in the form of tendrils from the corners of his mouth to ensnare his enemies. The bird with human attributes is sometimes used in precolumbian art as an icon to depict an empowered shaman's ability to fly in his vitalforce "soul." The claw elements along the tail and the clawed feet reinforce the aggressive, combative nature of the theme.
Courtesy of Museo Antropológico Reina Torres de Araúz.

35 POLYCHROME RING-BASED PLATE: BIRDS AND SAURIANS
Conte Style. Central Region, Panamá.
c. A.D. 600–800. Fired Clay, Paint.
1 3/4" h. x 10 7/8" d.
The saurian emanations coming from the bird's body indicate that this is no ordinary bird but rather a transformed shaman. Note that the artist has painted the upper wings purple and the lower portion red with white in between. This is a color pattern seen repeatedly in the art of the Central Region. It is reflected again in the blue upper jaw and red lower jaw seen on the saurian figures.
Anonymous Collection, San Francisco.

36 RING-BASED TRICOLOR PLATE: SHAMANIC TRANSFORMATION THEME
Conte Style. Central Region, Panamá.
c. A.D. 600–800. Fired Clay, Paint.
2" h. x 11 1/4" d.
Typical of the transformation theme are emanations pouring from the head in undulating bands, terminating in heads. In the precolumbian tropical forest cognitive model, the right emanation is associated with the male principle and the left with the female principle. Note the two additional and complementary emanations emerging from the chin of the figure's face.
Anonymous Collection, Los Angeles.

37 POLYCHROME PLATE: SOLAR MOTIF WITH FOUR SAURIAN PANELS
Conte Style. Central Region, Panamá.
c. A.D. 600–800. Fired Clay, Paint.
c. 10 1/5" d.
This design conforms to the basic circle-cross-X pattern that may have solar associations. The circle and cross were widely used to represent the sun in Amerindian art. The four intervening panels are decorated with saurian heads, with an ovoid element containing a claw sign.
Courtesy of Museo Antropológico Reina Torres de Araúz.

37a POLYCHROME SHALLOW BOWL: SAURIAN-HEADED CREATURES AT THE FOUR DIRECTIONS
Conte Style. Central Region, Panamá.
c. A.D. 600–800. Clay, Paint.
This composition incorporates the circle-cross-X design layout hypothetically associated with the movement of the sun along the horizon.
Courtesy of Robert T. Coffland and Mary Hunt Kahlenberg.

38 POLYCHROME PEDESTALED BOWL: STANDING FIGURE EMITTING STINGRAY SPINES
Macaracas Style. Central Region, Panamá.
c. A.D. 800–1000. Fired Clay, Paint.
7 3/4" h. x 11 5/8" d.
The design covers the interior and exterior of the bowl as well as the exterior surface of the base. The primary motif decorates the interior of the bowl and consists of a standing anthropomorphic figure emitting sting-ray spines from his body. This may be a depiction of a shaman in combat pose or may represent a specific mythic figure taken from indigenous mythology. The underside of the bowl consists of a quadrilateral design layout incorporating four saurian heads. The body of each head is highly abstracted and consists of a winding band ending in a Y. In essence, this design motif is a Y-scroll pattern with the scroll formed by the saurian head. The base is decorated with diamond and triangle patterns. Triangularly shaped cutouts were made in the base after the piece was fired. Two of the cutouts have apices pointing upward and two are pointing downward.
Anonymous Collection, San Francisco.

39 POLYCHROME PEDESTALED BOWL: SHAMAN IN COMBAT
Macaracas Style. Central Region, Panamá.
c. A.D. 800–1000. Fired Clay, Paint.
5 1/2" h. x 10 1/2" d.
The design is restricted to the interior of the bowl and rim. The central motif is a standing anthropomorphic saurian, shown in profile. Note the color coding of the body, predominantly purple on the right and red on the left. Note also the saurian head emanating from the left side of the body. Essentially, this composition appears to depict a shaman whose powers have been activated to engage in shamanic combat with a potential adversary.
Anonymous Collection, San Francisco.

40 POLYCHROME PEDESTALED PLATE: DOUBLE SAURIAN WITH SERPENTINE BODY
Macaracas Style. Central Region, Panamá.
c. A.D. 800–1000. Fired Clay, Paint.
4 1/2" h. x 12" d.
The design is restricted to the interior of the bowl and rim. The creature is characterized by two heads, clawed feet, and a long serpentine body.
Anonymous Collection, San Francisco.

PHOTO LISTINGS

41 POLYCHROME PEDESTALED BOWL: RUNNING SAURIANS
Macaracas Style. Central Region, Panamá.
c. A.D. 800–1000. Fired Clay, Paint.
The design is restricted to the interior of the bowl and consists of a bilateral layout incorporating saurians running in opposite directions. A median panel, decorated with alternately colored bands of zigzags, separates the animal forms. Note the saurians are not true saurians but composite creatures blending saurian traits with those more characteristic of mammals, such as a thick tail and a full supple body.
Anonymous Collection, Los Angeles.

42 POLYCHROME PEDESTALED BOWL: BIRDS
Macaracas Style. Central Region, Panamá.
c. A.D. 800–1000. Fired Clay, Paint.
6 3/4" h. x 10 3/4" d.
The design is restricted to the interior of the bowl. The layout is bilateral, with the two side panels mediated by a central panel. One bird has a red body with purple wings, the other has a purple body with red wings. The same color complementarity is evident in the intersecting zigzag patterns used to decorate the median panel. The intent appears clear. Paired male and female forms yield vitality and fertility, as symbolized by the zigzag lightning elements. Each bird is outlined utilizing serrated lines suggesting barbs such as are found in stingray spines. Postfired out-carving of two triangular elements is evident on base.
Anonymous Collection, San Francisco.

43 POLYCHROME PEDESTALED BOWL: STINGRAY-TAILED IGUANAS
Macaracas Style. Central Region, Panamá.
c. A.D. 800–1000. Fired Clay, Paint.
5 1/4" h. x 13" d.
These are composite creatures blending traits seen in different species. Note the Y scroll terminating in a claw at the abdomen. This may be a way of indicating a shamanic embryo or a latent potential within the creature to manifest shamanic power. Also note the yin-yang–like complementarity in the positioning of the creature.
Anonymous Collection, Texas.

44 RING-BASED POLYCHROME JAR WITH NECK AND FLARING RIM: TRANSFORMED SHAMAN IN RITUAL POSE
Macaracas Style. Central Region Panamá.
c. A.D. 800–1000. Fired Clay, Paint.
8 7/8" h. x 8" d.
The body of the vessel has a quadrilateral design layout with four panels. Each panel is decorated with a standing anthropomorphic saurian, probably representing a shaman. The pose is dynamic and depicts a transformed shaman in militant pose, or one ready for shamanic combat. Note that the figures are paired according to their predominant body color. Two have purple torsos, while two have red torsos. The neck of the vessel is decorated with saurian heads, abstracted from the fuller figures below. Two heads point upward, two downward.
Anonymous Collection, Los Angeles.

45 POLYCHROME CARINATED JAR: STANDING SAURIANS
Macaracas Style. Central Region, Panamá. Parita Bay Region.
c. A.D. 800–1000. Fired Clay, Paint.
10 5/8" h. x 13 3/4" d.
The shoulder of the jar is decorated with two standing saurian figures one on each side of the vessel. Each is facing in a direction opposite the other. Streams of energy emanate from the body of each figure ending in volutes or spirals. These figures are variations on the shaman-in-combat theme.
Anonymous Collection, Los Angeles.

46 POLYCHROME PEDESTALED BOWL: FISH
Parita Style. Central Region, Panamá.
c. A.D. 1000–1300. Fired Clay, Paint.
7" h. x 9" d.
The design covers the interior and rim of the bowl and the exterior of the pedestal base. The central motif is a fish placed in a central tondo. The artist has used purple and red to contrast both sides of the fish as well as the upper and lower planes of the head. The rim is decorated with complementary bilateral designs. Note the two highly abstract and stylized faces on opposite sides of the rim.
Thomas Collection.

128. Tricolor Dual-Spouted Jar Decorated with Bats

47 POLYCHROME CARINATED JAR IN THE FORM OF A STYLIZED TURTLE
Parita Style. Central Region, Panamá.
c. A.D. 1000–1300. Fired Clay, Paint.
11 1/3" h. x 13" d.
Only the head, tail, and legs are indicated. The carination of the vessel serves as the edge of the turtle's shell. The shoulder of the vessel is decorated with eight panels, four large and four small. As with other vessels of this style and genre, when viewed from above the layout is in the form of a cross with a circle at the center, in this case formed by the rim of the vessel.

In the context of some Amerindian traditions, this would be a solar symbol. The arms of the cross indicate the four directions and position of the sun along the horizon; rising sun in the east, zenith in the south, sunset in the west, and nadir in the north. Note that one red disc is unnucleated while the other three are nucleated.
Anonymous Collection, Los Angeles.

48 TRICOLOR PEDESTALED JAR IN THE FORM OF A STINGRAY
Parita Style. Central Region, Panamá.
c. A.D. 1000–1300. Fired Clay, Paint.
9 1/2" h. x 17 1/2" w. x 18 1/2" l.
The artist has skillfully modified the basic pedestaled jar form by means of modeling and paint to create the stingray.
Collection of James A. Greaves.

49 POLYCHROME PEDESTALED BOWL: STYLIZED ABSTRACT BIRDS
Early Parita Style. Central Region, Panamá.
c. A.D. 1000–1100. Fired Clay, Paint.
7 7/8" h.
This vessel is indicative of the shift from Macaracas Style to the Early Parita Style. The bird forms are highly abstract, which is in conformity with stylistic trends seen in Parita. The vessel form, however, is closer to Macaracas. The filling of the design field is also more characteristic of Macaracas.
Anonymous Collection, Santa Ana.

50 TRICOLOR CARINATED JAR WITH SOLAR MOTIF
Parita Style. Central Region, Panamá. Parita Bay region.
c. A.D. 1000–1300. Fired Clay, Paint.
12" h. x 15 3/4" w.
The primary design field comprises the rim and shoulder. The rim and accompanying bands form the central circle. The shoulder design layout yields a circle-cross-X pattern comprised of four smaller trapezoidal panels for the cross and four larger trapezoidal patterns for the X. The cross and circle in some Amerindian traditions represents the sun, with the four horizon directions implied. The X pattern could mark off the rising and setting points of the winter and summer solstices. The carination would represent the horizon or meeting of sky and earth. Often, the carination of vessels such as this is modified to represent a turtle, an animal icon widely used as an earth symbol in precolumbian America. The zigzag bands used to decorate the arms of the crosspattern in the same tradition symbolizes lightning and hence vital force. In most native traditions the sun is viewed as the source of vital force and the source of life on earth. Lightning was also closely associated with fertility in the indigenous mind.
Thomas Collection.

51 TRICOLOR FOOTED BOWL: TURTLE MOTIF
El Hatillo Style. Central Region, Panamá.
c. A.D. 1300–1520. Fired Clay, Paint.
5" h. x 9 1/2" d.
The artist appears to be conjoining two stylized bird forms seen in profile, in the composition of the turtle. Note that unlike true turtles, the shell is split and opened both at the front and back. The turtle's head results by joining the bird heads together. The birds' bodies form the turtle's shell. The emphasis on bilateralism is reinforced by the bilateral S motif, with similar flanges placed in yin-yang fashion.
Anonymous Collection, Los Angeles.

52 TRICOLOR VESSEL IN THE FORM OF A CROCODILIAN
El Hatillo Style. Central Region, Panamá, Veraguas Province.
c. A.D. 1300–1520. Fired Clay, Paint.
15 1/3" l. x 5 7/8" h.
The tendency to "load" a single form with multiple representations, a trait not uncommon in Panamanian art, is also evident in this artwork. The eyes of the crocodilian also serve as the eyes of a frog, the body of which has been painted on the top of the crocodilian's back. The black dots may be an allusion to eggs and hence may be a convention used by the artist to identify the frog as female. In the binary cognitive systems of tropical forest indians, a gender-based dualism pervades. Animals are routinely classified as representing male or female principles in the native cosmos, irrespective of the fact that such species naturally are represented by both genders. The crocodilian, being a primary predator, would be a natural choice as a male element. The down- and up-pointing triangles may also have fertility connotations. Hence, male (crocodilian) as well as female (frog) elements are united in the composition. This would have fertility connotations from the indigenous perspective.
Anonymous Collection, Los Angeles.

53 TRICOLOR FIGURAL VESSEL IN THE FORM OF A HORNED OWL
El Hatillo Style. Central Region, Panamá.
c. A.D. 1300–1520. Fired Clay.
c. 6 3/5" d.
Only the head of the owl is indicated by modeling.
Courtesy of Museo Antropológico Reina Torres de Araúz.

PHOTO LISTINGS

54 POLYCHROME JAR WITH STANDING HIERATIC FIGURE
Tonosí Style. Central Region, Panamá.
c. A.D. 200–400. Clay, Paint.
15" h. x 14 1/2" d.
Hourglass-shaped elements decorate the chest and abdomen of the figure. Figures such as this constitute a genre theme in Tonosí art. Commonly, long-legged birds are enveloped in loops formed by the tail of the figure. In this example there are two tails. This composition may possibly be a reference to the shaman's role as guardian of species or a reference to a personage akin to the Master of Animals.
Former Collection of Ben Johnson.

55 RING-BASED POLYCHROME BOWL WITH CRAB MOTIF
Conte Style . Central Region, Panamá.
c. A.D. 600–800. Fired Clay, Paint.
2 1/4" h. x 8 1/3" d.The artist has used red and purple colors to accent dimorphic dualism in the composition and complementarity in the appendages and formal characteristics of the crab.
Collection of James A. Greaves.

56 POLYCHROME PEDESTALED BOWL: SHAMAN-IN-COMBAT THEME
Macaracas Style. Central Region, Panamá.
c. A.D. 800–1000. Clay, Paint.
6" h. x 12 1/2" d.
Emanations can be seen at the head and at the right side of the figure. Note the stingray spines radiating from the body.
Anonymous Collection, San Francisco.

57 POLYCHROME RING-BASED JAR DECORATED WITH FANTASTIC CREATURES
Montijo Transitional Style. Central Region, Panamá.
c. A.D. 500–600. Fired Clay, Paint.
8 1/8" h. x 8 3/4" w.
The design is laid out in two decorative bands, one around the neck, the other extending from below the neck to within a few inches of the base. The larger, primary band consists of a series of alternating figures. One of these figures is a serpentine saurian, the other is a creature with large oval head, frog legs, and octopus-tentacled arms. Each figure alternates with the other, but each also alternates with itself, in that it is first positioned upward and then downward in its second rendition. There are a total of four serpentine saurians and four frog-legged, octopus-tentacled creatures. When viewed from above, the design layout yields the basic circle-cross-X pattern seen on other vessels with a large central spout. Duality and bilateralism is also denoted in the design along the neck.
Note: The saurians emanate from the froglike creature.
Anonymous Collection, Los Angeles.

129. Tricolor Dual-Spouted Figural Jar in Human Form

130. Figural Jar in the Form of a Human Figure

58 POLYCHROME PEDESTALED BOWL: STANDING SAURIAN SHAMAN-IN-COMBAT THEME
Macaracas Style. Central Region, Panamá.
c. A.D. 800–1000. Fired Clay, Paint.
5 1/3" h. x 10 1/8" d.
This composition lacks specific icons, such as animal familiar emanations, that would identify the figure as a shaman. Other characteristics, such as the standing posture in combination with an anthropomotphic body and saurian head in profile, relate it to the shaman-in-combat theme.
Anonymous Collection, San Francisco.

59 POLYCHROME PEDESTALED BOWL: MYTHIC CREATURE
Joaquín Polychrome. Central Region, Panamá. Azuero Peninsula.
c. A.D. 600–900. Fired Clay, Paint.
6" h. x 1" d.
The design field is restricted to the interior of the bowl and rim. The creature is characterized by a long serpentine body, with two clawed arms or feet, indicated close to the head. The head is utterly fantastic, consisting of two huge laterally positioned eyes. The equally oversized mouth is shown gaping and is lined with long sharp teeth. The tongue is long and bilaterally split.
Anonymous Collection, Los Angeles.

60 MYTHIC SHAMANIC CREATURE
Joaquín Polychrome. Central Region Panamá.
c. A.D. 700–900. Fired Clay, Paint.
Note the use of color coding in differentiating body parts. Left side is contrasted with the right side.
Anonymous Collection, Santa Ana.

61 POLYCHROME PEDESTALED BOWL DECORATED WITH A SCORPION
Joaquín Polychrome. Central Region, Panamá. Azuero Peninsula.
c. A.D. 600–900. Fired Clay, Paint.
5 3/4" h. x 9 1/2"
The design is restricted to the interior of the bowl and rim and consists of a scorpion with waves of energy radiating from the body. The emphasis on the complementarity and polarity of forces is reinforced by the positioning of the spurs or lines of force emanating from the body. Note that opposing sets of spurs emerge from each side. They create secondary waves, however, which appear to be a by-product of the two complementary oppositional forces. The body of the scorpion also seems to be intentionally shaped like female genitalia. The head appears to connote the "vagina dentata" of tropical forest mythology, replete with teeth and pubic hair. It is set in opposition to the benign fecund vulva formed by the body.
Anonymous Collection, Los Angeles.

62 POLYCHROME PEDESTALED BOWL: SHAMANIC BATS
Joaquín Polychrome. Central Region, Panamá.
c. A.D. 600–800.
6" h. x 11" d.
The layout is bilateral and consists of stylized bats with humanlike heads.
Anonymous Collection, Santa Ana.

62a POLYCHROME PEDESTALED PLATE: BIRDS
Parita Style. Central Region, Panamá.
c. A.D. 1000–1300. Fired Clay, Paints.
9 1/4" h. x 10" d.
The decoration covers the interior and exterior plate and the exterior base. The primary decorative field consists of a framed band with a series of six large birds possibly crassids. A solitary bird decorates a tondo at the center of the plate. The underside of the plate is also decorated with a framed band, but with a series of stylized motifs which in some Amerindian traditions would be interpreted as geometric birds. The lower base is decorated with a band of diamond-shaped elements.
Anonymous Loan, San Francisco.

132. Diminutive, Tricolor Figural Jar with Human and Avian Characteristics

63 POLYCHROME VESSEL WITH DEER'S HEAD
Montijo Transitional Style. Central Region Panamá.
c. A.D. 500–600. Fired Clay, Paint.
c. 7 4/5" w., at base.
The lower portion of the vessel has a bilaterally paneled design field, incorporating a mythic shamanic, or winged supernatural, creature. The shoulder is decorated with alternating bands of downward-pointing triangles in red

or purple. Bands of upward-pointing triangles are created as negative design in the intervening space. The top of the vessel is in the form of a deer's head with extended tongue.
Courtesy of Museo Antropológico Reina Torres de Araúz.

64   FIGURAL VESSEL INCORPORATING A BIRD
Conte Style. Central Region, Panamá.
c. A.D. 600–800. Fired Clay, Paint.
c. 9 3/4" d.
The body of the vessel is decorated with two panels, one with heavily clawed birds with humanlike limbs. This may be a representation of both shamanic flight and shamanic combat. The other two panels are decorated with saurian heads with serpentine bodies. The upper portion of the vessel has been modeled in the form of a bird with the lugs of the vessel forming the legs of the bird. Note the long impressive talons.
Courtesy of Museo Antropológico Reina Torres de Araúz.

73   TRICOLOR RING-BASED BOWL: MYTHIC FIGURE
Conte Style. Central Region, Panamá.
c. A.D. 600–800. Fired Clay, Paint.
3 1/3" h. x 11 1/4" d.
The design is restricted to the interior of the bowl. The central figure is painted in red with black outline and is drawn against a white ground. The figure is a composite creature, characterized by a head shown in profile. The head displays avian and crocodilian characteristics and is dominated by a single concentric eye. Both the upper and lower appendages have large claws or talons, four on each appendage. The torso of the creature is decorated with a large double Y scroll. Note the long Y scroll emanating from the tip of the creature's snout. Two phalliform appendages hang or emanate from each side of the torso. This composition may be a very early representation of the shaman-in-combat theme.
Anonymous Collection, Los Angeles.

74   COMPOSITE CREATURE COMBINING INSECT AND SERPENT CHARACTERISTICS
Conte Style. Central Region, Panamá.
c. A.D. 600–800. Fired Clay, Paint.
c. 11" d.
The central design consists of a creature with antenae on the head, a fierce mouth with bared teeth, insect wings, clawed arms and legs, and a serpenti-form body barbed with claws. This is no ordinary creature but one associated with myth, shamanism ,or the supernatural.
Courtesy of Museo Antropológico Reina Torres de Araúz.

75   POLYCHROME RING-BASED BOWL: SERPENT-FELINE CREATURES
Conte Style. Central Region, Panamá.
c. A.D. 700–800. Fired Clay.
4 3/4" h. x 17 1/2" d.
The artist has blended serpent and feline traits in the composition. The serpentine body and bifid tongue elements are clearly serpentlike, while the clawed feet and the shape of the head is more feline. The emphasis, however, is on the indigenous concept of duality. There are two creatures. Each serpent body is clearly divided in two by a median line. Two scrolls emanate from each head. The bifid tongue itself is a common icon suggesting duality, but here there are two bifid tongues per creature. Additionally, the creatures are arranged yin-yang fashion, emphasizing their complementarity.
Anonymous Collection, San Francisco.

76   POLYCHROME PLATE: BATS WITH OUT-STRETCHED WINGS
Conte Style. Central Region, Panamá.
c. A.D. 600–800. Fired Clay, Paint.
The decorative field is bilateral consisting of two opposing panels decorated with bats, separated from one another by a median panel decorated with alternating scrolls.
Courtesy of Museo Antropológico Reina Torres de Araúz.

77   POLYCHROME RING-BASED BOWL: DANCING COMPOSITE FIGURE
Conte Style. Central Region, Panamá. Veraguas Province.
c. A.D. 600–800. Fired Clay, Paint.
3 1/3" h. x 15 1/8" d.
The rim of this vessel is flat and clearly demarcated. The decorative field consists of a large tondo with a white ground. The central figure combines anthropomorphic and zoomorphic traits, for example an upright posture, distinct arms, legs, curved tail with birdlike head, and long-beaked mouth. The combative, predatory nature of the creature is indicated by the talons or spurs at the claws. Note: The distinctive hat is closely correlated with shamanic themes.
Anonymous Collection, Los Angeles.

78   TRICOLOR RING-BASED PLATE: POSSIBLY A SWORDFISH
Conte Style. Central Region, Panamá.
c. A.D. 600–800. Fired Clay, Paint.
2 1/3" h. x 11" d.
Anonymous Collection, San Francisco.

79   POLYCHROME RING-BASED PLATE WITH SCORPION OR CRAB AT THE CENTER
Conte Style. Central Region, Panamá.
c. A.D. 600–800. Fired Clay, Paint.
1 3/4" h. x 11" d.
There is a distinct emphasis on the number three in this composition. A scorpion or crab decorates the central tondo, which is encircled by a blue band, and a red band. The white ground of the tondo, the purple band and red band form three concentric ovoids. The outer ovoid is bordered by three double Y scroll patterns. These are encompassed by a trefoil undulating band painted purple. Three additional double Y-scrolls border the outer flow of the trefoil and complete the decoration.
Anonymous Collection, Los Angeles.

133. Tricolor Globular Jar with Serpent Motif

80 TRICOLOR RING-BASED BOWL WITH HAND-PRINT AT CENTER
Conte Style. Central Region, Panamá.
c. A.D. 600–800. Fired Clay, Paint.
2 1/2" h. x 10 1/4" d.
The design is restricted to the interior of the bowl and consists of a tondo decorated with a hand motif characterized by a palm, five realistically proportionate digits, and distinct fingernails. The tondo is encircled by a band of red outlined in black. Surrounding this is a quatrefoil meander marked by intermittent "talon" or "claw" elements. Above this is another quatrefoil meander incorporating Y scrolls.
Anonymous Collection, Los Angeles.

81 RING-BASED BOWL: FANTASTIC CREATURES WITH TENDRILS EMANATING FROM THEIR MOUTHS
Conte Style. Central Region, Panamá.
c. A.D. 600–800. Fired Clay, Paint.
3 1/8" h. x 11 1/2" d.
Although the specific identification of these creatures is unknown, they are clearly shamanic in nature. The head is somewhat feline in appearance, with eyes that seem to be the bird's-head-in-profile variety, which is closely related to shamanic figures. The two long filaments ending in spirals seem to fit the description in Venezuelan Warao ethnographic literature of tendril-like filaments that the shaman emits from his mouth to ensnare his enemy.
Anonymous Collection, New York.

82 POLYCHROME RING-BASED PLATE: SHAMANIC CREATURE WITH CRAB-LIKE CREATURES
Conte Style. Central Region, Panamá.
c. A.D. 600–800. Fired Clay, Paint.
1.5" h. x 10 1/2" d.
The design layout is bilateral, with a median panel incorporating six creatures with triangle-shaped bodies, pincers, and vagina dentata–type mouth. The larger opposing motifs are in the form of a shamanic creature with birdheads in profile for eyes and animal emanations at each side of the body.
Anonymous Collection, New York.

83 POLYCHROME DUAL-SPOUTED FIGURAL JAR IN THE FORM OF A STANDING FEMALE FELINE
Conte Style. Central Region, Panamá.
c. A.D. 600–800. Fired Clay, Paint.
9 1/3" h.
The addition of the phalliform spout at the back supports the gender based dimorphic symbolism associated with the dual-spouted vessels. The female genitalia is clearly indicated on the feline.
Collection of Denver Art Museum, Gift of the Nova Albion Foundation.

84 POLYCHROME DUAL-SPOUTED FIGURAL VESSEL IN THE FORM OF A FELINE
Conte Style. Central Region, Panamá.
c. A.D. 600–800. Fired Clay, Paint.
5 3/4"h. x 7 7/8 l.
Note how the feline's tail is formed by the spout. This example is a clear reinforcement of the importance of vulva symbolism in the dual-spouted forms. The tail-spout has been unnaturally drawn back upon itself so that the spout forms the clitoris, positioned just above the larger vulva spout atop the head, as seen in other dual-spouted forms.
Collection of the Denver Art Museum, museum purchase with funds from various donors.

85 POLYCHROME FIGURAL JAR IN THE FORM OF A FELINE
Conte Style. Central Region, Panamá.
c. A.D. 600–800. Fired Clay, Paint.
7 7/8" h. x 10 1/7" d.
The feline is characterized by a fierce aggressiveness typified by bared teeth and huge three-clawed paws. The tail of the feline serves as the handle of the jar. The design field is characterized by a trilateral layout when viewed from above and below.
Anonymous Collection, Los Angeles.

86 POLYCHROME PEDESTALED BOWL: NEEDLE-NOSED SERPENTIFORM CREATURE WITH LEGS
Early Macaracas Style. Central Region, Panamá.
c. A.D. 800–900. Fired Clay, Paint.
4 1/2" h. x 12 7/8" w.
The serpentlike body of this composite creature is segmented by alternating red, dashed, and purple bands. The eye is formed by concentric circles.
Anonymous Collection, Los Angeles.

87-88 POLYCHROME JAR WITH SAWFISH AND MYTHIC CREATURE

134. Tricolor Figural Jar: Feline-Headed Composite Animal

Early Macaracas Style. Central Region, Panamá.
c. A.D. 800–900. Fired Clay, Paint.
The large crocodilian-like creature's head is formed by two profile heads above and below. The creature's tail is barbed like a stingray spine. Note the embryonic saurian painted on the creature's body. It appears that the artist is giving us an X-ray view of the embryonic creature gestating within. In ancient Panamanian art embryos appear to be represented by creatures that are coiled or enfolded into themselves and lack distinct limbs, such as arms or legs. The form is also usually enclosed in an egg, sac, or some type of wrap. A sawfish-like creature is seen on the opposite side of the vessel.
Courtesy of Museo Antropológico Reina Torres de Araúz.

89   RING-BASED POLYCHROME BOWL: SHAMANIC SAWFISH
Conte Style. Central Region, Panamá.
c. A.D. 600–800. Fired Clay, Paint.
4" h. x 14 1/2" d.
These are not ordinary sawfish, but rather emblems of the shamanic universe. A close examination of the head of each creature reveals how the artist has formed the saw blade and eyes of the fish by conjoining two parrot heads, shown in profile. Barbs or claws, symbolic of shamanic power, line the head and body of the fish. Also note the yin-yang complementarity of the positioning of the fish.
Anonymous Collection, Texas.

90   TRICOLOR JAR: MYTHIC LIZARD
Late Tonosí Style (Ichon's Montevideo Style), Central Region, Panamá.
c. A.D. 400–500. Fired Clay, Paint.
11 1/4" h. x 11" d.
The primary design is laid-out in a band around the body of the vessel. The design field consists of two bilateral panels. Each panel is decorated with similar, yet slightly different scenarios. Each is dominated by a large lizard, likely a personage taken from an indigenous myth. Typical of Tonosí art are the rectangular parallel-lined panels seen in the background. The difference between the two sides of the vessel lie in the scroll-like design elements encompassed by the creature's tail. These combine the scroll-shaped tail, often associated with monkeys, and the paw-claw motif, sometimes used to connote an entire creature. These elements distinguish one side of the composition from the other. The neck of the vessel is decorated with a band of alternating curvilinear and parallel-lined rectilinear panels. Within the context of precolumbian thought, male-female dichotomies and interactions are suggested.
Note: The mythic lizard may represent the Solar Serpent motif more clearly discerned in other examples.
Anonymous Collection, San Francisco.

91   CARINATED JAR: BAT WITH ANIMAL EMANATIONS AS WINGS
Montijo Transitional Style. Central Region, Panamá.
c. A.D. 500–600. Clay, Paint.
The decoration is primarily composed of Tonosí Style design elements, although true Tonosí did not use blue paint as seen in this specimen. The animal emanations are more typical of the Conte and later styles. This is a very early expression of the use of emanations in Central Region painted ceramics.
Anonymous Collection, Los Angeles.

92   POLYCHROME JAR WITH GEOMETRIC DECORATION
Conte Style. Central Region, Panamá.
c. A.D. 600–800. Clay, Paint.
7" h. x 7 1/2" d.
Note how the spikes are made to interpenetrate the cavities of the adjacent forms. This, in addition to the color contrasts of red and blue, accentuates the underlying ideological dualism inherent in the precolumbian art of this period.
Anonymous Collection, Los Angeles.

93   POLYCHROME FIGURAL JAR: FELINE WITH SAURIAN DECORATION
Macaracas Style. Central Region, Panamá.
c. A.D. 800–1000. Fired Clay, Paint.
10 3/4" h. x 11 1/2" w.
The overall design layout is quadrilateral and incorporates a circle-cross-X pattern when viewed from above. The vessel has been modified in such a way that the head and front paws of a zoomorph, possibly a feline, is indicated. The body of the vessel is decorated with four primary panels incorporating saurian figures. If we begin on the right side of the feline's head, the first panel is relatively small and has an upside-down saurian. The next panel is the largest of all four and has an upright saurian with a predominantly purple body. The next

panel is somewhat smaller than the preceding panel and contains an upside-down saurian with a predominantly red body. The last panel adjacent to the left side of the feline has an upside-down saurian. Below each paw are stylized scroll patterns incorporating the claw motif. The dynamics of the layout suggest emergence, growth, maturity, and waning, as is suggested by the shape and size of the panels, possibly representing the rising sun, sun at the zenith, setting sun, and sun of transformation in the north.
Anonymous Collection, San Francisco.

94 POLYCHROME GLOBULAR FIGURAL JAR IN THE FORM OF A SHAMANIC BIRD
Conte Style. Central Region, Panamá.
c. A.D. 700–800. Fired Clay, Paint.
The large concentric eyes and the Y-scroll claw elements forming the wings indicate that this is no ordinary bird but one of shamanic significance. The style of this composition seems to be transitional between the Conte and Macaracas.
Anonymous Collection, Texas.

95 POLYCHROME JAR WITH MYTHIC, SHAMANIC, OR COSMOLOGICAL CREATURE
Macaracas Style. Central Region, Panamá.
c. A.D. 800–1000. Fired Clay.
The figure is characterized by spiral-shaped emanations at the head, a frontal view of the face with a wide distorted mouth, and a sinuous body with clawed appendages.
Courtesy of Museo Antropológico Reina Torres de Araúz.

96 POLYCHROME JAR WITH EGG-LAYING BIRD
Macaracas Style. Central Region, Panamá.
c. A.D. 800–1000. Fired Clay, Paint.
8 3/4" h. x 10 1/2" d.
An oval egg can be seen emerging from each bird's body. Each bird also appears to be swallowing an egg-shaped object indicated by the bulge in the neck. Additionally, when viewed from above, the arrangement of the birds forms a stylized "swastika" motif.
Anonymous Collection, Texas.

97 GLOBULAR POLYCHROME JAR: RUNNING SAURIANS
Macaracas Style. Central Region, Panamá.
c. A.D. 800–1000. Fired Clay.
11 1/2"h. x 13 1/3"d.
The central design is laid out within one large circumferential band. The dominant motifs are running saurians and double saurians within triangular and lozenge-shaped panels. There is no doubt that the saurians are shamanic in nature and not representative of any real species. The saurians represent various stages of shamanic transformation and manifestation. Some are characterized by long, spiral tails terminating in a claw element. Others have long, bifurcated tails. Some are

135. Polychrome Figural Jar in the Form of a Horned Standing Figure

upright, while others are upside down. The entire composition is highly kinetic with frenetic shamanic activity.
Anonymous Collection, Texas.

98 FIGURAL PENDANT IN THE FORM OF A FELINE WITH FOOT IN MOUTH
Veraguas-Gran Chiriquí Group. Costa Rica/Panamá.
c. A.D. 700–1520. Gold.
3 7/8" l.
The Edythe L. Broad Collection.

99 FIGURAL PENDANT: SHAMAN UNDERGOING TRANSFORMATION
International Group. Parita, Azuero Peninsula, Central Region, Panamá.
c. A.D. 400–900. Gold.
1 3/4 "
Note the figure's legs are in the form of bird heads, icons that are associated with the shaman's animal allies and assistants or reference the shaman's ability to fly in his spirit body.
Formerly in the collection of the late Count and Countess Guy du Boisrouvray.
The Edythe L. Broad Collection.

100 FIGURAL PENDANT: SHAMAN UNDERGOING EMPOWERMENT
International Group. Parita, Azuero Peninsula, Central Region, Panamá.
c. A.D. 400–900. Gold.
4 1/4"h.

PHOTO LISTINGS

136. Pedestaled Polychrome Figural Bowl in the Form of a Highly Abstracted Turtle

137. Carinated Zoomorphic Figural Jar with Lid: Turtle and Bird

The body of the figure is characterized by a crocodilian body with human head. Emanations can be seen at the head and tail. Formerly in the collection of the late Count and Countess Guy du Boisrouvray.
The Edythe L. Broad Collection.

101a FIGURAL PENDANT: FROG WITH SAURIAN EMANATIONS
Costa Rica/Panamá.
c. A.D. 800–1500. Gold.
3 1/8" l.
Saurian emanations can be seen at the mouth and at the knee joints. Figures such as this show the iconographic consistency in varying art mediums. Similar iconography is found in ceramics, bone, stone, and shell. Formerly in the collection of the late Count and Countess Guy du Boisrouvray.
The Edythe L. Broad Collection.

101b FIGURAL PENDANT IN THE FORM OF A SHAMANIC FROG
Veraguas-Gran Chiriquí Group. Central Region, Panamá
c. A.D. 700–1520. Gold.
2 1/4" l.
Note the serpent emanations at each side of the mouth of the frog. Also observe how each serpent has been longitutinally divided into two streams. The serpent is an icon used to represent vital force, which has a male and female aspect.
The Edythe L. Broad Collection.

101c FIGURAL PENDANT IN THE FORM OF A CROCODILIAN

Veraguas-Gran Chiriquí Group. Panamá.
c. A.D. 700–1520. Gold.
3 7/8" l.
The Edythe L. Broad Collection.

102a FIGURAL PENDANT RATTLE: JOINED SHAMANIC ZOOMORPHS
Veraguas-Gran Chiriquí Group. Panamá.
c. A.D. 700–1520. Gold.
3 3/8" w.
Note the serpentine emanations at the back of the figures. One of the emanations is shared. Although the creatures have animal-like bodies, their heads are birdlike. They are depicted grasping a double-headed serpent with their claws and beaks. Formerly in the collection of the late Count and Countess Guy du Boisrouvray.
The Edythe L. Broad Collection.

102b FIGURAL PENDANT: SHAMANIC ZOOMORPH
Veraguas-Gran Chiriquí Group. Veraguas Province, Panamá.
c. A.D. 700–1520. Gold.
4 " l.
The emanations at the end of the body indicate that this is a shamanic animal. The creature has a turtlelike body with a bird-beaked head. Formerly in the collection of the late Count and Countess Guy du Boisrouvray.
The Edythe L. Broad Collection.

103a FIGURAL PENDANT IN THE FORM OF A SHAMANIC EAGLE
Veraguas-Gran Chiriquí Group. Panamá.
c. A.D. 700–1520. Gold.

5 1/4" w.
Note the saurian emanations at each side of the bird's head, indicative of its shamanic associations.
The Edythe L. Broad Collection.

103b FIGURAL PENDANT IN THE FORM OF A SHAMANIC EAGLE
Veraguas-Gran Chiriquí Group. Panamá.
c. A.D. 700–1520. Gold.
6" w.
Note the shamanic animal emanations at each side of the bird's head.
The Edythe L. Broad Collection.

104 SHAMANIC FROG FIGURAL PENDANT
Openwork Group. Panamá.
c. A.D. 400–700. Gold.
3 3/8" l.
Emanations in the form of saurian heads flank the sides of the frog's body, which is decorated with openwork scroll patterns.
The Edythe L. Broad Collection.

105 FIGURAL PENDANT IN THE FORM OF A SHAMANIC HIERATIC SAURIAN
Panamá.
c. A.D. 700–1520. Gold.
5 1/8" l.
Note the saurian head emanations at the head and bottom of the figure. The lower emanations form an elongated vulva. Also observe the finlike appendages at the sides of the central figure. Each of these emanations and protrusions are indicative of the shamanic nature of this figure, which may be a gold version of the Master of Animals, a prominent figure in the ethnographic literature of many neotropical forest groups. The Master of Animals is responsible for the replenishment of species. The large vulva characteristic of this figure would seem to reflect a female, procreative, fecund aspect of this mythic personage.
The Edythe L. Broad Collection.

106 POLYCHROME PEDESTALED PLATE: SHAMANIC TRANSFORMATION THEME
Macaracas Style. Central Region, Panamá.
c. A.D. 800–1000. Fired Clay, Paint.
4 1/3" h. x 11 1/3" d.
The interior of the bowl is decorated with a standing figure. Saurian figures emanate from his head and arms. An additional saurian stands between his legs. This composition is of ancient origin in South America and is recorded for Chavín, Paracas, and many later cultures in both Perú and Colombia. The composition most likely represents a shaman with activated shamanic powers. The diagnostic elements are a central figure in frontal standing pose flanked by animal familiars, which are placed at the head, waist, and feet. The saurian emanating from the figure's right arm has a purple body with head in red outline, while that on the left has a red body with head in blue outline. Note the manner in which the artist has color coded other parts of the central figure's body and other components.
Anonymous Collection, San Francisco.

107 POLYCHROME PEDESTALED BOWL: SHAMANIC TRANSFORMATION THEME

138. Polychrome Pedestaled Bowl: Long-Beaked Birds

139. Polychrome Pedestaled Bowl: Saurian or Crocodilian Embros

Macaracas Style. Central Region, Panamá.
c. A.D. 800–1000. Fired Clay, Paint.
5 1/8" h. x 13 1/2" w.
The design is restricted to the interior of the bowl and rim. The primary motif consists of a standing, frontally facing, anthropomorphic figure. The figure's legs are fluid and terminate in saurian heads. Its arms are shaped like bird wings. At its chest, a white spiral and purple spiral come together in yin-yang fashion. A smaller rendition of this motif in red and white can be seen below, where the genitalia would be indicated. The large concentric eyes gaze menacingly at the onlooker. This figure conforms to all the criteria associated with the themes called "shaman empowered" and "shaman in flight." In shamanic lore, a shaman's powers must be activated by ritual preparation prior to undertaking such shamanic tasks as combating illness, malevolent spirits, or other hostile shamans. It was also believed that a shaman could fly in his soul body. The convention of placing wings on a human figure or rendering the figure as a bird-man was employed as an artistic device to represent the theme of shamanic flight.
Anonymous Collection, San Francisco.

109 POLYCHROME PEDESTALED BOWL: SHAMANIC TRANSFORMATION THEME
Macaracas Style. Central Region Panamá.
c. A.D. 800–1000. Fired Clay, Paint.
7" h. x 10 3/4" d.

140. Polychrome Pedestaled Bowl: Alternating Panels of Birdlike Saurians

The bowl of the vessel is decorated with a frontably facing anthropomorphic figure representing a transformed shaman prepared for ritual combat. An abstract long-beaked zoomorphic head emanates from his body at the waist. His ear spools are also shaped like stylized long-beaked bird heads. Typical of this genre is the dynamic combative pose of the central figure. The underside of the bowl is decorated with a band of four trapezoid panels. The two larger panels incorporate abstract bird heads in profile.
Anonymous Collection, Los Angeles.

110 POLYCHROME PEDESTALED BOWL: SHAMANIC TRANSFORMATION THEME
Macaracas Style. Central Region, Panamá.
c. A.D. 800–1000. Fired Clay, Paint.
6 5/8" h. x 10 1/3" d.
The pedestal and interior bowl are decorated. The central motif of the interior of the bowl is a dynamic figure, with frontal view of the face. Serpentine saurians emanate from the head of the figure. Purple is used to outline the right side of the figure's face, while red is used to outline the left side. Stingray spine–like elements appear to emanate from the sides of the body. These are alternately red and purple, colors used by the artist to accentuate the complementarity of forces expressed in the composition. This is also evident at the neck; one half of which is red, white, and purple, the other half a mirror image.
Anonymous Collection, Los Angeles.

111 POLYCHROME SPOUTED JAR: SHAMAN-IN-COMBAT THEME
Macaracas Style. Central Region, Panamá.
c. A.D. 800–1000. Fired Clay, Paint.
c. 4 3/4" w.
Courtesy of Museo Antropológico Reina Torres de Araúz.

112 TRICOLOR RING-BASED BOWL: DOUBLE-HEADED MYTHIC FISH AND SWORDFISH
Conte Style/Macaracas Style. Central Region, Panamá.
c. A.D. 700–850. Fired Clay, Paint.
5" h. x 17 1/4" d.
The design is restricted to the interior of the bowl. The central figure is a mythic being with two heads and a body that blends serpent and fish qualities. The eyes of this being are formed by bird heads in profile. Swordfish can be seen about the head. This figure may represent a mythic figure, such as the Master of Fish, who controls the manifestation of fish in the human world. The Master of Fish is a prominent personage in some neotropical Indian cosmologies.
Anonymous Collection, San Francisco.

113 POLYCHROME JAR: SPLIT IMAGE FISH/SAURIAN/BIRD
Late Macaracas Style. Central Region, Panamá.
c. A.D. 900–1000. Fired Clay, Paint.
10" h. x 10 1/2" d.

GUARDIANS OF THE LIFE STREAM

141. Polychrome Pedestal Bowl: Fish

142. Tricornered Jar: Shaman-In-Combat Theme

The design layout is bilateral as well as quatrilateral, consisting of four decorative panels. Two panels are joined together at the mouth to create a frontal view of a fish. Each decorative panel, however, also incorporates the head of a long-beaked bird and the head of a saurian. The stylized bird head is configured by the eye and a long protruding element that forms a beak. Connected to the bird's head, complementing it, and at the same time opposed to it, is a saurian head. The overall layout yields the circle-cross-X pattern seen in other jar forms.
Anonymous Collection, Carmel.

114 TRICOLOR RING-BASED BOWL. COMPOSITE ANIMAL: DEER, BIRD, AND OTHER ANIMALS
Conte Style. Central Region Panamá, Coclé Province type.
c. A.D. 600–800. Fired Clay, Paint.
c. 8" d.
The vessel is decorated with a creature that combines deer, bird, and other animal characteristics. Note the ambiguous rendering of the deer's tail, which also looks like the head and long beak of a bird in profile. The bird aspect of the composition is given added emphasis by the wing-shaped element seen on the deer's body.
Courtesy of Museo Antropológico Reina Torres de Araúz.

115 POLYCHROME DUAL-SPOUTED FIGURAL JAR IN THE FORM OF A BIRD
Conte Style. Central Region, Panamá.
c. A.D. 600–800. Fired Clay, Paint.
8 1/3" h. x 7 5/8'
The gender-based dualism of dual-spouted vessels is also evident in this example. The formation of the wings and juxtaposition of the phalliform spout conjoin to form a very realistic rendition of the female genitalia when viewed from above.
Anonymous Collection, Los Angeles.

116 TRICOLOR SPOUTED FIGURAL JAR IN THE FORM OF A DEER
Possibly Cubitá Style. Central Region, Panamá.
c. A.D. 500–600. Fired Clay, Paint.
5 1/4" h. x 9 1/2" l.
The animal is characterized by horns and black spots.
Anonymous Collection, Los Angeles.

117 POLYCHROME FIGURAL JAR IN THE FORM OF A CROCODILIAN
Conte Style. Central Region, Panamá.
c. A.D. 600–800 . Fired Clay, Paint.
17 3/4" l. x 8" w.
The body of the crocodilian is decorated with checkerlike patterning. The tail, however, has a red band, demarcating the left and right sides. Each side is decorated with alternating white and black vertical bands.
Anonymous Collection, Los Angeles.

118 POLYCHROME DUAL-SPOUTED FIGURAL JAR IN THE FORM OF A CRAB
Conte Style. Central Region, Panamá.

c. A.D. 600–800. Fired Clay, Paint.
8 1/8" h. x 8 1/2" w.
The mouth of the crab is greatly exaggerated and connotes a "vagina dentata." Interestingly, the vessel incorporates two spouts. The rear spout is attenuated and phalliform. While the phalliform spout gets narrower toward the opening, the central spout gets wider. The artist has intentionally connected the "male" spout to the "female" spout. Coincidentally, this gives the "female" spout a distinctly vaginal appearance, replete with clitoris when viewed from above.
Thomas Collection.

119 "NIPPLE-SPOUTED" BOTTLE WITH GEOMETRIC DESIGN
Conte Style. Central Region, Panamá. Coclé Province Type.
c. A.D. 600–800. Fired Clay, Paint.
c. 9" d.
The design consists of alternating red, white, and purple bands of chevron design elements. The artist is contrasting red with purple. The white bands result as negative design. Among some Amerindian groups the connotations of this composition are fertility, which results from the interaction of male and female elements, here represented by color coding the bands in red and purple. The negative white zigzag band would represent the dynamic energy (lightning) that results from male-female interactions.
Courtesy of Museo Antropológico Reina Torres de Araúz.

120 POLYCHROME RING-BASED BOWL: SQUARE AND ROSETTE DESIGN
Conte Style. Central Region, Panamá.
c. A.D. 600–800. Fired Clay, Paint.
2 1/4" h. x 11 1/2" d.
The design is restricted to the bottom of the bowl and consists of complementary geometric patterns in solid colors with black outline.
Anonymous Collection, San Francisco.

121 "NIPPLE-SPOUTED" BOTTLE WITH GEOMETRIC DESIGN
Conte Style. Central Region Panamá.
c. A.D. 600–800. Fired Clay, Paint.
c. 8 4/5" d.
The design incorporates bilateral and quadrilateral arrangements of YC scrolls and similar arrangements of claw motifs.
Courtesy of Museo Antropológico Reina Torres de Araúz.

122 TRICOLOR RING-BASED BOWL: ABSTRACT EYE MOTIF
Conte Style. Central Region, Panamá.
c. A.D. 600–800. Fired Clay, Paint.
2 1/4" h. x 7 3/4" d.
Concentric circles with a border are commonly used in precolumbian Panamanian art as an artistic convention to depict eyes. Normal eyes are usually configured by a circle with a dot at the center. The concentric eye motif appears to be especially associated with composite animal forms and shamanic transformation themes, or depictions of shamans, hierophants, and mythic personages.
Anonymous Collection, San Francisco.

123 POLYCHROME CARINATED JAR: SOLAR PATTERN WITH SAURIAN DECORATIVE PANELS
Macaracas Style. Central Region, Panamá. Parita Bay region.
c. A.D. 800–1000. Fired Clay.
11" h. x 13 5/8" d.
Typical of this genre is the circle-cross-X pattern formed by the design on the upper half of the vessel. These patterns suggest symbols for the sun and solstice points. The circle-and-cross, or sun symbol, is indicated in black, the solstice points may be suggested by the quatrefoil panels decorated with saurians. Note that two of the upper saurians have purple bodies while two have red bodies. In relation to the solar symbol, these form an X. The carination of the vessel may mark off the horizon line. The design below the shoulder appears to complement the upper design. Note, however, that the arms of the cross are upside down in the lower design and interface with the upper saurian panels rather than with the arms of the upper cross. Additionally, instead of panels with saurians, the lower panels contain double-scroll designs in which the scroll incorporates claw motifs. Moreover, they are positioned just below the arms of the upper cross. Anonymous Collection, San Francisco.

124 POLYCHROME CARINATED JAR IN THE FORM OF A STYLIZED TURTLE
Parita Style. Parita Bay Region. Central Region, Panamá.
c. A.D. 1000–1300. Fired Clay, Paint.
Only the head and legs of the turtle are indicated. The carination, a sharp ridge demarcating the shoulder from the base of the vessel, is used to signify the edge of the turtle shell. The turtle is shown in the swimming mode. The shoulder of the vessel is divided into eight uneven decorative panels. When viewed from above, the cross pattern with a circle is formed by the black ground. Within the context of some Amerindian traditions, this would symbolize the sun. In fact, the panels with red discs, of which there are four, may symbolize the sun at the four directions. The four intermediate panels may indicate sunrise, zenith, sunset, and nadir, respectively. In the Southwestern and Mesoamerican contexts, the earth is often imaged as a turtle. The above imagery may refer to the relationship of Sun to Earth and, hence, sky and earth.
Thomas Collection.

125 POLYCHROME CARINATED FIGURAL JAR: TURTLE
Parita Style. Central Region, Panamá.
c. A.D. 1000–1300. Fired Clay, Paint.
10 1/3" h. x 14" d.
Like many carinated jars of this particular form, the

143. Polychrome Pedestaled Bowl: Stylized Serpent

vessel has been slightly modified to represent a turtle. Although the significance and meaning is unclear, other vessels of this type generally have motifs that appear to represent the sun. Perhaps the orange discs are solar in intent. The turtle in most precolumbian cultures in which it is used iconographically has uterine, female connotations and is often used to represent the earth. Since the primary relationship with the earth is that of the sun, a male entity associated with the sky, the placement of solar icons on top of the turtle's shell would be in conformity with indigenous perspectives.
Anonymous Collection, San Francisco.

126 POLYCHROME PEDESTALED PLATE: SOLAR SHAMANS
Macaracas Style. Central Region, Panamá.
c. A.D. 800–1000. Fired Clay, Paint.
3 1/3" h. x 13 1/2" d.
The design is restricted to the interior plate and rim. Essentially quadrilateral in layout, it appears to be a variant of the cross with X pattern, possibly associated with the sun and solstices. Two panels are decorated with standing bird-beaked anthropomorphic figures. Significantly, the head also contains the circle-cross-X pattern. Note how the body of each figure appears to be eclipsing a disc. In one scene the disc is orange and white with black trim, and in the other the disc is orange and black with black trim. The panels on the other axis of the composition are decorated with a bird-beaked serpentine creature. Four discs, which appear to represent movement or turning action, decorate the space between panels. These elements are also associated with the sun in other traditions. Overall, the composition seems to be representing activity associated with the sun, possibly including eclipses.
Anonymous Collection, San Francisco.

127 TRICOLOR DOUBLE JAR: FROGS IN NEGATIVE DESIGN
Zahina Polychrome. Central Region, Panamá.
c. A.D. 200–400. Fired Clay, Paint.
10" h. x 11" d.

The design layout is bilateral. The primary design motif, which is repeated on each side of the vessel, consists of a highly stylized froglike creature effected as negative design in black outline.
Anonymous Collection, New York.

128 TRICOLOR DUAL-SPOUTED JAR DECORATED WITH BATS
Zahina Polychrome. Central Region, Panamá.
c. A.D. 200–400. Fired Clay, Paint.
7 7/8" h. x 7 5/8" d.
The design consists of a decorative band divided into two primary and two much smaller secondary panels that separate the primary panels from each other. The primary panels are decorated with bats. This vessel, like others of this form, appears to incorporate a dimorphic gender-based symbolism in the spouts.
Anonymous Collection, Los Angeles.

129 TRICOLOR DUAL-SPOUTED FIGURAL JAR IN HUMAN FORM
Late Tonosí Style (Ichon's Montevideo Style). Central Region, Panamá.
c. A.D. 400–500. Fired Clay, Paint.
7 5/8" h. x 7 1/2" w.
Anonymous Collection, Los Angeles.

130 FIGURAL JAR IN THE FORM OF A HUMAN FIGURE
Late Tonosí (Ichon's Montevideo Style). Central Region, Panamá. Tonosí Area.
c. A.D. 400–500. Fired Clay, Paint.
c. 9 2/5" d.
Only the head and face are modeled. Other details—such as arms, breasts, and navel—are painted.
Courtesy of Museo Antropológico Reina Torres de Araúz.

131 TRICOLOR JAR: GEOMETRICS AND FACES
Tonosí Style. Central Region, Panamá.
c. A.D. 200–400. Clay, Paint.
11" h. x 11 1/2" d.
The design is laid out in two decorative bands, one below the rim, the other covering the shoulder and body of the vessel. Each band is demarcated by framing lines. The primary band is bilateral, with two primary decorative panels and two spacer panels between the primary panels. The primary panels consist of ticked rectilinear meanders. There are two meanders per panel. The point of interface between the two meanders has been used by the artist to paint in two faces, one above and one below, which are connected. The exact significance of these motifs is unclear.
Anonymous Collection, San Francisco.

132 DIMINUTIVE, TRICOLOR FIGURAL JAR WITH HUMAN AND AVIAN CHARACTERISTICS
Cubitá Style. Central Region, Panamá.
c. A.D. 500–600. Fired Clay, Paint.
5" h. x 5 1/8" l.

The vessel combines human and animal traits in its composition. The female gender seems to be implied by the vulvalike element below the navel. The arms are bent, with hands at the navel. Seen in profile, however, the body appears more birdlike than human. The back of the figure is decorated with two large YS scrolls. It is possible that a hunchback is also intended in this composition.
Anonymous Collection, Los Angeles.

133 TRICOLOR GLOBULAR JAR WITH SERPENT MOTIF
Montijo Transitional Style. Central Region, Panamá. Azuero Peninsula.
c. A.D. 500–600. Fired Clay, Paint.
The serpent encircles the entire vessel in three balanced bands, marking off the four cardinal directions. The serpent's body is characterized by outer framing lines in black and a median body line in black. Two bands of red form the rest of the body. In other examples, the spiral-shelled nautilus is a key design of this thematic motif. Here Y scrolls either are used in its place or may be schematized representations of the nautilus. Four scrolls also mark off the cardinal directions and, as in other similar compositions, an additional scroll is placed near the head in line with the tail.
Anonymous Collection, Los Angeles.

134 TRICOLOR FIGURAL JAR: FELINE-HEADED COMPOSITE ANIMAL
Cubitá Style. Central Region, Panamá.
c. A.D. 500–600. Fired Clay, Paint.
10 1/2" h. x 11 1/4" l.
Although the head appears to be that of a feline, the tail is not. The clawed paws appear to emerge, as does the head and tail, from a carapace or shell body. The design layout, however, as viewed from above, repeats the basic circle-cross-X pattern associated with the sun, four directions, and solstice rising and setting points seen in other vessels.
Anonymous Collection, Los Angeles.

135 POLYCHROME FIGURAL JAR IN THE FORM OF A HORNED STANDING FIGURE
Conte Style. Central Region, Panamá.
c. A.D. 600–800. Fired Clay, Paint.
13" h. x 8 5/8" w.
The figure cannot be sexed as to gender and is characterized by an absence of arms. Also of note are the two small spurs or horns atop the head. The body of the figure is elaborately painted with four Y scrolls that terminate in the form of some unspecified zoomorphic form. Two of these are at front, two at back.
Anonymous Collection, Los Angeles.

136 PEDESTALED POLYCHROME FIGURAL BOWL IN THE FORM OF A HIGHLY ABSTRACTED TURTLE
Conte Style. Central Region, Panamá.
c. A.D. 600–800. Fired Clay, Paint.
4 1/8" h. x 13" l. x 10 1/4" w.
The interior of the bowl is decorated with trefoil compositions, YC scrolls, and Y elements terminating in claws. The central tondo is painted black. The underside of the vessel is decorated with white, blue, white, and red bands from the top to the base.
Collection of Denver Art Museum, Gift of Jan and Frederick Mayer.

137 CARINATED ZOOMORPHIC FIGURAL JAR WITH LID: TURTLE AND BIRD
Conte Style. Central Region, Panamá.
c. A.D. 600–800. Fired Clay, Paint.
c. 8 2/5" d.
The artist has used the carination of the vessel to serve as the edge of the shell of the turtle. Note the turtle's head. The lid of the vessel is in the form of a bird's head. The turtle was a widely used icon representing the earth. Birds are clearly animals associated with the sky. The union of the two in this composition would seem to be a reference to the relationship between earth and sky. Note the turtle is below and the bird is above.
Courtesy of Museo Antropológico Reina Torres de Araúz.

138 POLYCHROME PEDESTALED BOWL: LONG-BEAKED BIRDS
Macaracas Style. Central Region, Panamá.
c. A.D. 800–1000. Fired Clay, Paint.
5" h. x 12 1/4" d.
The design is restricted to the interior and rim of the vessel. The design layout is quadrilateral and comprises four large ground-dwelling birds, possibly crassids, placed directionally astride a central tondo of undetermined significance. Four triangular panels, decorated

145. Polychrome Pedestaled Figural Jar: Bird

GUARDIANS OF THE LIFE STREAM

146a. Ring-Based Polychrome Jar with Four Lugs
146b. Ring-Based Polychrome Jar with Four Lugs

with colored chevron patterns, mark off the space between each bird.
Anonymous Collection, Los Angeles.

139 POLYCHROME PEDESTALED BOWL: SAURIAN OR CROCODILIAN EMBRYOS
Macaracas Style. Central Region, Panamá.
c. A.D. 800–1000. Fired Clay, Paint.
5" h. x 11 1/4" w.
That embryos are artistically intended is based on the following observations: legs or other appendages are not indicated; the tail is incurved and faces the head, creating a fetallike posturing of the body; the mouth is enclosed and unopened. Six embryos are indicated. Note that two have purple outlines for the outer curve of the body, while two have red outlines with only the end of the tail indicated in purple. This may be a convention used by the artist to gender type the embryos that is, as two males and two females. One of the embryos has a red outline for the head and purple outline for the back and tail, while the sixth figure has a purple outline for the head, red for the back, with the tail in purple. The figures with purple outlines have red bodies. The figures with predominantly red outlines have purple bodies, while the figure with purple head and purple tail but red back has a red body. The indigenous dimorphic gender-based model will suggest that tails and predatory snouts are essentially male organs, whether they are found in males or females. In many indigenous color schemes, red is a color associated with females—blood, copper, etc. We might expect, therefore, that blue is being used by the artist to suggest maleness or male energy. But since in the indigenous perception male and female energies are blended in any single form, a preponderance of one over the other could be used to suggest gender, lacking other more definitive icons.
Collection of James A. Greaves.

140 POLYCHROME PEDESTALED BOWL: ALTERNATING PANELS OF BIRDLIKE SAURIANS
Macaracas Style. Central Region, Panamá.
c. A.D. 800–1000. Fired Clay, Paint.
12 1/8" h. x 8" d.
The animal forms on the panels incorporate saurian and avian characteristics. In two panels the figures are upright. In the two alternate panels the figures are upside down and face in opposite directions from the upright panels. The base of the vessel also has a quadrilateral layout.
Anonymous Collection, Los Angeles.

141 POLYCHROME PEDESTAL BOWL: FISH
Macaracas Style. Central Area, Panamá.
c. A.D. 900–1000. Fired Clay, Paint.
6 3/4" h. x 9 1/3" d.
The bowl of the vessel is decorated with a fish, possibly a form of sea catfish or hammerhead shark. Note the use of contrasting bands of red and purple to form the body. The fish is depicted with its belly side facing the viewer. There is no decoration on the underside of the bowl. The pedestal is decorated with geometrics. Rim is quadrated into four unequal segments, demarcated by

bands of white split by black.
Anonymous Collection, Los Angeles.

142 TRICORNERED JAR: SHAMAN-IN-COMBAT THEME
Macaracas Style. Central Region, Panamá.
c. A.D. 800–1000. Fired Clay.
Anonymous Collection, New York.

143 POLYCHROME PEDESTALED BOWL: STYLIZED SERPENT
Early Parita Style. Central Region, Panamá.
c. A.D. 1000–1100. Fired Clay Paint.
7 1/7"h.
This vessel is indicative of the shift from Macaracas Style design traits to the Parita Style. The design occupies little of the design field, which remains white. The serpent is already on the way to becoming abstracted. Purple is only sparingly used. All of these are early Parita stylistic traits.
Anonymous Collection, Los Angeles.

144 POLYCHROME DOUBLE-HEADED FIGURAL VESSEL
El Hatillo Style. Central Region, Panamá.
c. A.D. 1300–1520. Fired Clay, Paint.
15 1/4" l. x 8 1/3" h.
The vessel depicts two conjoined figures, each distinguished by a separate head though they appear to share one body. Both are facing in the same direction. The original intent of the artist is unclear. Whether the front or back figure is intended to be male or female is difficult to discern, although the front figure is distinguished from the back figure by dots and added black lines below the nose, while the back figure has multiple bands around the neck.
Anonymous Collection, Los Angeles.

145 POLYCHROME PEDESTALED FIGURAL JAR: BIRD
Parita Style. Central Region, Panamá.
c. A.D. 1000–1300. Fired Clay, Paint.
9 1/8" h. x 8 5/8" w.
Although the vessel is in the shape of a bird, female genitalia seem to be implied by the overall design, when seen from above. The base of the vessel is decorated with a band of concentric diamond motifs. In some South American Indian groups, such as the Tukanoans of the northwest Amazon, the concentric diamond motif is itself a symbol for female genitalia. This vessel is unusual in the number of triangular post-fired cutouts on the base.
Anonymous Collection, San Francisco.

146a RING-BASED POLYCHROME JAR WITH FOUR LUGS
Parita Style. Central Region, Panamá.
c. A.D. 1000–1300. Fired Clay, Paint.
8 1/4"h. x 10 1/3" w.
The design is highly abstract and only the color combinations are reminiscent of the previous Macaracas Style. The lugs are also highly abstract animal forms, no longer clearly discernible as to species. In other vessels, similarly shaped lugs are in the form of small frogs.
Anonymous Collection, Texas.

146b RING-BASED POLYCHROME JAR WITH FOUR LUGS
Parita Style. Central Region, Panamá.
c. A. D. 1000–1300. Fired Clay, Paint.
7 7/8"h, x 10 1/4"w.
This vessel appears to be a companion piece to vessel 146a. The designs on this vessel are equally abstracted and stylized.

144. Polychrome Double-Headed Figural Vessel

INDEX OF PHOTOS ACCORDING TO APPEARANCE IN TEXT

Photo No.	Page No.	Photo No.	Page No.	Photo No.	Page No.	Photo No.	Page No.
1.	p. 10	43.	p. 42	88.	p. 85	131.	p. 126
2.	p. 10	44.	p. 43	89.	p. 82	132.	p. 134
3.	p. 11	45.	p. 43	90.	p. 78	133.	p. 136
4.	p. 16	46.	p. 44	91.	p. 80	134.	p. 137
5.	p. 20	47.	p. 44	92.	p. 83	135.	p. 138
6.	p. 21	48.	p. 45	93.	p. 86	136.	p. 139
7.	p. 22	49.	p. 45	94.	p. 88	137.	p. 139
8.	p. 25	50.	p. 45	95.	p. 90	138.	p. 140
9.	p. 25	51.	p. 48	96.	p. 93	139.	p. 140
10.	p. 26	52.	p. 49	97.	p. 94	140.	p. 141
11.	p. 27	53.	p. 49	98.	p. 98	141.	p. 142
12.	p. 28	54.	p. 53	99.	p. 99	142.	p. 142
13.	p. 28	55.	p. 53	100.	p. 99	143.	p. 144
14.	p. 28	56.	p. 54	101a.	p. 100	144.	p. 147
15.	p. 29	57.	p. 55	101b.	p. 100	145.	p. 145
16.	p. 29	58.	p. 56	101c.	p. 100	146a.	p. 146
17.	p. 29	59.	p. 56	102a.	p. 100	146b.	p. 146
18.	p. 30	60.	p. 56	102b.	p. 100	147.	p. 168
19.	p. 30	61.	p. 57	103a.	p. 101		
20.	p. 31	62.	p. 57	103b.	p. 101		
21.	p. 31	62a.	p. 59	104.	p. 101	Map	p. 24
22.	p. 31	63.	p. 52	105.	p. 102	Table of Chronological	
22a.	p. 32	64.	p. 60	106.	p. 104	Periods	p. 50
23.	p. 33	65.	(Table)	107.	p. 107	Table A.	p. 61
24.	p. 33	66.	(Table)	109.	p. 107	Table B.	p. 62
25.	p. 34	67.	(Table)	110.	p. 107	Table 1.	p. 63
26.	p. 34	68.	(Table)	111.	p. 108	Table 2.	p. 64
27.	p. 34	69.	(Table)	112.	p. 109	Table 3.	p. 65
28.	p. 35	70.	(Table)	113.	p. 110	Table 4.	p. 65
29.	p. 35	71.	(Table)	114.	p. 110	Table 5.	p. 66
29a.	p. 35	72.	(Table)	115.	p. 111	Table 6.	p. 66
29b.	p. 35	73.	p. 68	116.	p. 111		
30.	p. 36	74.	p. 69	117.	p. 111		
31.	p. 37	75.	p. 70	118.	p. 112		
32.	p. 37	76.	p. 70	119.	p. 114		
33.	p. 38	77.	p. 71	120.	p. 115		
34.	p. 38	78.	p. 71	121.	p. 116		
35.	p. 39	79.	p. 72	122.	p. 117		
36.	p. 39	80.	p. 72	123.	p. 118		
37.	p. 39	81.	p. 72	124.	p. 118		
37a.	p. 40	82.	p. 72	125.	p. 120		
38.	p. 40	83.	p. 74	126.	p. 120		
39.	p. 41	84.	p. 75	127.	p. 128		
40.	p. 41	85.	p. 76	128.	p. 131		
41.	p. 41	86.	p. 84	129.	p. 133		
42.	p. 41	87.	p. 85	130.	p. 133		

BIBLIOGRAPHY

Acosta, Joaquín
1848 *Compendio Histórico del Descubrimiento y Colonización de la Nueva Granada en el Siglo Décimo Sexto.* Paris.

Adam, Richard
1956 Cultural Components of Central America. *American Anthropologist.* 58(5):881-907.

Aguilera Patiño, Luisita
1952 *Leyendas y Tradiciones Panameñas.* Panamá: Imprenta Nacional.

Alba, C.
1928 *Etnología y Población Histórica de Panamá.* Panamá.

Alphonse, Ephraim S.
1956 Guaymi Grammar and Dictionary, with Some Ethnological Notes. *Smithsonian Institution, Bureau of American Ethnology Bulletin 162.* Washington, D.C.

Andagoya, Pascual de
1829 Provincias de Tierra firme o Castilla del Oro. In *Fernandez de Navarette: 1825, 1837.* Tomo III:393, et seq.
1865 *Narrative of the Proceedings of Pedrarias Dávila.* C. R. Markham, trans. and ed. London: Hakluyt Society.
1913 Relación de los sucesos de Pedrarias Dávila en las Provincias de Tierra Firme. In *El descubrimiento del Océano Pacífico: Vasco Núñez de Balboa, Fernando de Magallanes y sus Compañeros: Documentos Relativos a Núñez de Balboa.* J. T. Medina, ed. Tomo II. Santiago de Chile: Imprenta Universitaria. Pp. 191-207.

Anderson, C. L. G.
1914 *Old Panama and Castilla del Oro.* Boston.

Anghera, Peter Martyr d' (Pietro Martire d'Anghiera)
1912 *De Orbe Novo: The Eight Decades of Peter Martyr D'Anghera.* Francis Augustus MacNutt, trans. New York: G. P. Putnam.

Araúz, Reina Torres de
1963 La Ceremonia de la Pubertad Femenina en Dos Culturas Indígenas Panameñas. *Tareas* (2):63-69.
1972a The Anthropology of Eastern Panama: The Panamic Biota: Some Observations Prior to a Sea-Level Canal. *Bulletin of the Biological Society of Washington.* (2):229-46.
1972b *Arte Precolombino de Panamá.* Instituto Nacional de Cultura y Deportes, Dirección de Patrimonio Histórico. Panamá: La Editora de la Nación.
1972c *Nata Prehispánico.* Centro de Investigaciones Antropológicas. Panamá Ciudad: Universidad de Panamá; Panamá Ciudad Instituto Nacional de Cultura y Deportes. Publicación Especial No. 3.
1982 *Panamá Indígena.* Panamá: Instituto Nacional de Cultura y Deportes.

Arbin, Arne
1950 A Journey up the Sambu River to Visit the Choco Indians. *Kroeber Anthropological Society Papers.* University of California, Berkeley. 2:79-88.

Arcand, Bernard
1974 *Making Love Is Like Eating Honey or Sweet Fruit; It Causes Cavities: Essays on Cuiva Symbolism.* Unpublished manuscript, McGill University.

Arsandaux, H. and P. Rivet
1923 *L'orfèvrerie du Chiriqui et de Colombie.* Socíete des Americanistes de Paris. 15:169-82.

Aveni, Anthony
1980 *Skywatchers of Ancient Mexico.* Austin: University of Texas Press.

Bailey, Robert C., G. Head, M. Jenike, B. Owen, R. Rechtman, and E. Zechenter
1989 Hunting and Gathering in Tropical Rain Forests: Is It Possible? *American Anthropologist.* 91:59-82

Bancroft, Hubert Howe
1886 The Works of Hubert Howe Bancroft. In *The Native Races:* Vol. 3, *Myths and Languages.* San Francisco: History Co.

Barral, Padre Basilio de
1960 *Guarao Guarata: Lo que cuentan los Indios Guaraos.* Caracas: Fundación Creole.

Barrantes, Ramiro, P. E. Smouse, J. V. Neel, H. W. Mohrenweiser, and H. Gershowitz
1982 Migration and Genetic Infrastructure of the Central American Guaymi and Their Affinities with Other Tribal Groups. *American Journal of Physical Anthropology.* 58:201-14.

Barrantes, Ramiro, P. E. Smouse, H. W. Mohrenweiser, H. Gershowitz, J. Azofeifa, T. Arias, and J. V. Neel
1990 Microevolution in Lower Central America: Genetic Characterization of Chibcha-Speaking Groups of Costa Rica and Panama, and a Taxonomy Based on Genetics, Linguistics and Geography. *American Journal of Human Genetics.* 46:63-84.

Barrett, John
1904a Facts about Panama. *Monthly Bulletin of the Bureau of American Republics.* February.
1904b Historical Sketch of the Isthmus of Panama. Written in Spanish. *Monthly Bulletin of the Bureau of American Republics.* July.

Bartlett, Alexandra S., and E. S. Barghoorn
1973 Phytogeographic History of the Isthmus of Panama, During the Past 12,000 Years: A History of Vegetation, Climate and Sea-Level Change. In *Vegetation History of Northern South America.* A. Graham, ed. New York: Elsevier Scientific Publishing Co. Pp. 233-47.

Bartlett, Alexandra S., E. S. Barghoorn, and R. Berger
1969 Fossil Maize from Panama. *Science.* 165:389-390.

Bateman, John F.
1860-61 Account of a Visit to the Huacas or Ancient Graveyards of Chiriqui. *Bulletin of the American Ethnological Society.* No. 1.

Baudez, Claude F.
1963 Cultural Development in Lower Central America. In Aboriginal Cultural Development in Latin America: An Interpretative Review. Vol. 1. *Smithsonian Miscellaneous Collections Bulletin 146.*
1967 Recherches archeologiques au Costa Rica. *Travaux et Memoires de l'Institut des Hautes Etudes d'Amerique Latine.* Vol. 18. Paris.

Baudez, Claude F., and Michael D. Coe
1962 *Archaeological Sequences in Northwestern Costa Rica.* Proceedings of the 34th International Congress of Americanists, Vienna. Vol. 1. Pp. 366-373.

Bell, Eleanor Yorke
1909 The Republic of Panama and Its People with Special Reference to the Indians. *Smithsonian Institution Annual Report.* Washington D.C. Pp. 607-37.

Bennett, Charles F.
1962 The Bayano Cuna Indians of Panama: An Ecological Study of Livelihood and Diet. *Annals of the Association of American Geographers.* 52:32-50.
1968 *Human Influences on the Zoogeography of Panama.* Berkeley: University of California Press.

Bierhorst, John
1988 *The Mythology of South America.* New York: William Morrow and Company, Inc.

Biese, Leo P.
1960 Spindle Whorls from Panama Viejo. *Panama Archaeologist.* 3(1):35-44.
1961 The Frog Effigy and Large Polychrome Vessels from Parita. *Panama Archaeologist.* 4(1):31-41.
1962a Arqueología de Panamá. Bibliografía de Trabajos Publicados, 1859-1961. *Publicación Revista Lotería.* (Panamá). 7(77):70-84.
1962b La Arena de Quebra: A Mixed Cultural Site on the Azuero Peninsula. *Panama Archaeologist.* 5(1):28-35.
1962c The Archaeological Society of Panama Site Report System. *Miscellaneous Publications in Isthmian Archaeology.* No. 1. Canal Zone, Panama.
1964 The Prehistory of Panama Viejo. Anthropological Papers No. 58. *Smithsonian Institution, Bureau of American Ethnology Bulletin 191.* Washington, D.C.
1967 Cerro Largo: An Atypical Gravesite in Central Panama. *Ethnos.* (4):26-34.
n.d. Rio Cative Geometric Ware: A New Pottery Type from Panama. *Ethnos.* Pp. 90-95.

Bird, Junius B., and R. G. Cooke
1977 Los artefactos más antiguos de Panamá. *Revista Nacional de Cultura.* Panamá. 6:19-31.
1978a *La Cueva de los Ladrones: Datos preliminares sobre la ocupación Formativa.* Actas del V Symposium Nacional de Antropología, Arqueología y Etnohistoria de Panamá. Panamá: Instituto Nacional de Cultura. Pp. 283-304.
1978b The Occurrence in Panama of Two Types of Paleoindian Projectile Points. In *New Evidence for the Pleistocene Peopling of Americas.* A. L. Bryan, ed. Orono, Maine: Center for the Study of Early Man. Pp. 263-72.

Bird, Robert McK.
1980 Maize Evolution from 500 B.C. to the Present. *Biotropica.* 12:30-41.
1984 South American Maize in Central America? In *Pre-Columbian Plant Migration.* D. Z. Stone, ed. Cambridge: Massachusetts. Papers of the Peabody Museum of Archaeology and Ethnology. 76:39-65.

Bischof, Henning
1966 *Canapote: An Early Ceramic Site in Northern Colombia.* Preliminary Report. Proceedings of the 36th International Congress of Americanists, Madrid. Vol. I. Pp. 484-91.
1972 *The Origins of Pottery in South America: Recent Radiocarbon Dates from Southwest Ecuador.* Proceedings of the 40th International Congress of Americanists. Vol. I. Pp. 269-81.

Bolian, Charles E.
1973 Seriation of the Darien Style Anthropomorphic Figure. In *Variations in Anthropology: Essays in Honor of John C. McGregor.* D. W. Lathrap and J. Douglas, eds. Champaign: Illinois. Pp. 213-32.
1970 *Similarities in the Pre-Columbian Gold Work of Colombia and Central America.* Paper read at the XXXIX Congreso International de Americanistas, Lima.

BIBLIOGRAPHY

Bollaert, William
1859 Ancient Indian Tombs of Chiriqui. *American Ethnological Society Transactions.* 2:151-59.
1859 On Golden Objects Found in the Ancient Huacas of Chiriqui. Proceedings of the Society of Antiquarians. London. Pp. 36-38.

Borland, Francis
1779 *The History of Darien, Giving a Short Description of that Country and an Account of the Attempts of the Scotch Nation to Settle a Colony There.* Glascow: J. Brice.

Bray, Warwick M.
1977 Maya Metalwork and Its External Connections. In *Social Process in Maya Prehistory.* Norman Hammond, ed. New York: Academic Press. Pp. 365-403.
1981 Gold Work. In *Between Continents, Between Seas: Precolumbian Art of Costa Rica.* E. P. Benson, ed. New York: Harry N. Abrams, Inc. Pp. 153-66.
1984 Across the Darien Gap. In *The Archaeology of Lower Central America.* F. W. Lange and D. Z. Stone, eds. Albuquerque: University of New Mexico Press. Pp. 305-38.

Briggs, Peter S.
1993 Fatal Attractions: Interpretations of Prehistoric Mortuary Remains from Lower Central America. In *Reinterpreting the Prehistory of Central America.* M. M. Graham, ed. Colorado: University of Colorado Press.
n.d. *Re-Conquest Mortuary Arts and Status in the Central Region of Panama.* Ph.D. Dissertation, University of New Mexico. Ann Arbor, Michigan: University Microfilms, Inc.

Brown, Charles Melville
1909 Tisingal: The Lost Mine of Panama. *Bulletin of the International Bureau of American Republics.* No. 30.

Brown, Michael F.
1985 Tsewa's Gift, Magic and Meaning in an Amazonian Society. In S*mithsonian Series in Ethnographic Inquiry.* Washington, D.C.: Smithsonian Institution Press.

Brush, Charles F.
1965 Pox Pottery: Earliest Identified Mexican Ceramic. *Science.* 149:194-95.

Bull, Thelma H.
1958 Excavations at Venado Beach: Canal Zone. *Panama Archaeologist.* 1(1):6-14.
1959 Preliminary Report on an Archaeological Site: District of Chame, Province of Panama. *Panama Archaeologist.* 2(1):91-137.
1961 An Urn Burial: Venado Beach. *Panama Archaeologist.* 4:42-47.
1965 *The Archaeological Society of Panama Site Report List.* Revised Report of December 1931. Republic of Panama.

Bullis, Harvey R. and Edward F. Klima
1972 The Marine Fisheries of Panama. The Panama Biota: Some Observations Prior to a Sea-Level Canal. *Bulletin of the Biological Society of Washington.* Pp. 167-77.

Burr, Wm. H.
1904 The Republic of Panama. *National Geographic Magazine.* February. Pp. 57-73.

Bush, Mark, and P. Colinvaux
1990 A Pollen Record of a Complete Glacial Cycle from Lowland Panama. *Journal of Vegetation Science.* 1:105-18.

Bushnell, Geoffrey and Adrian Digby
1955 *Ancient American Pottery.* London: Faber and Faber.

Carles, Rubén Darío
1953 Los Monolitos de Barriles. *Panamá American.* December 20.
1949 *220 años del período Colonial en Panamá.* 1st edition. Panamá: Los Talleres de The Star & Herald Co..

Carneiro, Robert L.
1981 The Chiefdom: Precursor of the State. In *The Transition to Statehood in the New World.* G. D. Jones and R. R. Kautz, eds. Cambridge: Cambridge University Press. Pp. 37-79.

Casas, Bartolomé de las
1927 *Historia de las Indias.* 3 Vols. M. Aguilar, ed. Madrid: J. Pueyo.

Casimir de Brizuela, Gladys
1971 *Informe preliminar de las excavaciones en el sitio arqueológico Las Huacas, distrito de Sona, Veraguas.* II Symposium Nacional de Antropología y etno-historia de Panamá (non publié).

Castillero, Calvo, Alfredo
1967 *Estructuras sociales y económicas de Veragua desde sus orígines históricos, siglos XVI y XVII.* Panamá: Editora Panamá.
1968 *Azuero y la zona Chiriquí-Veraguas: Análisis comparativo de dos estructuras económico-sociales.* Conference faite le 8 avril 1968 á la Dirección General de Planificación y Administración (non publié).
1971 *La Fundición de la Villa de los Santos y los Orígenes Históricos de Azuero.* Edición de la Dirección Nacional de Cultura. Panamá.

Castillero R., and J. Ernesto
1951 Descubrimientos Arqueológicos en la República de Panamá. *Revista de Indias* (Madrid). 11:281-85.
1952 Descubrimientos Arqueológicos en la República de Panamá. *Revista de Indias* (Madrid). 12:337-41.

Chamberlain, Von Del
1982 When Stars Came Down to Earth, Cosmology of the Skidi Pawnee Indians of North America. *Ballena Press Anthropological Papers.* No. 26.

Chapin, Mac
1970 *Pab Igala: Historias de la Tradición Kuna.* Centro de Investigaciones Antropológicas. Panamá City: Universidad de Panamá Press.

Chaumeil, Jean-Pierre
1983 *Voir, Savoir, Pouvoir, Le chamanisme chez les Yagua du nord-est peruvien*. Editions de l'Ecole des Hautes Etudes en Sciences Sociales. Paris.

Cieza de León, Pedro de
1864 *The Travels of Pedro de Cieza de León, A.D. 1532-1550, Contained in the First Part of His Chronicle of Peru*. C. R. Markham, trans. and ed. London: Hakluyt Society.

Civrieux, Marc de
1980 *Watuna: An Orinoco Creation Cycle*. San Francisco: North Point Press.

Clary, James, P. Hansell, A. Ranere, and T. Buggey
1984 The Holocene Geology of the Western Parita Bay Coastline of Central Panama. In *Recent Developments in Isthmian Archaeology*. F. W. Lange, ed. Oxford: BAR International Series 212. Pp. 55-83.

Coe, Michael D.
1960 Archaeological Linkages with North and South America at La Victoria, Guatemala. *American Antiquity*. 62:363-93.
1962 Costa Rican Archaeology and Mesoamerica. *Southwestern Journal of Anthropology*. 18:170-83.

Coe, Michael, and Claude Baudez
1961 The Zoned Bichrome Period in Northwest Costa Rica. *American Antiquity*. Vol 26.

Colón, Fernando
1959 *The Life of the Admiral Christopher Colombus by His Son Ferdinand*. B. Keen, trans. and annot. New Brunswick, New Jersey: Rutgers University Press.

Constenla, Alfredo
1981 *Comparative Chibchan Phonology*. Ph.D. Dissertation, University of Pennsylvania.
1985 Clasificación Lexicoestadística de las Lenguas de la Familia Chibcha. Tomo IV. *Estudios de Linguística Chibcha, Serie Anual* (Universidad de Costa Rica). Pp. 155-97.

Consultores e Ingenieros de Panamá, S. A.
1966 *Estudio de factibilidad para el control combinado de avenidas y drenaje, y de irrigación. Valle de Tonosí. Informe preliminar*. Dirección General de Planificación y Administración de la República de Panamá. San Francisco: McKoretsky Engineers.

Cooke, Richard G.
1972 *The Archaeology of the Western Coclé Province of Panama*. Ph.D. Dissertation, University of London.
1976a Panamá: Región Central. *Indice de Vínculos*. 2(1):122-41.
1976b *Nuevos Análisis de Carbono-14 para Panamá al Este de Chiriquí: Una Actualización de los Cambios Culturales Prehistóricos*. Pp. 88-115.
1976c El hombre y la tierra en el Panamá prehistórico. *Revista Nacional de Cultura*. Instituto Nacional de Cultura, Panamá. 2:17-38.
1979 *Los impactos de las comunidades agrícolas precolombinas sobre los ambientes del Trópico estacional: Datos del Panamá prehistórico*. Actas del IV Simposio Internacional de Ecología Tropical. Tomo 3. Pp. 917-73.
1982 Los guaymíes sí tienen historia. In *El Pueblo Guaymí y su Futuro*. CEASPA y Comité Patrocinador del Foro sobre el Pueblo Guaymí y su Futuro, eds. Panamá: Impretex, S.A. Pp. 27-64.
1984a Archaeological Research in Central and Eastern Panama: A Review of Some Problems. In *The Archaeology of Lower Central America*. F. W. Lange and D. Z. Stone, ed. Albuquerque: University of New Mexico Press. Pp. 263-304.
1984b *El rescate arqueológico en Panamá: historia, análisis y recomendaciones*. Colección El Hombre y su cultura, Tomo 2. Panamá: Instituto Nacional de Cultura, Dirección Nacional de Patrimonio Histórico, Proyecto de Desarrollo Cultural.
1985 Ancient Painted Pottery from Central Panama. *Archaeology*. 8(4).
1986 *La arqueología del Panamá precolombino y su importancia para los estudios de los pueblos de habla Chibcha*. In Memorias del Primer Simposio Científico sobre Pueblos Indígenas de Costa Rica. R. Barrantes, M. E. Bozzoli, and P. Gudiño, eds. San José, Costa Rica: Ministerio de Obras Públicas y Transporte y Instituto Geográfico. Pp. 81-95.
1987 El motivo del ave de las alas desplegadas en la metalurgia de Panamá y Costa Rica. *Metalurgia Precolombina*. C. Plazas, ed. Bogotá: Banco de la República. Pp. 139-53.
1988 Some Social and Technological Correlates of Coastal Fishing in Formative Pacific Panama. In *Diet and Subsistence: Current Archaeological Perspectives*. B. V. Kennedy and G. LeMoine, eds. Calgary: Chacmool (the Archaeological Association of the University of Calgary). Pp. 127-39.
1993 Animal Icons and Pre-Columbian Society: The Felidae, with special reference to Panama. In *Reinterpreting Prehistory of Central America*. Colorado: University Press.
Manuscript in work Field Symbolism in Precolumbian Panama. In *Field Symbolism in the New World*. N. Saunders, ed.

Cooke, Richard G., and Anthony J. Ranere
1984 The "Proyecto Santa María": A Multidisciplinary Analysis of Prehistoric Adaptations to a Tropical Watershed in Panama. In *Recent Developments in Isthmian Archaeology: Advances in the Prehistory of Lower Central America*. F. W. Lange, ed. Oxford: BAR International Series 212. Pp. 3-30.
1989a *Changing Responses to Lagoon-Estuary Systems in Prehistoric Central Panama*. Paper presented at the Circum-Pacific Prehistory Conference in Seattle on August 1-6, 1989 (available in reprint proceedings).
1989b Hunting in Prehistoric Panama: A Diachronic Perspective. In *The Walking Larder: Pattern of Domestication, Pastoralism and Predation*. J. Clutton-Brock, ed. London: Unwin Hyman. Pp. 295-315.
In press The Relation of Fish Resources to the Location, Diet Breadth, and Procurement Technology of a Preceramic and a Ceramic Site in an Estuarine Embayment on the Pacific

Coast of Panama. In *Development of Hunting-Fishing-Gathering Societies on the Central and South American Pacific Coast*. Proceedings of the Circum-Pacific Prehistory Conference. M. Blake, ed. Seattle: Washington State University Press.
1992a Prehistoric Human Adaptations to the Seasonally Dry Forests of Panama: Colonization of Tropical Regions (The Humid Tropics). *World Archaeology*. 24(1).
1992b The Origin of Wealth and Hierarchy in the Central Region of Panama (12,000-2,000 B.P.) with Observations on Its Relevance to the History and Phylogeny of Chibchan-Speaking Polities in Panama and Elsewhere. In *Wealth and Hierarchy in the Intermediate Area*. F. W. Lange, ed. Washington, D.C.: Dumbarton Oaks Research Library and Collection.

Cooke, Richard G., and Junius Bird
1974 *Excavaciones arqueológicas en la Cueva de los Ladrones, Distrito de la Pintada, Coclé, Panamá*. Manuscript in the archives of the Patrimonio Histórico. Panamá.

Cooke, Richard G., and Warwick M. Bray
1985 The Goldwork of Panama: An Iconographic and Chronological Perspective. In *The Art of Precolumbian Gold: The Jan Mitchell Collection*. J. Jones, ed. Boston: Little, Brown. Pp. 39-45.

Corrales, Francisco U.
1985 Prospección y excavaciones estratigráficas en el sitio Curré (P-62-Ce). *Vínculos* (Valle del Diquís, Costa Rica). 11:1-16.
1989 *La ocupación agrícola temprana del sitio arqueológico Curré, Valle del Diquís, Costa Rica*. Tésis de Licenciatura, Universidad de Costa Rica.

Correal, Gonzalo
1987 Aguazuque: Una Estación y Complejo Funerario Precerámico. *Boletín de Arqueología* (Colombia). 3:3-24.
1989 *Aguazuque: Evidencias de cazadores, recolectores y plantadores en la altiplanicie de la cordillera oriental*. Fundación de Investigaciones Arqueológicas Nacionales. Bogotá: Banco de la República.

Creamer, Winifred, and J. Haas
1985 Tribe Versus Chiefdom in Lower Central America. *American Antiquity*. 50:738-54.

Creighton, J. M.
1925 Hermit Tribe: The San Blas Indians of Panama. *The Mentor*. February, 55.

Crusoe, Donald Lewis
1968 *Archaic Formative Cultures Along the Western Coast of the Gulf of Panama*. Florida State University (unpublished).

Cruxent, José, and Irving Rouse
1959 *Venezuela and Its Relationship with Neighboring Areas*. Proceedings of the 33rd International Congress of Americanists, Juy 20-27, San José, Costa Rica. Pp. 173-83.
1964 *Arqueología cronológica de Venezuela*. Washington, D.C.: Union Panamericana.

Cruxent, José María
1956-57 Informe Sobre un Reconocimiento Arqueólogico en el Darién, Panamá. *Boletín Museo de Ciencias Naturales* (Caracas). 1:1-2.

Curtis, Beatrice
1960 The Cucua Costume. *Panama Archaeologist*. 3(1):95-99.

Curtis, Karl P.
1959 Agate Beads and Pendant. *Panama Archaeologist*. 2(1):87-88.

Curtis, K. P. and G. R. Willey
1949 A Veraguas Grave. *Journal of the Washington Academy of Sciences*. 39(1).

Dade, Philip L.
1959a Tomb Burials in Southeastern Veraguas. *Panama Archaeologist*. 2(1):16-34.
1959b Humpback Figures from Panama. *Ethnos*. 24(1-2):38-44.
1960 Rancho Sancho de la Isla: A Site in Cocle - Province, Panama: A Preliminary Report. *Panama Archaeologist*. 3(1):66-87.
1961a The Provenance of Polychrome Pottery in Panama. *Ethnos*. 26(4):172-97.
1961b A Ceramic Art Form from Western Panama. *Panama Archaeologist*. 4(1):48-55.
1962a Another Ceramic Art Form from Western Panama: The Crane. *Panama Archaeologist*. 5(1):36-38.
1962b Falsified Gold Guacas. *Panama Archaeologist*. 5(1):10-15.
1970 Veraguas: Heartland of Panama's Pre-Columbian Art. *Ethnos*. Pp. 16-39.
1972 Archaeology and Pre-Columbian Art in Panama. *Ethnos*.

DeBoer, Warren R.
1975 The Archaeological Evidence for Manioc Cultivation: A Cautionary Note. *American Antiquity*. 40:419-33.

DeCicco, Gabriel
1969 The Chatino. *Handbook of Middle American Indians*. Vol. 7. Austin: University of Texas Press. Pp. 360-66.

Rocha, Fray Antonio de la
1964 Del Padre Fray Antonio de la Rocha y de la conversión de los Indios de la provincia de San Salvador de Austria de los Doraces y Zuríes en el reino de Panamá, hecha por su grande celo. (Transcribed by Sonia Menéndez). *Hombre y Cultura* (Panamá). 3:87-132.

Densmore, Frances
1926 Music of the Tule Indians of Panama. *Smithsonian Miscellaneous Collections, Vol. 77, No. 11*. Washington D.C.: Smithsonian Institution.

Dere, Christopher
1981 *The Geological and Paleogeographic Setting of an Archeological Site on the Southwestern Coast of Parita Bay, Panama*. M.A. Thesis, Temple University, Pennsylvania.

DeSmidt, Leon S.
1948 *Among the San Blas Indians of Panama*. Troy, New York. Pp. 15-21.

Doyle, Gerald A.
1960 Metal and Pottery Associations. *Panama Archaeologist.* 3:48-51.

Drolet, Robert
1984 Community Life in a Late Phase Chiefdom Village, Southwestern Costa Rica. In *Recent Developments in Isthmian Archaeology.* F. W. Lange, ed. Oxford: BAR International Series 212. Pp. 123-52.
1986 Social Grouping and Residential Activities within a Late Phase Polity Network: Diquis Valley, Southeastern Costa Rica; In *Prehistoric Settlement Patterns in Costa Rica.* F. W. Lange and L. C. Norr, eds. Journal of the Steward Anthropological Society, Vol. 14, Nos. 1-2. Steward Anthropological Society, University of Illinois, Urbana. Pp. 325-38.
1980 *Cultural Settlement along the Moist Caribbean Slopes of Eastern Panama.* Ph.D. Dissertation, University of Illinois. Ann Arbor, Michigan: University Microfilms, Inc.

Earle, Sylvia
1972 A Review of the Marine Plants of Panama - The Panama Biota: Some Observations Prior to a Sea Level Canal. *Bulletin of the Biological Society of Washington.* Pp. 69-87.

Earle, Timothy K.
1987 Chiefdoms in Archaeological and Ethnohistorical Perspective. *Annual Review of Anthropology.* 16:332-41.

Easby, Elizabeth Kennedy
1981 Jade. In *Between Continents, Between Seas: Pre-Columbian Art of Costa Rica.* New York: Harry N. Abrams, Inc. Pp. 135-51.

Eidt, Robert C.
1959 Aboriginal Chibcha Settlement in Colombia. *Annals of the Association of American Geographers.* 49:374-92.

Elliot, D. H.
1965 Panama's Parita Pyramids. *Panama Archaeologist.* 6(1):66-67.

Emboden, William
1979 *Narcotic Plants.* New York: Collier Books.

Ereira, Alan
1993 *The Elder Brothers: A Lost South American People and Their Wisdom.* New York: Vintage Books.

Espinosa, Gaspar de
1892 Relación hecha por Gaspar de Espinosa, Alcalde Mayor de Castilla del Oro, dada a Pedrarias de Avila, Lugar Teniente General de aquellas Provincias, de todo lo que sucedió en la entrada que hizo en ellas de orden de Pedrarias. *Documentos Inéditos de Colombia* (Bogotá). Tomo II.
1913b Relación hecha por Gaspar de Espinosa, Alcalde Mayor de Castilla de Oro, dada a Pedrarias Dávila. In *El descubrimiento del Océano Pacífico: Vasco Núñez de Balboa, Fernando de Magallanes y sus Compañeros.* J. T. Medina, ed. Tomo II. Santiago de Chile: Editorial Universitaria. Pp. 272-304.
1913c Relación del Proceso quel Licenciado Gaspar de Espinosa, alcalde mayor, hizo en el viaje mandado por el muy magnífico señor Pedrarias Dávila... desde esta ciudad a las Provincias de Natá e París e a las otras provincias Comarcanas. In *El descubrimiento del Océano Pacífico: Vasco Núñez de Balboa, Fernando de Magallanes y sus Compañeros.* J. T. Medina, ed. Tomo II. Santiago de Chile: Editorial Universitaria. Pp. 154-83.

Evans, C. H.
1910 Note on the Gilded Metal-Work of Chiriqui. *Nature.* Vol. 82.

Feriz, Hans
1956 *Bericht Uber eine Ausgrabund an der "Venado Beach" Panama, Canal Zone.* Vienna: Wiener Volkerkundliche Mittheilungen Volkerkunde. Pp. 191-97.
1959a *Die Tabasarakultur.* Amsterdam: Kononkluk Instituut voor Tropen.
1959b Zeugnisse Einer Unbekannten Vorkolumbischen Kultur in Panama. *Ausgrabungen am Rio Tabasara (West Panama); Die Umschau in Wissenschaft und Tecnik,* Jahrganf 59, Jeft 23, Frankfurt. Pp. 728-32.
1959c Ausgraben bei Parita: Provinz Herrera, República de Panama. *Zeitschrift fur Ethnologie, Braunschweig.* Bd. 84, Heft 1. Pp. 62-69.

Fernández de Oviedo y Valdés, Gonzalo
1852-53 *Historia General y Natural de las Indias.* Vols. 1-3. Madrid: La Real Academia de la Historia.
1959 *Natural History of the West Indies.* S. A. Stoudemire, trans. and ed. Chapel Hill: University of North Carolina Press.

Ferrero, A. Luis
1981 Ethnohistory and Ethnography in the Central Highlands: Atlantic Watershed and Diquis. In *Between Continents/Between Seas: Precolumbian Art of Costa Rica.* New York: Harry N. Abrams, Inc. Pp. 93-103.

Fewkes, Jesse Walter
1973 *Designs on Prehistoric Hopi Pottery.* New York: Dover Publications.

Floyd, Troy S.
1967 *The Anglo-Spanish Struggle for Mosquitia.* Albuquerque: University of New Mexico Press.

Ford, James A.
1969 *A Comparison of Formative Cultures in the Americas: Diffusion or the Psychic Unity of Man?* Washington, D.C.: Smithsonian Institution Press.

Galinat, Walton C.
1980 The Archeological Maize Remains in Volcan, Panama: A Comparative Perspective. *Adaptive Radiations in Prehistoric Panama.* O. F. Linares and A. J. Ranere, eds. Peabody Museum Monograph. Cambridge, Massachusetts: Harvard University Press. Pp. 175-80.

Garay, Narciso
1930 *Tradiciones y cantares de Panamá, ensayo folklorico.* Bruxelles: Presses de l'Expansion Helge.

BIBLIOGRAPHY

Gebhart-Sayer, Angelika
1986 Una terapia estética, los diseños visionarios del Ayahuasca entre los Shipibo-Conibo. *América Indígena* (Mexico). 46(1):189-218.

Geertz, Clifford
1957 Ethos, World-View and the Analysis of Sacred Symbols. *Antioch Review.* 17:421-37.
1966 Religion as a Cultural System. In *Anthropological Approaches to the Study of Religion.* Michael Banton, ed. A. S. A. Monographs. Vol. 3. London: Tavistock Publications. Pp. 1-46.

Gentry, Howard Scott
1948 Land plants collected by the Allan Hancock Atlantic Expedition of 1939. *Allan Hancock Atlantic Expedition Report.* Los Angeles: University of Southern California Press. Pp. 36.

Gisborne, Lionel
1853 *The Isthmus of Darien in 1852.* London: Saunders and Stanford.

Glynn, Peter W.
1972 Observations on the Ecology of the Caribbean and Pacific Coasts of Panama - The Panamic Biota: Some Observations Prior to a Sea-Level Canal. *Bulletin of the Biological Society of Washington.* No. 2. Washington, D.C.: National Museum of Natural History, Smithsonian Institution. Pp. 13-30.

Goddard, Pliney E.
1932 The Golden Graves of Cocle. *Popular Mechanics.* December.

Goldman, Edward Alphonso
1920 Mammals of Panama. *Smithsonian Miscellaneous Collection, Vol. 69, No. 5.* Washington, D.C.: Smithsonian Institution.

González, Raúl
1971 Informe sobre Excavaciones Arqueológicas en El Cafetal. *II Symposium Nacional de Antropología, Arqueológia y etno Historia de Panamá* (non publié).

González Cháves, Alfredo, and Fernando González Vásquez
1989 *La Casa Cósmica Talamanqueña y sus Simbolismos.* San José: Costa Rica. Editorial de la Universidad de Costa Rica.

González-Zuleta, Fabio
1960 Dos Melodías Aborígenes del Choco. *Revista Colombiana de Folklor* (Bogotá). 2(4):121-26.

Gordon, B. Leroy
1962 Notes on Shell Mounds Near the Caribbean Coast of Western Panama. B. L. Gordon, ed. *Panama Archaeologist.* 5(1):1-9.
1982 *A Panama Forest and Shore.* Pacific Grove, CA: The Boxwood Press.

Gordon, Burton Leroy
1957-61 *Notes on the Chiriqui Lagoon District and Regions of Panama.* Berkeley, California: University of California, Department of Geography.

Graham, Mark Miller
1992 *Displacing the Center: Constructing Prehistory in Central America.* M. M. Graham, ed. Niwot, Colorado: University Press of Colorado.

Greenberg, Joséph H.
1987a *Language in the Americas.* Palo Alto: Stanford University Press.
1987b Language in the Americas (Author's Precis). *Current Anthropology.* 28:647-52.

Grieder, Terence
1975 The Interpretation of Ancient Symbols. *American Anthropologist.* 77:849-55.

Gunn, Robert
1980 Clasificación de los Idiomas Indígenas de Panamá con un Vocabulario Simple de los Mismos. In *Lenguas de Panamá.* Tomo VII. Panamá: Instituto Lingüístico de Verano/Instituto Nacional de Cultura.

Gunn, Robert, and Mary Gunn
1974 Fonología bocotá. *Lenguas de Panamá.* Tomo II. Panamá: Instituto Lingüístico de Verano/Instituto Nacional de Cultura. Pp. 31-48.

Guzmán, David Joaquín
1957 Excavations in Costa Rica and Panama. *Archaeology.* 10:258-63.

Haberland, Wolfgang
1955 Preliminary Report on the Aguas Buenas Complex, Costa Rica. *Ethnos.* (4).
1957 Black-on-Red Painted Ware and Associated Features in the Intermediate Area. *Ethnos.* 22:148-61.
1959a *A Re-Appraisal of Chiriquian Pottery Types.* Proceedings of the 33rd International Congress of Americanists, July 20-27, San José, Costa Rica. Vol. 2. Pp. 339-46.
1959b Chiriqui Pottery Types. *Panama Archaeologist.* 2(1):7-21
1960a Cien Años de Arqueología en Panamá. *Publicación Revista Lotería.* (Panamá). 12:7-16.
1960b Villalba, Part 1: A Preliminary Report. *Panama Archaeologist.* 4(1):7-21.
1960c Die Steinfiguren von Barriles in Panama. *Die Umschau in Wissenschaft und Technik* (Frankfurt). 60(23):720-22.
1961a New Names for Chiriquian Pottery Types. *Panama Archaeologist.* 4(1): 56-60.
1961b Two Shaman Graves in Central America. *Archaeology.* 14(3):154-60.
1961c Archaeologische Untersuchungen in der Provinz Chiriqui, Panama. *Acta Humboldtiana, Series Geographia et Ethnographica* (Wiesbaden). 3:73.
1962 *The Scarified Ware and the Early Cultures of Chiriqui, Panama.* Proceedings of the 34th International Congress of Americanists, Vienna. Pp. 381-89.
1966 *Early Phases on Ometepe Island, Nicaragua.* Proceedings of the XXXVI International Congress of Americanists, Madrid. Vol. 1. Pp. 399-403.
1969 *Early Phases and Their Relationship in Southern Central America.* Proceedings of the 38th International Congress of Americanists, Stuttgart. Vol. 1. Pp. 229-42.
1978 Lower Central America. In *Chronologies in New World Archaeology.* R. E. Taylor and C. W.

Meighan, eds. New York: Academic Press. Pp. 395-430.
1984 The Archaeology of GreaterChiriqui. In *The Archaeology of Lower Central America*. F. W. Lange and D. Z. Stone, eds. Albuquerque: University of New Mexico Press. Pp. 233-54.

Habicht-Mauche, Judith, John W. Hoopes, and Michael Geselowitz
1987 *Where's the Chief? The Archaeology of Complex Tribes.* Paper presented at the 52nd annual meeting of the Society for American Archaeology in Toronto in May.

Handley, Charles O.
1942 Mammalogy in Panama - The Panamic Biota: Some Observations Prior to a Sea-Level Canal. *Bulletin of the Biological Society of Washington* (The Smithsonian Institution). (2):217-27.

Hansell, Patricia
1987 The Formative in Central Pacific Panama: La Mula-Sarigua. In *Chiefdoms in the Americas.* R. D. Drennan and C. A. Uribe, eds. New York: University Press of America. Pp. 119-40.
1988 *The Rise and Fall of an Early Formative Community: La Mula-Sarigua, Central Pacific Panama.* Ph.D. Dissertation, Temple University. Ann Arbor, Michigan: University Microfilms, Inc.
1988 *Resource Accessibility and Control(?): An Example from Central Panama.* Paper presented at the 46th International Congress of Americanists, Amsterdam.

Harte, Eva
1958a Mountain-Top Burials. *Panama Archaeologist.* 1(1):29-31.
1958b Guacamayan Indian Culture. *Panama Magazine* (Panama). February.
1959 Petroglyphs in Panama. *Panama Archaeologist.* 2(1):58-69.

Harte, Neville H.
1958 A Madden Lake Cave. *Panama Archaeologist.* 1(1):21-24.
1960 *Preliminary Report on Petroglyphs of the Republic of Panama*: Panamá: Impresión Privada.

Harte, Neville, and Eva Harte
1966 El Sitio Guacamayo. *Boletín del Museo Chiricano.* 3:3-7.

Hayans, Guillermo
1952 New Cuna Myths, According to Guillermo Hayans. S. H. Wassen, ed. *Etnologiska Studier* (Goteborg). Pp. 85-105.

Helms, Mary W.
1976 Competition, Power and Succession to Office in Pre-Columbian Panama. In *Frontier Adaptations in Lower Central America*. M. W. Helms and F. L. Loveland, eds. Philadelphia: Institute for the Study of Human Issues. Pp. 25-35.
1977 Iguanas and Crocodilians in Tropical American Mythology and Iconography with Special Reference to Panama. *Journal of Latin American Lore.* 3(1): 51-132.
1979 *Ancient Panama.* Austin: University of Texas Press.
1981a Precious Metals and Politics: Style and Ideology in the Intermediate Area and Peru. *Journal of Latin American Lore.* (7):215-38.
1981b *Cunas, Molas, and Cocle Art Forms: Reflections on Panamanian Design Styles and Symbols.* Philadelphia: Institute for the Study of Human Issues.
1981c Succession to High Office in Pre-Columbian Circum-Caribbean Chiefdoms. *Man.* 15: 718-31.
1991 *Cosmological Chromaticism: Color and Symbolism in the Ceramic Art of Ancient Panama.* Paper Presented at a symposium held at the University of North Carolina at Greensboro.
1992 Thoughts on Public Symbols and Distant Domains Relevant to the Chiefdoms of Lower Central America. In *Wealth and Hierarchy in the Intermediate Area.* F. W. Lange, ed. Washington, D.C.: Dumbarton Oaks Research Library and Collection.
1993 Cosmological Chromatics: Color-Related Symbolism in the Ceramic Art of Ancient Panama. In *Reinterpreting Prehistory of Central America.* Denver: University of Colorado Press.

Helms, Mary W., and Franklin O. Loveland, eds.
1976 *Frontier Adaptations in Lower Central America.* Philadelphia: Institute for the Study of Human Issues.

Herlihy, Peter
1986 *A Cultural Geography of the Embera and Waunaan (Choco) Indians of Darien, Panamá, with Emphasis on Recent Village Formation and Economic Diversification.* Ph.D. Dissertation, Louisiana State University.

Herrera, Francisco
1970 La zona indígena del Distrito de Las Palmas, Veraguas, y el proceso de politización. *Hombre y Cultura* (Panamá). 2:97-105.

Herrera, Francisco A., and Raúl González
1964 Informe Sobre una Investigación Etnográfica entre los Indios Bogotá de Bocas del Toro. *Hombre y Cultura* (Panamá). 1(3):56-81.

Herrera, Leonor, W. M. Bray, M. Cardale De Schrimpff, and Pedro Botero
1988 *Nuevas Fechas de Radiocarbono para el Precerámico en la Cordillera Occidental de Colombia.* Paper presented at the 46th International Congress of Americanists, Amsterdam.

Holdridge, L. R., and Gerardo Holdridge
1956 Report of an Ecological Survey of the Republic of Panama. *Caribbean Forester.* 17:92-110.

Holloman, Regina E.
1969 *Developmental Change in San Blas.* Ph.D. Dissertation, Northwestern University.
1976 Cuna Household Types and the Domestic Cycle. In *Frontier Adaptions in Lower Central America.* Mary W. Helms and Franklin O. Loveland eds. Philadelphia: Institute for the Study of Human Issues. Pp. 131-50.

Holmer, Nils M., and
S. Henry Wassen, trans.
1947 *Mu-Igala, or the Way of the Muu: A Medicine Song from the Cuna Indians of Panama*. From original recording by Guilermo Haya. Göteborg: Elanders Boktyckeri Aktiebolag.
1953 The Complete Mu-Igala in Picture Writing: A Native Record of a Cuna Indian Medicine Song. *Ethnologiska Studier* (Göteborg). (21).
1963 Dos Cantos Shamanísticos de los Indios Cuna. *Ethnologiska Studier* (Göteborg). (27).

Holmes, William H.
1887 The Use of Gold and Other Metals Among the Ancient Inhabitants of Chiriqui, Isthmus of Darien. *Smithsonian Institution, Bureau of American Ethnology Bulletin 3*. Washington, D.C. Pp. 27.
1888 Ancient Art of the Province of Chiriqui. In *Smithsonian Institution, Bureau of American Ethnology, 6th Annual Report, 1884-1885*. Pp. 1-187.

Hoopes III, John Wilton
1987 *Early Ceramics and the Origins of Village Life in Lower Central America*. Ph.D. Dissertation, Harvard University. Ann Arbor, Michigan: University Microfilms, Inc.
1988 *The Complex Tribe in Prehistory: Sociopolitical Organization in the Archaeological Record*. Paper presented at the 53rd Annual Meeting of the Society for American Archaeology in Phoenix.

Hoover, F. Louis
1969 *Molas from the San Blas Islands*. New York: Art Gallery, Center for Inter-American Relations.

Howarth, David
1966 *Panama: Four Hundred Years of Dreams and Cruelty*. New York: McGraw-Hill.

Howe, James
1974 *Village Political Organization among the San Blas Cuna*. Ph.D. Dissertation, University of Pennsylvania. Ann Arbor, Michigan: University Microfilms, Inc.
1976 Smoking Out the Spirits: A Cuna Exorcism. In *Ritual and Symbolism in Native Central America*. P. Young and J. Howe, eds. University of Oregon Anthropological Papers. Vol. 9. Pp. 67-76.
1977 Carrying the Village: Cuna Political Metaphors. In *The Social Use of Metaphor*. C. Crocker and J. D. Sapir, eds. Philadelphia: University of Pennsylvania. Pp. 132-63.
1978 Algunos problemas no resueltos de la etnohistoria del este de Panamá. *Revista Panameña de Antropología*. 2:3-47.
1986 *The Kuna Gathering: Contemporary Village Politics in Panama*. Austin, Texas: University of Texas Press.

Howe, James, and Philip Young, eds.
1976 Ritual and Symbol in Native Central America. *University of Oregon Anthropological Papers*. No. 9.

Hrdlicka, Alex
1926 The Indians of Panama: Their Physical Relationship to the Mayas. *American Journal of Physical Anthropology*. 9(1).

Hudson, Travis, Armand J. Labbé, and Christopher Moser
1983 *Skywatchers of Ancient California*. Santa Ana, California: Bowers Museum Foundation.

Hudson, Travis, and Ernest Underhay
1978 Crystals in the Sky: An Intellectual Odyssey Involving Chumash Astronomy, Cosmology and Rock Art. *Ballena Press Anthropological Papers*. No. 10.

Hugh-Jones, Stephen
1974 *Barasana Initiation and Cosmology Among the Barasana Indians of the Vaupés Area of Colombia*. Ph.D. Dissertation, Cambridge University (unpublished).

Hugh-Jones, Christine
1982 *From the Milky River*. Cambridge: University Press.

Humphries, Frank Theodore
1944 *The Indians of Panama: Their History and Culture*. Panama American Publishing Co.

Ibarra, R. Eugenia
1984 *Los cacicazgos indígenas de la vertiente Atlántica y Valle Central de Costa Rica: un intento de reconstrucción etnohistórica*. Tésis. Universidad de Costa Rica.

Ichon, Alain
1968a La mission archéologique française au Panamá. *Journal de la Société des Américanistes* (Musée de l'Homme, Paris). LVII:139-43.
1968b *Informe preliminar sobre las investigaciones arqueológicas en el sur de la Península de Azuero*. Actas del Primer Symposium Nacional de Arqueología y Etno-Historia de Panamá, Universidad de Panamá.
1970 Vases funéraires d'El Indio, District de Tonosí, Panamá. *Objets et Mondes* (Musée de l'Homme, Paris). 10:29-36.
1975 Tipos de Sepultura en el Sur de la Península de Azuero. *Publicación Especial de la Dirección Nacional de Patrimonio Histórico, Instituto de Cultura*. Panamá: La Editora de la Nación.
1980 L'archéologie du Sud de la Péninsule d'Azuero, Panamá. *Etudes Mesoaméricaines - Serie II*. Mexico City: Mission Archéologique et Ethnologique Française au Méxique.

Isaza, Ilean
1994 Desarrollo estilístico de la cerámica Pintada del Panamá central con énfasis en el Período 500 A.C. - 500 D.C. M.A. Tésis, Departamento de Arqueología, Universidad Autónoma de Guadalajara.

Jaen Arosemena, Agustin
1955 Nociones Históricas de Coclé. *Centenario de la Provincia, 1855, 12 de Septiembre, 1955*. Panamá: Ediciones del Ministerio de Educación, Departamento de Bellas Artes y Publicaciones.
1961 Siluetas biográficas de ilustres coclesaños. *Centenario de la Provincia de Coclé, Septiembre de 1855-1955*. Panamá.

Janiger, Oscar, and
Marlene Dobkin de Ríos
1973 Suggestive Hallucinogenic Properties of Tobacco. *Medical Anthropology Newsletter.* No. 4.

Johnson, Frederick
1948 Central American Cultures: An Introduction. Vol. 4. *Smithsonian Institution, Bureau of American Ethnology Bulletin 145.* Washington, D.C. Pp. 43-68.

Joly, L. G., S. Guerra, R. Septimo, P. N. Solis, and others
1990 Ethnobotanical Inventory of Medicinal Plants Used by the Guaymi Indians in Western Panama. Part II. *Journal of Ethnopharmacology.* 28:191-206.

Keeler, Clyde E.
1953 The Archaeology of a Medicine Basket. *Archaeology.* New York. 6(2):95-98.
1954 Cuna Indian Beliefs Concerning the Afterlife. *Journal of the Tennessee Academy of Science.* 29.
1955 Cuna Uchus and Catholic Saints. *Journal of the Tennessee Academy of Science.* 30:203-11.
1956 *Land of the Moon-Children. The Primitive San Blas Culture in Flux.* Athens: University of Georgia Press.
1956 The Worship of Ishtar Among the Cuna Indians of San Blas. *Bulletin of the Georgia Academy of Science.* 19:1-26.
1960 *Secrets of the Cuna Earth Mother: A Comparative Study of Ancient Religions.* New York: Exposition Press.
1961 *Apples of Immortality from the Cuna Tree of Life: The Study of a Most Ancient Ceremony and a Belief That Survived 10,000 Years.* New York: Exposition Press.
1969 *Cuna Indian Art: The Culture and Craft of Panama's San Blas Islanders.* New York: Exposition Press.

Kinney, Bob, ed.
1976 *Extensive Inaugural Exhibit Focuses on Art and Artifacts of Cuna Indians.* Granville, Ohio.

Krieger, Herbert W.
1926 Material Culture of the People of Southeastern Panama, Based on Specimens in the U.S. National Museum. *Smithsonian Institution Bulletin 134.* Government Printing Office: Washington, D.C.

Kroeber, Alfred Louis
1949 Esthetic and Recreational Activities. Vol. 5. *Smithsonian Institution, Bureau of American Ethnology Bulletin 143.* Washington, D. C. Pp. 411-92.

Labbé, Armand J.
1982 *Religion, Art, and Iconography: Man and Cosmos in Prehispanic Mesoamerica.* Santa Ana, California: Bowers Museum Foundation Press.
1986a *Art, Myth, and Cognition: An Exploration of the Esoteric Content of Southwest Indian Geometric Art.* Unpublished Manuscript.
1986b *Colombia Before Columbus: The People, Culture, and Ceramic Art of Prehispanic Colombia.* New York: Rizzoli International Publications.
1988 *Colombia Antes de Colón: el pueblo, la cultura y el arte de la cerámica en Colombia prehispánica.* Bogotá, Colombia: Carlos Valencia, editores.
1992 *Images of Power: Masterworks of the Bowers Museum of Cultural Art.* Santa Ana, California: Cultural Arts Press.

Labbé, Armand J., Clemencia Plazas and Ana Maria Falchetti
1992 *Tribute to the Gods: Treasures of the Museo del Oro.* Santa Ana, California: Cultural Arts Press.

Labbé Armand J., D. Travis Hudson and Christopher Moser
1983 *Skywatchers of Ancient California.* Santa Ana, California: Bowers Museum Press.

Ladd, John
1957 A Stratigraphic Trench at Sitio Conte, Panama. *American Antiquity.* 22(2):65-271.
1964 Archaeological Investigations in the Parita and Santa Maria Zones of Panama. *Smithsonian Institution, Bureau of American Ethnology Bulletin 193.* Washington, D.C.

Lagrotta Garces, Roque
1967 *Inventario de los recursos humanos de los corregimientos Tonoso y el Bebedero del area de desarrollo del valle de Tonoso en Panamá.* Instituto Interamericano de Ciencias Agrícolas de la D. E. A. Centro de Enseñanza e Investigación Costa Rica: Turrialba (non publié).

Lange, Frederick W.
1980 The Formative Zoned Bichrome Period in Northwestern Costa Rica (800 B.C. to A.D. 500), Based on Excavations at the Vidor Site, Bay of Culebra. *Vinculos.* 6:33-42.
1984a Cultural Geography of Pre-Columbian Lower Central America. In *The Archaeology of Lower Central America.* Albuquerque: University of New Mexico Press. Pp. 233-62.
1984b The Greater Nicoya Archaeological Sub-Area. In *The Archaeology of Lower Central America.* F. W. Lange and D. Z. Stone, eds. Albuquerque: University of New Mexico Press. Pp. 165-94.
1992 The Intermediate Area: An Introductory Overview of Wealth and Hierarchy Issues. In *Wealth and Hierarchy in The Intermediate Area.* Washington, D.C.: Dumbarton Oaks Research Library and Collection.

Lange, Frederick W., and Doris Z. Stone, eds.
1984 *The Archaeology of Lower Central America.* Albuquerque: University of New Mexico Press.

Lange, Frederick W., Ronald L. Bishop, and Lambertus van Zelst
1981 Perspectives on Costa Rican Jade: Compositional Analyses and Cultural Implications. In *Between Continents/Between Seas: Precolumbian Art of Costa Rica.* New York: Harry N. Abrams, Inc. Pp. 167-75.

Lathrap, Donald W.
1963 Possible Affiliations of the Machalilla Complex of Coastal Ecuador. *American Antiquity.* 29:239-41.

1966 Relationships between Mesoamerica and the Andean Areas. In *Handbook of Middle American Indians*. Vol. 4. Gordon F. Ekholm and Gordon R. Willey, eds. Austin: University of Texas Press. Pp. 265-76.
1970 *The Upper Amazon*. London: Thames and Hudson.
1973 The Antiquity and Importance of Long Distance Trade Relationships in the Moist Tropics of Pre-Columbian South America. *World Archaeology*. 5:170-86.
1977 Our Father the Cayman, Our Mother the Gourd: Spinden Revisited or a Unitary Model for the Emergence of Agriculture in the New World. In *Origins of Agriculture*. Charles A. Reed, ed. Mouton: The Hague. Pp. 713-52.

Lehmann, Henri
1959 *Pre-Columbian Ceramics*. New York: Viking Press.

Leon, Jorge
1959 *Origen del Cultivo del Cacao*. Actas y Memorias del XXXIII Congreso Internacional de Americanistas, San José, California. Tomo 1. Pp. 251-58.

Leon-Portilla, Miguel
1978 *Aztec Thought and Culture*. Norman, Oklahoma: University of Oklahoma Press.

Levi-Strauss, Claude
1978 *Tristes Tropiques*. John Russell, trans. Antheneum Series 48. New York: Anthenaeum Press
1983a *The Raw and the Cooked*. John and Doreen Weightman, trans. Levi-Strauss, Claude Mythologiques Series, Vol. 1. Chicago: University of Chicago Press.
1983b *From Honey to Ashes*. John and Doreen Weightman, trans. Levi-Strauss, Claude Mythologiques Series, Vol. 2. Chicago: University of Chicago Press.

Linares de Sapir, Olga F.
1962 *The Archaeology and Ethnohistory of Panama*. Unpublished seminar paper. Cambridge, Massachusetts: Harvard University.
1966 *La cronología arqueológica del golfo de Chiriquí, Panamá*. Actas y Memorias del XXXVI Congreso Internacional de Americanistas, Madrid.
1968a Ceramic Phases for Chiriqui, Panama, and Their Relationship to Neighboring Sequences. *American Antiquity*. 33(2):216-25.
1968b *Cultural Chronology of the Gulf of Chiriquí, Panamá*. Washington, D.C.: Smithsonian Institution Press.
1968c *Coclé and the Cuna: A Mistaken Association*. Paper presented at the 33rd Annual Meeting of the Society for American Archaeology held in Santa Fe, New Mexico. May.
1971a Cerro Brujo, A Tiny Guaymi Hamlet of the Past. *Expedition*. 13(2).
1971b Cocle Culture and the Cuna. *Bulletin of the University of Pennsylvania Museum*. 3:10-15.
1975 *Differential Exploitation of Lagoon-Estuary Systems in Panama*. Paper presented at the 40th Annual Meeting of the Society for American Archaeology, Dallas. May.
1976a Animals That Were Bad to Eat Were Good to Compete With: An Analysis of the Conte Style from Ancient Panama. *Ritual and Symbol in Native Central America: University of Oregon Anthropological Papers 9*:1-20.
1976b Current Research: Central America. *American Antiquity*. 41(2):225-26.
1976c *From the Late Preceramic to the Early Formative in the Intermediate Area: Some Issues and Methodologies*. Proceedings of the First Puerto Rican Symposium on Archaeology. Report 1. San Juan: Fundación Arqueológica, Antropológica e Histórica de Puerto Rico. Pp. 65-77.
1977 Ecology and the Arts in Ancient Panama: On the Development of Social Rank and Symbolism in the Central Provinces. *Studies in Pre-Columbian Art and Archaeology*. Washington, D.C.: Dumbarton Oaks.
1977a Adaptive Strategies in Western Panama. *World Archaeology*. 8:304-19.
1979 What Is Lower Central American Archaeology? *Annual Review of Anthropology*. 8:21-43.
1980 *Adaptive Radiations in Prehistoric Panama*. Cambridge, Massachusetts: Peabody Museum of Archaeology and Ethnology, Harvard University.
1980b Ecology and Prehistory of the Aguacate Peninsula. In *Bocas del Toro, Part I: Adaptive Radiations in Prehistoric Panama*. Peabody Museum Monograph. Olga F. Linares and A. J. Ranere, eds. Vol. 5. Cambridge, Massachusetts: Harvard University Press. Pp. 57-66.

Linares, Olga, and Anthony R. Ranere
1962 Información sobre el proyecto arqueológico en Costa del Pacífico del oeste de Panamá. *Publicación Revista Lotería* (Panamá). 7(74): 49-50
1971 Human Adaptation to the Tropical Forests of Western Panama. *Archaeology*. 24(4):346-55.
1980 *Adaptive Radiations in Prehistoric Panama: Peabody Museum Monograph*. No. 5. Cambridge, Massachusetts: Harvard University Press.

Linares, Olga F., P. D. Sheets, and E. J. Rosenthal
1975 Prehistoric Agriculture in Tropical Highlands. *Science*. 187: 137-45.

Linné, Sigval
1936 Archaeological Field Work in Chiriqui, Panama. *Ethnos*. 1(4): 95-102.

Loewen, Jacob
1960 A Choco Miraculous Escape Tale. *América Indígena* (México). 20(3):207-16.
1962 A Choco Indian in Hillsboro, Kansas. *Practical Anthropology* (Tarrytown, New York). 9(3): 129-33.
1963 Choco I: Introduction and Bibliography. *International Journal of American Linguistics*. 29.

Lothrop, Samuel Kirkland
1919 The Discovery of Gold in the Graves of Chiriqui, Panama. *Indian Notes and Monographs, Vol. 2*. New York: Museum of the American Indian, Heye Foundation. Pp. 23-36.

1932 Aboriginal Navigation Off the West Coast of South America. *Journal of the Royal Anthropological Institute of Great Britain and Ireland.* LXII:229-56.

1934 Archaeological Investigation in the Province of Coclé, Panama. *American Journal of Archaeology.* 38(2):207-11.

1935 Aboriginal Gilding in Panama. *American Antiquity.* 26(1):106-8.

1936 *Zacala: A Study of Ancient Quiche Artifacts.* Monograph 472. Washington, D.C.: Carnegie Institution of Washington.

1937 Cocle: An Archaeological Study of Central Panama. Part 1, No. 7. *Memoirs of the Peabody Museum of Archaeology and Ethnology.* Cambridge, Massachusetts: Harvard University.

1940 *Cuatro Antiguas Culturas de Panamá.* Actas y Memorias del XXVII Congreso Internacional de Americanistas, Lima. Pp. 205-09.

1942a Cocle: An Archaeological Study of Central Panama. Part 2, No. 8. *Memoirs of the Peabody Museum of Archaeology and Ethnology.* Cambridge, Massachusetts: Harvard University.

1942b *The Sigua: Southernmost Aztec Outpost.* Proceedings of the Eighth American Scientific Congress, Washington, D.C. Vol. 2. Pp. 109-16.

1948 The Archaeology of Panama. In *Handbook of South American Indians.* J. Steward, ed. Vol. 4. Smithsonian Institution, Bureau of American Ethnology Bulletin 43. Washington, D.C. Pp. 43-168.

1950 Archaeology of Southern Veraguas, Panama. Vol. 9, No. 3. *Memoirs.* Cambridge, Massachusetts: Peabody Museum, Harvard University.

1954 Suicide, Sacrifice and Mutilations in Burials at Venado Beach, Panama. *American Antiquity.* 19:226-34.

1956 Jewelry from the Panama Canal Zone. *Archaeology.* IX(1):34-40.

1957 *Pre-Columbian Art: The Robert Woods Bliss Collection.* New York: Phaidon Press, Garden City Books.

1959a A Re-Appraisal of Isthmian Archaeology. *Americanistische Miszellen, Mitteilungen aus dem Museum für Völkerkunde in Hamburg.* Hamburg: Museum für Völkerkunde. 25:85-91.

1959b *The Archaeological Picture in Southern Central America.* Vol. 1. Proceedings of the 33rd International Congress of Americanists, July 20-27, San José, Costa Rica. Pp. 166-72.

1959c Ceramic Style and Sequence at Sitio Conte, Panama. In *Archaeologist at Work.* Robert Heizer, ed. New York: Harper & Bros. Pp. 425-41.

1960 C-14 Dates for Venado Beach, Canal Zone. *Panama Archaeologist.* 3(1):96.

1961 Peruvian Stylistic Impact on Lower Central America. *Essays in Pre-Columbian Art and Archaeology.* Cambridge, Massachusetts. Pp. 258-65.

1963 Archaeological Remains in the Diquís Delta, Costa Rica. Vol. LI. *Peabody Museum Papers.* Cambridge, Massachusetts.

1964 *Treasures of Ancient America: The Arts of the Pre-Columbian Civilizations from Mexico to Peru.* Geneva: Albert Skira.

1966 Archaeology of Lower Central America. Vol. 4. *Handbook of Middle American Indians.* Robert Wauchope, ed. Austin: University of Texas Press. Pp. 180-208.

1976 *Pre-Columbian Designs from Panama: 591 illustrations from Coclé Pottery.* New York: Dover Publications.

Lothrop, Samuel K. and Paul Bergsoe
1960 Aboriginal Gilding in Panama. *American Antiquity.* 26(1):106-08.

Lothrop, Samuel Kirkland, and E. B. Lothrop
1934a Treasures Which the Spanish Conquistadores Missed. Gold, Jewelry and Pottery from Cocle, Panama: One of the Richest Archaeological Discoveries in the New World. *Illustrated London News.* March 31.

1934b An Ancient Culture is Brought to Light: Panama Graves Yield Golden Treasures of a Vanished People Who Attained a High Degree of Art and Workmanship Centuries Ago. *New York Times Magazine.* February 25.

Lothrop, Samuel K., et al.
1964 *Essays in Pre-Columbian Art and Archaeology.* Cambridge: Harvard University Press.

Luna, Luis Eduardo, and Pablo Amaringo
1991 *Ayahuasca Visions, The Religious Iconography of a Peruvian Shaman.* Berkeley, California: North Atlantic Books.

MacCurdy, G. G.
1906 *The Armadillo in the Ancient Art of Chiriqui.* Vol. 2. 15th Congrès International des Americanistes, Québec. Pp. 7-23.

1908 *The Alligator in the Ancient Art of Chiriqui.* 16th International Congess of the Americas, Vienna.

1911 A Study of Chiriquian Antiques. Vol. 3. *Memoirs of the Connecticut Academy of Arts and Sciences.* New Haven.

1912 Notes on the Ancient Art of Central America. *American Anthropologist.* 14(2).

1913 Notes on the Archaeology of Chiriqui. *American Anthropologist.* 15(4):661-67.

1916 The Octopus Motive in Ancient Chiriquian Art. *American Anthropologist.* 18(3):366-83.

1919 Ancient Panama Art. *Natural History.* 9(2).

MacLeod, Murdo J.
1973 *Spanish Central America.* Berkeley: University of California Press.

Mahler, Joy
1961 Grave Associations and Ceramics in Veraguas, Panama. *Essays in Pre-Columbian Art and Archaeology.* Cambridge, Massachusetts: Harvard University Press.

Mallery, Garrick
1972 *Picture-Writing of the American Indians.* Vols. I-II. New York: Dover Publications.

Marshall, Donald S.
1949 Archaeology of Far Fan Beach, Panama Canal Zone. *American Antiquity.* 15(2):124-32.

BIBLIOGRAPHY

Mason, John Alden
1940 Ivory and Resin Figurines from Coclé. *University Museum Bulletin*. Philadelphia: University of Pennsylvania. 8(4):13-21.
1942 *New Excavations at the Sitio Conte, Coclé, Panama*. Proceedings of the 8th American Scientific Congress, Washington D. C., May 10-18, 1940. Vol. 2. Pp. 103-7.
1943 The American Collections of the University Museum. *University Museum Bulletin*. 10(1-2):49-56.

McGimsey III, Charles R.
1956 Cerro Mangote: A Preceramic Site in Panama. Part 1. *American Antiquity*. 22(2):151-61.
1958 Further Data and a Date for Cerro Mangote, Panama. *American Antiquity*. 23(4):434-35.
1959 *A Survey of ArchaeologicallyKnown Burial Practices in Panama*. Vol. 2. Proceedings of the 33rd International Congress of Americanists, July 20-27, San José, Costa Rica. Pp. 347-56.
1960 Arqueología Panameña. *Arkansas Archaeological Society Newsletter* (Fayetteville). 1(10): 12-14.
1964 Investigaciones Arqueológicas en Panamá: Informe preliminar sobre las temporadas de 1961-62. *Hombre y Cultura* (T. I., Centro de Investigaciones de la Universidad Nacional, Panamá). 3:39-55.
1968 *A Provisional Dichotomization of Regional Styles in Panamanian Goldwork*. Proceedings of the 37th International Congress of Americanists, Buenos Aires, Argentina. Vol. 4. Pp. 45-55.

McGimsey III, Charles R., M. B. Collins, and T. W. McKern
1986-87 Cerro Mangote and Its Population. *Journal of the Steward Anthropological Society*. 16(1-2): 125-57.

McNiel, J. A.
1887 Gold and Bronze Relics, and Guaymi Indians. *American Antiquarian* (Chicago). 9.

Means Philip, Ainsworth
1940 The Philosophic Interrelationship Between Middle America and Andean Religions (An essay discussing the intellectual and emotional differentiation between the religions of Middle America and those of the Andes). *The Maya and Their Neighbors*. New York: Appleton-Century. Pp. 430-40.

Meggers, Betty J. and Clifford Evans
1967 *Potsherds Language and How to Speak it*. Washington, D.C.: Smithsonian Institution.

Meggers, Betty, Clifford Evans, and Emilio Estrada
1965 *Early Primitive Culture of Coastal Ecuador: The Valdivia and Machalilla Phases*. Washington, D.C.: Smithsonian Institution.

Menard de Saint, Maurice E.
1888 *Les Poteries des Sepultures Indiennes du Chiriqui*. Chatillon Sur-Seine.

Méndez, Alejandro
1947 El Hallazgo de Barriles, Panamá. *Epocas*. June 25.

Mercado y Sousa, Elsa
1959 *El hombre y la tierra en Panamá (S. XVI) según las primeras fuentes*. Madrid.

Merritt, J. King
1860 *Report on the Huacas or Ancient Grave Yards of Chiriqui*. New York: American Ethnological Society.

Miller, Mary and Karl Taube
1993 *The Gods and Symbols of Ancient Mexico and the Maya: An Illustrated Dictionary of Mesoamerican Religion*. New York: Thames and Hudson.

Minelli, Laura L.
1976 Mesoamerican Influences Among Talamanca and Western Guaymí Indians. In *Frontier Adaptations in Lower Central America*. M. Helms and F. Loveland, eds. Philadelphia: Institute for the Study of Human Issues. Pp. 55-65.

Mitchell, Russell H.
1959a An Unreported Pottery Vessel from Panama. *Panama Archaeologist*. 2:35-38.
1959b Projectile Points from Panama. *Panama Archaeologist*. 2(1):70-83.
1960a Panama Projectile Points. *Panama Archaeologist*. 3(1):22-34.
1960b Stone Mask from Panama. *Panama Archaeologist*. 3(1):88-93.
1961a Recent Discoveries in Northern Panama. *Archaeology*. 14(3):198-204.
1961b Máscara de Piedra Encontrada en Panamá. *Publicación Revista Lotería* (Panamá). 6(73):37-40.
1961c An Unusual Pottery Vessel from the Campana Mountains. *Panama Archaeologist*. 4:69-70.
1961d Preliminary Report on Wooden Artifacts from Cave Urn Burials in the Madden Lake Area, Panama. *Ethnos*. 1(2):30-39.
1962 A Pre-Colombian (siq.) Burial in Panama. *Archaeology*. 15(4):227-32.
1963a A Possible Gold Pectoral from Panama. *American Antiquity*. 28(4):549.
1963b An Unfinished Metate from Panama. *American Antiquity*. 28(3):401-402.
1964a *Burial Practices and Shellwork of La Tranquilla (CZ-3), Canal Zone*. Proceedings of the 35th International Congress of Americanists, Mexico.
1964b Limestone Figure from Tumba Vieja. *Panama Archaeologist*. 5(1):24-27.

Mitchell, Russell H., and James F. Heidenreich
n.d. New Developments on the Azuero Peninsula, Province of Los Santos, Republic of Panama. *Panama Archaeologist*. 2(1):13.

Mitchell, Russell H. and John Acker
1961 A New Pottery Type from the Province of Herrera, Panama. *Panama Archaeologist*. 4(1):61-65.

1961a A Pottery Collection from Parita. *Panama Archaeologist*. 4(1):4-30.

Morales, Padrón
1958 Histiografía y Bibliografía Americanista. *Anuario de Estudios Americanos* (Escuela de Estudios Hispano-Americanos de Sevilla). Tomo XV:551-83.

Myers, Thomas P.
1978 Formative Period Interaction Spheres in the Intermediate Area: Archaeology of Central America and Adjacent South America. In *Advances in Andean Archaeology*. David L. Browman, ed. Mouton, The Hague. Pp. 203-04.

Navarette, Martín Fernández de
1829 *Colección de los Viajes y Descubrimientos que Hicieron por mar los Españoles Desde Fines del Siglo XV*. Tomo III, capítulo VII. Madrid.

Neal, Avon
1968 The Witchery of Stitchery. *CIBA Journal*. Spring:17-23.

Nordenskiöld, Erland
1929 Les rapports entre l'arte, la religion et la magie chez les Indiens Cuna et Choco. *Journal Societé Americaine* (Paris). 21:141-58.
1930 *Cuna Indian Religion*. Proceedings of the 23rd International Congress of Americanists, New York.
1931 Faiseurs de miracles et voyants chez les Indiens Cuna. *Revista del Institute de Etnología* (Tucumán). 2:459-69.
1938 *An Historical and Ethnological Survey of the Cuna Indians*. No. 10. Comparative Ethnographical Studies. Göteborg: Etnografiska Museum.

Norr, Lynette C.
1984 Prehistoric Subsistence and Health Status of Coastal Peoples from the Central American Isthmus. In *Paleopathology at the Origins of Agriculture*. George J. Armelagos and Mark Cohen, eds. New York: Academic Press. Pp. 463-90.
1990 *Nutritional Consequences of Prehistoric Subsistence Strategies in Lower Central America*. Ph.D. Dissertation, University of Illinois at Champaign.

Osgood, Cornelius
1935 The Archaeological Problem in Chiriqui. *American Anthropologist*. 37(2):234-43.

Otis, Fessenden N.
1859 The New Gold Discoveries on the Isthmus of Panama. *Harper's Weekly*. 3(136):499-500.
1860 Los Nuevos Descrubrimientos de Oro en el Istmo de Panamá. *Publicación Revista Lotería*. 12:3-6.
1867 *Isthmus of Panama*. New York: Harper & Bros.

Oviedo, Fernández de
1944 *Historia natural y general de los indias*. J. Natalico, ed. 14 Vols. Asunción, Paraguay: Editorial Guaranía.

Oyuela, Augusto, and J. Zeidler
1990 *The Early Formative Cultures of Northwestern South America: Ceramic Change and Assemblage Diversity Compared*. Paper presented at the 55th Annual Meeting of the Society for American Archaeology, Las Vegas, Nevada, April 18-22.

Parker, Ann and Avon Neal
1977 *Molas: Folk Art of the Cuna Indians*. Barre, Massachusetts: Barre Publishers.

Pearsall, Deborah M.
1986 La circulación primitiva del maíz entre Mesoamérica y Sudamérica. In *Arqueología de la Costa Ecuatoriana: Nuevos enfoques, Vol. 1*. J. Marcos, ed. Ecuador: Escuela Politécnica del Litoral, Centro de Estudios Arqueológicos y Antropológicos. Pp. 231-58.
1988 An Overview of Formative Period Subsistence in Northern South America: Paleoethnobotanical Data and Perspectives. In *Diet and Subsistence: Current Archaeological Perspectives*. B. V. Kennedy and G. M. LeMoine, eds. Calgary: University of Calgary.
In Press The Origins of Plant Cultivation in South America. In *Origins of Agriculture in World Perspective*. P. J. Watson and C. W. Cowan, eds. Washington, D.C.: Smithsonian Institution Press.

Pickersgill, Barbara, and C. B. Heiser
1987 Origins and Distributions of Plants Domesticated in the New World Tropics. In *The Origins of Agriculture*. C. A. Reed, ed. Mouton, The Hague. Pp. 803-35.

Pinart, Alphonse L.
1875 Noticias de los indios del departmento de Veraguas, y vocabulario de las lenguas Guaymí, norteño, sabanero y dorasque. In *Bibliotheque de linguistique et d'ethnographie Americaines, Numero 4*. San Francisco.
1882a *Colección de Lingüística y Etnografía Americanas*. Tomo 4. San Francisco: Imprenta de A. L. Brancroft y ca.
1882b *Vocabulario de las lenguas Guaymí-Sabanero y Dorasque*. Paris: Imprenta Lehmann.
1885 Chiriquí. Bocas del Toro, Valle Miranda. *Bulletin de la Societe de Geographie de Paris*. 6:433.
1887 Les Indiens de l'etate de Panama. *Revue d'ethnographie* (Paris). Mars-Avril.
1890 *Vocabulario Castellano-Cuna*. Paris: Ernest Leroux.
1892 *Vocabulario Castellano-Guaymie*. Paris: Ernest Leroux.
1897 *Vocabulario Castellano-Chocoe*. Paris: Ernest Leroux.
1900 *Notes sur les Tribus Indiennes de Familles Guarano-Guaymies de l'Isthme de Panama et du Centre-Amerique*. Chartres Imprimiere Durand Rue Fulbert.

Pineda Giraldo, R., and V. Gutiérrez de Pineda
1959 En el mundo espiritual del Indio Choco. *Miscellanea Paul Rivet*. (Octogenario Dicata), Vol. 2. Universidad Autónoma Nacional de México. Pp. 435-62.

Piperno, Dolores R.
1981 First Report on the Phytolith Analysis of the Vegas Site (OGSE-80), Ecuador. In *The Vegas Culture: Early Prehistory of Southwestern Ecuador*. K. Stothert, ed. Guayaquil, Ecuador: Museo Anthropologico del Banco Central de Ecuador.

1988 *Phytolith Analysis: An Archaeological and Geological Perspective.* San Diego: Academic Press.

1989a Non-affluent Foragers: Resource Availability, Seasonal Shortages and the Emergence of Agriculture in Panamanian Tropical Forests. In *Foraging and Farming: The Evolution of Plant Domestication.* D. R. Harris and G. Hillman, eds. London: George Allen and Unwin, Ltd. Pp. 538-54.

1989b *The Origins and Development of Food Production in Pacific Panama.* Proceedings of the Circum-Pacific Prehistory Conference, Seattle, August. Seattle: Washington State University Press.

Piperno, Dolores P., and Karen H. Clary
1984 Early Plant Use and Cultivation in the Santa Maria Basin, Panama: Data from Phytoliths and Pollen. In *Recent Developments in Isthmian Archaeology: Advances in the Prehistory of Lower Central America.* F. W. Lange, ed. Oxford: BAR International Series 212. Pp. 85-122.

Piperno, Dolores R., Karen H. Clary, Richard J. Cooke, Anthony J. Ranere, and Doris Weiland
1985 Preceramic Maize in Central Panama: Phytolith and Pollen Evidence. *American Anthropologist.* 87:871-78.

Piperno, Dolores R., Mark B. Bush, and Paul A. Colinvaux
1988 Man-Land Relationships in the Humid Tropics of Panama: The Past 13,000 Years. Paper presented at the 46th International Congress of Americanists, Amsterdam.

1990 Paleoenvironments and Human Settlement in Late-Glacial Panama. *Quaternary Research.* 33:108-16.
In Press Paleoecological Perspectives on Human Adaption in Panama. Part I: The Late Glacial and Early Holocene. *Geoarchaeology.*
In Press Paleoecological Perspectives on Human Adaptions in Central Panama. Part II: The Holocene. *Geoarchaeology.*

Plazas, Clemencia, and Ana María Falchetti
1986 Cerámica arcaica en las sábanas de San Marcos, Sucre. *Boletín de Arqueología, Fundación de Investigaciones Arqueológicas Nacionales* (Bogotá, Colombia). 1(2):16-23.

Puls, Herta
1988 *Textiles of the Kuna Indians of Panama.* Cromwell House, United Kingdom: Shire Publications, Ltd.

Ranere, Anthony J.
1980a Human Movement into Tropical America at the End of the Pleistocene. In *Anthropological Papers in Memory of Earl H. Swanson.* L. B. Harten, C. N. Warren, and D. R. Tuohy, eds. Pocatello, Idaho: Museum of Natural History. Pp. 41-47.
1980b Preceramic Shelters in the Talamancan Range. In *Adaptive Radiations in Prehistoric Panama.* O. F. Linares and A. J. Ranere, eds. *Peabody Museum Monograph.* Cambridge, Massachusetts: Harvard University. 5:316-53.
In Press Implements of Change in the Holocene Environments of Panama. Proceedings of the 46th International Congress of Americanists: Archaeology and Environment. O. Ortiz-Troncoso and T. van der Hammen, eds. Amsterdam, July 12, 1994.
n.d. The Re-excavation and Reinterpretration of Cerro Mangote: A Ceramic Shellmidden in Central Panama. Manuscript on file at the Smithsonian Tropical Research Institute, Panama.

Ranere, Anthony J., and Pat Hansell
1978 Early Subsistence Patterns along the Pacific Coast of Central Panama. In *Prehistoric Coastal Adaptations: The Economy and Ecology of Maritime Middle America.* New York: Academic Press. Pp. 3-59.

Ranere, Anthony J., and Richard G. Cook
In Press Paleoindian Occupation in the Central American Tropics. In *Clovis: Origins and Human Adaptation.* R. Bonnichsen and K. Fladmark, eds. Orono, Maine: Center for the Study of the First Americans.
1989 Early Human Migrations through the Isthmus of Panama. In *Human Occupation of the Pacific Continents/Islands: Routes into the New World.* R. Ackerman, ed. Proceedings of the Circum-Pacific Prehistory Conference, August 1-6. Seattle: Washington State University Press.

Reclus, Armand
1888 *Panamá et Darien voyages d'exploration 1876 to 1878.* Paris: Hatchette et cie.

Reichel-Dolmatoff, Gerardo
1950-51 *Los Kogi: Una tribu indígena de la Sierra Nevada de Santa Marta, Colombia.* 2 Vols. Bogotá.
1960 Notas etnográficas sobre los Indios del Choco. *Revista Colombiana de Antropología.* (Bogotá, Colombia). 11:75-158.
1965a *Colombia.* London: Thames and Hudson.
1965b Excavaciones arqueológicas en Puerto Hormiga, Departamento de Bolívar. Vol. 2. *Publicaciones de la Universidad de Los Andes, Antropología.* Bogotá, Colombia.
1971 *Amazonian Cosmos: The Sexual and Religious Symbolism of the Tukano Indians.* Chicago, Illinois: University of Chicago Press.
1975 *The Shaman and the Jaguar.* Philadelphia: Temple University Press.
1982 Astronomical Models of Social Behavior Among Some Indians of Colombia. In *Ethnoastronomy and Archaeoastronomy in the American Tropics.* New York: Academy of Sciences. Pp. 165-82.
1985a *Monsú: Un sitio arqueológico.* Bogotá, Colombia: Fondo de Promoción de la Cultura del Banco Popular.
1985b *Basketry as Metaphor: Arts and Crafts of the Desana Indians of the Northwest Amazon.* Los Angeles: Museum of Cultural History, University of California.
1988 *Goldwork and Shamanism.* Medellin, Colombia: Compañía Litográfica Nacional.

Reichel-Dolmatoff, Gerardo, and Alicia Reichel-Dolmatoff
1951 Investigaciones arqueológicas en el Departamento de Magdalena, Colombia, 1946-1950. *Boletín de Arqueología* (Bogotá). III(1-6).

Resquejo Salcedo, Padre Juan
1908 Relación geográfica e histórica de la provincia de Panamá. Tomo VIII. In *Colección de libros y documentos referentes a la historia de América: Relaciones históricas y geográficas de América Central*. Librería General de Victoriano Sánchez, Madrid. Pp. 87-136.

Restrepo Tirado, Ernesto
1888 Costumbres de los Indios Darienitas. In *Viajes de Lionel Wafer al Istmo del Darién (Cuatro meses entre los Indios)*. Vincente Restrepo, trans. and annot. Bogotá. Pp. 113-29.

1892 *Estudios sobre los aborígenes de Colombia*. Bogotá, Colombia.

Riesanz, John Berry
1955 *The People of Panama*. New York: Colombia University Press.

Roe, Peter G.
1982 *The Cosmic Zygote, Cosmology in the Amazon Basin*. New Brunswick, New Jersey: Rutgers University Press.

Romoli, Kathleen
1987 *Los de la lengua Cueva: Los grupos indígenos del Istmo Oriental en la época de la Conquista Española*. Bogotá: Instituto Colombiano de Antropología y Instituto Colombiano de Cultura.

Roosevelt, Anna C.
1979 The Goldsmith: The Cocle Style of Central Panama. In *The Ancestors: Native Artisans of the Americas*. A. C. Roosevelt and J. G. E. Smith, eds. New York: Museum of the American Indian. Pp. 68-101.
1984 Problems in Interpreting the Diffusion of Cultivated Plants. In *Pre-Columbian Plant Migration*. D. Z. Stone, ed. Papers of the Peabody Museum of Archaeology and Ethnology, Vol. 76. Cambridge, Massachusetts: Harvard University Press. Pp. 2-18.

Roth, Walter E.
1915 An Inquiry into the Animism and Folklore of the Guiana Indians. *30th Annual Report of the Bureau of American Ethnology, 1908-1909*. Washington, D.C.: Smithsonian Institution Press. Pp. 103-386.

Roys, Ralph L.
1931 The Ethno-Botany of the Maya. *Middle American Research Series*. No. 2. New Orleans: Tulane University.

Sabloff, Jeremy A., and Robert E. Smith.
1969 The Importance of Both Analytic and Taxonomic Classification in the Type-Variety System. *American Antiquity*. 34(3).

Salcedo, Juan Requejo, ed.
1908 Relación Histórica y Geográfica de la Provincia de Panamá (Año 1640). In *Relaciones Históricas y Geográficas de América Central*. Madrid: Colección de Libros y Documentos Referentes a la Historia de América, Vol. 8.

Sander, Dan
1959 The Circular Problematicals of the Azuero Peninsula, Panama. *Panama Archaeologist*. 2(1):1-6.
1959 Fluted Points from Madden Lake. *Panama Archaeologist*. 2(1):39-52.
1960 Report on Pottery Stamp, Chiriqui Province, Panama. *Panama Archaeologist*. 3(1):99.
1961 An Archaeological Discovery: Rio Negro. *Panama Archaeologist*, 4(1):1-3.
1964 *Lithic Material from Panamá: Fluted Points from Madden Lake*. Proceedings of the 35th International Congress of Americanists, Mexico. Vol. 1. Pp.183-92.

Sander, Dan and R. H. Mitchell
1960 Report on Fabric and Figurine, Venado Beach, Canal Zone, Panama. *Panama Archaeologist*. 3(1):52-53.

Sander, Dan, Russell H. Mitchell, and R. G. Turner
1958 Report on Venado Beach Excavations, Panama. *Archaeological Society of Panama* (Panama). 1:26-28.

Sanders, William, and David Webster
1978 Unilinealism, Multilinealism and the Evolution of Complex Societies. In *Social Archaeology*. New York: Academic Press. Pp. 249-302.

Santos, Gustavo S.
1989 Las etnias indígenas prehispánicas y de la conquista en la región del Golfo de Urabá. *Boletín de Antropología* (Universidad de Antioquía). 6(22).

Sauer, Carl O.
1950 Cultivated Plants of South and Central America. Vol. 6. *Smithsonian Institution, Bureau of American Ethnology Bulletin 143*. Washington, D.C. Pp. 487-543.
1966 *The Early Spanish Main*. Berkeley: University of California Press.

Seeman, Berthold
1853 The Aborigines of the Isthmus of Panama. *Transactions of the American Ethnological Society*. Vol. 3. New York.

Selfridge, T. O.
1874 *Reports of Explorations, Surveys, etc*. Washington, D.C.

Severin, Kurt
1936 Evil Spirits in the Jungles of Panama. *Travel* (Floral Park, New York). 67(6):22-23.

Sharer, Robert J.
1984 Lower Central America as Seen from Mesoamerica. In *The Archaeology of Lower Central America*. F. W. Lange and D. Z. Stone, eds. Albuquerque: University of New Mexico Press.

Shelton, Catherine Norell
1984 *Formative Settlement in Western Chiriqui, Panama: Ceramic Chronology And Phase Relationships*. Ph.D. Dissertation, Temple University, Philadelphia.

Shepard, Anna O.
1968 *Ceramics for the Archaeologist.* Publication No. 609. Washington, D.C.: Carnegie Institution.

Shook, Edwin M.
1965 *Anthropological Bibliography of Aboriginal Panama.* San José, Costa Rica: Tropical Science Center.

Smith, J. H., and Dr. McDowell
1884 A Paper on Chiriquian Antiquities. *Journal of the Geographic Society.* 14:256.

Smith, Marjorie B.
1959 *Progress Report on the Study of African Influences in the Music of Panama.* Proceedings of the 33rd International Congress of Americanists, July 20-27, San José, Costa Rica. Vol. 2. Pp. 639-46.

Snarskis, Michael J.
1979 Turrialba: A Paleo-Indian Quarry and Workshop Site in Eastern Costa Rica. *American Antiquity.* 44:125-38.
1981 The Archaeology of Costa Rica. In *Between Continents/Between Seas: Pre-Columbian Art of Costa Rica.* E. P. Benson, ed. New York: Harry N. Abrams, Inc. Pp. 15-84.
1984 Central America: The Lower Caribbean. In *Archaeology of Lower Central America.* F. W. Lange and D. Z. Stone, eds. Albuquerque: The University of New Mexico Press.
1987 The Archaeological Evidence for Chiefdoms in Eastern Central Costa Rica. In *Chiefdoms in the Americas.* R. D. Drennan and C. A. Uribe, eds. New York: University Press of America. Pp. 105-18.

Spielman, Richard S., E. C. Migliazza, J. V. Neal, H. Gershowitz, and R. Torres
1979 The Evolution of Two Populations: A Study of the Guaymi and Yanomama. *Current Anthropology.* 20:377-88.

Squier, E. G.
1859 More About the Gold Discoveries of the Isthmus. *Harper's Weekly.* August.

Stevens-Arroyo, Antonio M.
1988 *Cave of the Jaguar: The Mythological World of the Tainos.* Albuquerque: University of New Mexico Press.

Stewart, T. D.
1959 Skeletal Remains from Venado Beach, Panama: Cranial Deformity. Proceedings of the 33rd International Congress of Americanists, July 20-27, San José, Costa Rica. Vol. 2. Pp. 45-54.

Stier, Francis R.
1979 *The Effect of Demographic Change on Agriculture in San Blas.* Ph.D. Dissertation, University of Arizona. Ann Arbor, Michigan: University Microfilms, Inc.

Stirling, Matthew William
1949 The Importance of Sitio Conte. *American Anthropology.* 51:514-17.
1953 Hunting Pre-History in Panama Jungles. *National Geographic Magazine.* 104(2):271-90.
1964 Archaeological Notes on Almirante Bay, Bocas del Toro, Panama. *Smithsonian Institution, Bureau of American Ethnology Bulletin 191.* Washington, D.C. Pp. 255-284.

Stirling, M. W. and Stewart, R. H.
1949 Exploring the Past in Panama. *National Geographic.* 95(3): 373-99.
1950 Exploring Ancient Panama by Helicopter. *National Geographic.* 97(2):227-46.

Stirling, Matthew W. and Marion Stirling
1964 El Limón, An Early Tomb Site in Coclé Province, Panama. *Smithsonian Institution, Bureau of American Ethnology Bulletin 191* Washington, D.C.: Smithsonian Institution Pp. 247-254.

Stone, Doris
1966 Panama. *Encyclopedia of World Art.* Vol. XI. London: McGraw-Hill Publishing Co.

1966 Synthesis of Lower Central American Ethnohistory. In *Handbook of Middle American Indians.* Robert Wauchope, ed. Austin: University of Texas Press.

Stone, Doris Z.
1961 *Las tribus talamanqueñas de Costa Rica.* San José, Costa Rica: Editorial Antonio Lehmann.

Stothert, Karen E.
1985 The Preceramic Las Vegas Culture of Coastal Ecuador. *American Antiquity* 50(3): 613-637.

Stout, David B.
1947 *San Blas Cuna Acculturation: An Introduction.* New York: Viking Fund Publication.
1948 The Choco. Vol 4. *Smithsonian Institution, Bureau of American Ethnology Bulletin 143.* Washington, D.C. Pp. 269-76.
1952 Persistent Elements in the San Blas Cuna Social Organization. In *Indian Tribes of Aboriginal America.* Chicago: University of Chicago Press. Pp. 262-65.

Tastevin, P. C.
1925 La légende de Bóyusú en Amazonie: Texte Tupy ou neengatu. *Revue d'Ethnographie et des Traditions Populaires.* 6(2):172-207.

Taylor, Alfred B.
1867 Golden Relics from Chiriqui. In *Proceedings of Numismatic and Antiquarian.* Philadelphia: Society of Philadelphia. Pp. 75-80.

Taylor, R.E., and Clement W. Meighan
1978 *Chronologies in New World Archaeology.* New York: Academic Press.

Tomes, Robert
1855 *Panama in 1855.* New York: Harper & Bros.

Toral, Demetrio
1963 El problema arqueológico de Panamá. *Publicación Revista Lotería* (Panamá). 8(94):49-65.
1971 Análisis estilístico de la cerámica de la cultura Tonose. *II Símposio Nacional de Antropología, arqueología y etno-historia de Panamá* (non publié).

Torres, Reina C.
1958 Aspectos culturales de los Indios Cunas. *Anuario de Estudios Americanos.* Sevilla: Escuela de Estudios Hispano-Americanos de Sevilla. XV:515-47.
1972 *Nata Prehispánico.* Publicación Especial No. 3. Centro de Investigaciones Antropológicas. Panamá: Universidad de Panamá.

Townsend, Richard Fraser
1979 *State and Cosmos in the Art of Tenochtitlan.* Washington, D.C.: Dumbarton Oaks.

Tozzer, Alfred Marsten
1941 Middle American Archaeology: The Greater Cultures. *Bulletin of the Museum of Art* (Rhode Island School of Design, Providence). 29(1-2).
1941 Landa's relación de las cosas de Yucatán: A Translation. *Papers of the Peabody Museum of American Archaeology and Ethnology.* Vol. 18. Cambridge, Massachusetts: Harvard University Press.

Trustees for Harvard University
1963 *Handbook of the Robert Woods Bliss Collection of Pre-Columbian Art.* Washington, D.C.: Dumbarton Oaks.

Tyler, Hamilton
1984 *Pueblo Gods and Myths.* Norman: University of Oklahoma Press.

Uhle, Max
1924 Cronología y Relaciones de las Antiguas Civilizaciones Panameñas. *Boletín de la Academia Nacional de Historia* (Quito). 9:24-26.

Universidad de Panamá
1973 *Actas del IV Simposium Nacional de Antropología, Arqueología y Ethnohistoria de Panamá.* Centro de Investigaciones Antropológicas, Instituto Nacional de Cultura, Dirección Nacional del Patrimonio Histórico, Universidad de Panamá. October.

University of Pennsylvania
1943 The Lesser Archaeological Cultures of Mexico and Central America. *University Museum Bulletin.* 10(1-2):49-56.

Valdes, Ramon M.
1898 *Geografía del Istmo de Panamá.* Bogotá, Colombia: Imprenta Nacional.

Valerio, Wilson A.
1985 Investigaciones preliminares en dos abrigos rocosos en la Región Central de Panamá. *Vínculos.* 11:17-30.
1987 *Análisis funcional y estratigráfico de SF-9 (Carabalí), un abrigo rocoso en la Región Central de Panamá.* Vol. 1. Tésis de Grado, Universidad de Costa Rica.

Verrill, A. Hyatt
1924 Ethnological Collections from Darien. Vol. 1. In *Indian Notes.* New York: Heye Foundation, Museum of the American Indian. Pp. 194-200.
1927a Excavations in Coclé Province, Panama. Vol. IV, No. 1. *Indian Notes.* New York: Heye Foundation, Museum of the American Indian. Pp. 47-61.
1927b The Pompeii of Ancient America: A Vast Settlement Destroyed Centuries Before Christ. *The World's Work.* LIII(3):279-88.
1928 A Mystery of the Vanished Past in Panama: Newly Discovered Relics of a Vanished Civilization Destroyed by Earthquake or Volcanic Eruption. *Illustrated London News.* 173(4669).

Verrill, A. Hyatt, and Ruth Verrill
1953 The Puzzling Culture of Cocle, Chapter III. In *America's Ancient Civilizations.* New York: Capricorn Books.

Vinton, Kenneth W.
1959 Rising Coastline in Panama Bay Permits Unique Archaeological Studies. *Panama Archaeologist.* 2:6-13.
1960 Pre-Ceramic Engineers. *Panama Archaeologist.* 3:55-65.

Wassén, Henry
1933 Cuentos de los Indios Chocos recogidos por Erland Nordenskiöld durante su expedicion al Istmo de Panamá en 1927 y publicados con notas y observaciones comparativas. *Journal Societé des Américanistes de Paris.* 25:103-37.
1934a Mitos y Cuentos de los Indios Cunas. *Journal Societé des Américanistes de Paris.* 26:103-37.
1934b The Frog in Indian Mythology and Imaginative World. *Anthropos.* Vol. XXIX.
1935 Notes on Southern Groups of Choco Indians in Colombia. *Etnologiska Studier* (Göteborg). 1:35-182.
1937 Some Cuna Indian Animal Stories with Original Texts. *Etnologiska Studier* (Göteborg). 4:69-79.
1940 An Analogy Between A South American and Oceanic Myth Motif and Negro Influence in Darien. *Etnologiska Studier* (Göteborg). 10:69-79.
1949 Contributions to Cuna Ethnography. Some Archaeological Observations from Boquete. *Etnologiska Studier* (Göteborg). 16.
1949 Some Archaeological Observations from Boquete, Chiriqui, Panama. *Etnologista Studier* (Göteborg). 16:145-92.
1952 New Cuna Myths, According to Guillermo Hayans. *Etnologiska Studier* (Göteborg). 20:87-106.
1960 *A Find of Cocle-Style Pottery in a Single Veraguas Grave, Panama, 1957-1958.* Göteborg, Arstryck: Etnografiska Museet. Pp. 62-81.

Waters, Frank
1963 *Book of the Hopi.* New York: Ballantine Books.

Wauchope, Robert
1948 *Excavations at Zacualpa, Guatemala,* Louisiana: Tulane University. Middle American Research Institute.

Weiland, Doris
1984 Prehistoric Settlement Patterns in the Santa Maria Drainage of Panama: A Preliminary Analysis. In *Recent Developments in Isthmian Archaeology.* Frederick W. Lange,

ed. Oxford: BAR International Series 212. Pp. 31-53.
1985 *Preceramic Settlement Patterns in the Santa Maria Drainage of Panama*. Revised version of a paper presented at the 45th International Congress of Americanists, Bogotá, Colombia.

Weiss, Gerald
1975 Campa Cosmology: The World of a Forest Tribe in South America. *Anthropological Papers*. Vol. 52, No. 5. New York: American Museum of Natural History.

Wetmore, Alexander
1972 The Birds of the Isthmus of Panama, The Panama Biota: Some Observations Prior to a Sea-Level Canal. *Bulletin of the Biological Society of Washington*. 2:211-216.

Whitten Jr., Norman E.
1976 *Sacha Runa: Ethnicity and Adaptation of Ecuadorian Jungle Quichua*. Champaign: University of Illinois Press.

Wilbert, Johannes
1972 Tobacco and Shamanistic Ecstacy among the Warao Indians of Venezuela. In *Flesh of the Gods*. Peter T. Furst, ed. New York: Praeger Publications Pp. 55-83.

Wilbert, Johannes and David M. Guss.
1980 Navigators of the Orinoco: River Indians of Venezuela. *University of California Pamphlet Series*. No. 11. Los Angeles: Museum of Cultural History.

Willey, Gordon Randolph
1951 A Preliminary Report on the Monagrillo Culture of Panama. In *The Civilizations of Ancient America*. Sol Tax, ed. Selected papers of the 29th International Congress of Americanists held in 1949. Pp. 173-180.
1958 Estimated Correlations and Dating of South and Central American Culture Sequences. Part 1. *American Antiquity*. 23(4):353-378.
1959 The Intermediate Area of Nuclear America: Its Prehistoric *Relationships to Middle America and Peru*. Proceedings of the 33rd International Congress of Americanists, July 20-27, San José, Costa Rica.
1971 *An Introduction to American Archaeology, Volume II: South America*. New Jersey: Prentice Hall.
1984 A Summary of the Archaeology of Lower Central America. In *The Archaeology of Lower Central America*. F. W. Lange and D. Z. Stone, eds. Albuquerque: University of New Mexico Press. Pp. 341-380.

Willey, Gordon R. and
Charles R. McGimsey III
1952 Archaeology in Western Panama. *Archaeology*. 5(3):173-181.
1954 The Monagrillo Culture of Panama: With an Appendix on Archaeological Marine Shells by Robert E. Greengo. *Papers of the Peabody Museum of Archaeology and Ethnology*. Vol. 49, No. 2. Cambridge, Massachusetts: Harvard University Press.
1959 Stratigraphy at the Monagrillo Site. In *The Archaeologist at Work*. New York: Harper & Bros. Pp. 281-302.

Willey, Gordon R., and
Theodore L. Stoddard
1954 Cultural Stratigraphy in Panama: A Preliminary Report of the Girón Site. *American Antiquity*. 19(4):332-343.

Wilson, David J.
1992 Modeling the Role of Ideology in Societal Adaptation: Examples from the South American Data. In *Ideology and Pre-Columbian Civilizations*. Santa Fe, New Mexico: School of American Research Press.

Wolf, Carolyn E., and Karen R. Folk
1977 *Indians of North and South America: A Bibliography Based on the Collection at the Willard E. Yager Library-Museum, Hartwick College, Oneonta, N.Y.* New Jersey: The Scarecrow Press, Inc.

Young, Philip
1971 Ngawbe: Tradition and Change among the Western Guaymi. *Illinois Studies in Anthropology* (Urbana), No. 7.
1976 The Expression of Harmony and Discord in Guaymi Ritual. In *Frontier Adaptations in Lower Central America*. M. W. Helms and F. Loveland, eds. Philadelphia: Institute for the Study of Human Issues. Pp. 37-53.

Young, Philip, and James Howe, eds.
1976 Ritual and Symbol in Native Central America. *University of Oregon Anthropological Papers, No. 9*. Eugene: Department of Anthropology, University of Oregon.

Zelsman, James M.
1959 A Rio Grande Burial. *Panama Archaeologist*. 2(1):89-91.

Zucchi, Alberta R.
1968 Algunas hipótesis sobre la población aborigen de los llanos occidentales de Venezuela. *Acta Cien Venezolana* (Venezuela). 19:135-139.

147. Sunset, Panamá